PRAISE FOR ADVENTURE DIVAS

"Hilarious . . . a delightful triangulation of adventure travel, telecommuting and self-reinvention . . . Morris is not afraid to show her everyday self on the page, which is invigorating in a genre that too often has only two speeds: turbo self-aggrandizement and ambling naturalist introspection. The female perspective is also refreshing: how many men could survive not one but two international waxing appointments—Brazilian and Persian?"   —*The New York Times Book Review*

"In this fascinating book, Morris offers vicarious thrills and more than just a little bit of inspiration for desk-bound people everywhere."
    —*Chicago Tribune*

"With her trademark candor, guts, wit and insight, [Morris's memoir] is a sweet song to the questing, world-engaged life on the move that stops at no national boundaries or geographic hazards."   —*Seattle Post-Intelligencer*

"Ever insightful and unpretentiously brilliant, Morris inspires her readers as the divas themselves have inspired her. . . . [A] literary gem [that] takes many steps beyond the labels 'travel writing' and 'memoir.' . . . This armchair adventure will unquestionably make you want to get up off the couch, get on a plane and explore international divadom for yourself. Be forewarned."   —Fredericksburg *Free Lance-Star*

"Obvious pick [for a] feisty friend."   —*Good Housekeeping*

"A meaningful and inspiring book."   —*The Salt Lake Tribune*

"Only a few women warriors have successfully stormed prime time. There's Xena. And the Femme Nikita. Now travel temptress Holly Morris is giving it a try." —*Orange County Register*

"The Adventure Divas have some advice for firing up your soul!"
—*USA Today*

"Between film shoots, Morris hunts boar in Borneo, races camels in the Sahara, and climbs the Matterhorn—escapades that prove her to be just as inspiring as her subjects." —*Condé Nast Traveler*

"Morris chases down her subjects and exacts a story that is fresh and idea-driven." —*Mother Jones*

"Writing with compassion, humor, and activism, Morris empowers women to follow their dreams by showing that determined women can indeed effect change in their lives. Highly recommended."
—*Library Journal*

"Morris's writing is clean, rhythmic and full of both storytelling flair and journalistic pragmatism. The story of the spunky [Adventure Divas] project itself . . . is as inspiring as the divas." —*Publishers Weekly*

"This is not just about travel, although it's as adventurous as can be. . . . Morris's interviews . . . are thoughtful and probing, [and] her text adds context—and humor—to the project, warts and all." —*Booklist*

"Genuinely interesting subject matter . . . Morris shows an admirable fearlessness." —*Kirkus Reviews*

"Smart, sexy, inspiring! Holly Morris is the ultimate Adventure Diva. Whether she's deconstructing Cuban politics, finding meaning in a Brazilian bikini wax, or succumbing to the pleasures of a Tehran security pat-down, Holly lives and writes like a brainy bad girl. I loved reading *Adventure Divas*—it's like riding shotgun on a high-octane global road trip."

—CAMERON TUTTLE, author of *The Bad Girl's Guide to the Open Road*

"Let us celebrate Holly Morris and all of the other amazing, hilarious, tough, and tender Adventure Divas in this book. There is no substitute for the old-fashioned adventurer with frequent flier miles, dirt on her boots, and new ideas." —SHERMAN ALEXIE, author of *The Lone Ranger and Tonto Fistfight in Heaven*

"Holly Morris is hip, wise, concerned, endlessly curious, fearless, and fiercely independent." —NICK LYONS, author of *Full Creel*

"The Adventure Divas really do go where angels fear to tread. Meet the eighty-one-year-old Cuban poet and her forty-one-year-old husband; the rebellious spirit behind Iran's foremost women's magazine; a female Maori bandleader. Holly Morris has written a lively and fascinating old-girl's-guide paean to never holding back on life. Move over, Mr. Hemingway." —JACKI LYDEN, *National Public Radio*

"Beware. If you read this remarkable book, you will pack your bags and go. And you will want to take Holly Morris with you as your friend and guide—she notices everything and she's wickedly funny." —SUSAN FOX ROGERS, editor of *Solo: On Her Own Adventure*

"Holly Morris has given us a fresh and individualistic take on the American tradition of lighting out for the territory." —HOWELL RAINES, author of *Fly Fishing Through the Midlife Crisis*

"Find your passport to excitement, enlightenment, intelligence and ingenuity in Holly Morris's spirited exploration of the global sisterhood. *Adventure Divas* is what the world needs now!" —EVELYN C. WHITE, author of *Alice Walker: A Life*

"*Adventure Divas* will inspire you to set out on your own journey. Holly Morris is a delightful and trustworthy guide." —JENNIFER BAUMGARDNER and AMY RICHARDS, co-authors of *Grassroots: A Field Guide for Feminist Activism*

ADVENTURE DIVAS

VILLARD

NEW YORK

ADVENTURE DIVAS

SEARCHING THE GLOBE FOR WOMEN WHO ARE CHANGING THE WORLD

Holly Morris

AUTHOR'S NOTE

Aided by notes, transcripts, and memory, I have re-created events and conversations to the best of my ability. That said, memory is both capricious and dodgy—you know the spiel. The exact chronology of my travels has been altered somewhat for the sake of the narrative. I take responsibility for all errors and omissions herein.

2006 Villard Books Trade Paperback Edition

Copyright © 2005 by Holly Morris

All rights reserved.

Published in the United States by Villard Books, an imprint of
The Random House Publishing Group, a division of Random House, Inc., New York.

VILLARD and "V" CIRCLED Design are registered trademarks of Random House, Inc.

Originally published in hardcover in the United States by Villard Books, an imprint of
The Random House Publishing Group, a division of Random House, Inc., in 2005.

"Cud, Sweat, and Fears" was previously published, in slightly different form, in *A Woman Alone: Travel Tales from Around the Globe,* ed. by Faith Conlon et al. (Seattle: Seal Press, 2001). Excerpts from "Paradox Found" were previously published, in slightly different form, in *Two in the Wild: Tales of Adventure from Friends, Mothers, and Daughters,* ed. by Susan Fox Rogers (NY: Vintage, 1999), and in *Cuba in Mind,* ed. by Maria Finn Dominguez (NY: Vintage, 2004).

*Grateful acknowledgment is made to the following for permission
to reprint previously published material:*

Adventure Divas, Inc.: "when my grandmother came . . ." by Carilda Oliver Labra. Recited for camera. Reprinted by permission of Adventure Divas, Inc. Copyright © Carilda Oliver Labra.

Adventure Divas, Inc.: Instinto rap lyrics (performed for camera) reprinted by permission of Adventure Divas, Inc. Copyright © Instinto.

Cross Cultural Communications: "Declaration of Love" from *Dust Disappears* by Carilda Oliver Labra, translated by Enildo A. García and Daniela Gioseffi. Copyright © 1988, 1995 by Enildo A. García and Daniela Gioseffi. *Latin American Writers, Chapbook 1.* Reprinted by permission of the publisher on behalf of the author and the translators.

Pooran Farrokhzad: "Another Birth" by Forough Farrokhzad from *Az Past O Bolande.* Reprinted by permission of Pooran Farrokhzad.

Photograph and Illustration Credits:
Adventure Divas, Inc., page 50; Barbara Bachman, page 2; the collection of Mark and Carolyn Blackburn, Kamuela, Hawaii, page 180; Julie Costanzo, title page and page 222; Cheryl Dunn, page 84; Ellen Forney, page xx; Michael Gross, page 162; Tim Knight, page 204; Holly Morris, page 140; Rusty Scott, page 264

ISBN 0-375-76063-6

Printed in the United States of America

www.villard.com

2 4 6 8 9 7 5 3 1

Book design by Barbara M. Bachman

For Jeannie / Mom

THEY WERE NOTHING MORE THAN PEOPLE, BY THEMSELVES. . . .

BUT ALL TOGETHER, THEY HAVE BECOME THE HEART AND

MUSCLES AND MIND OF SOMETHING PERILOUS AND NEW,

SOMETHING STRANGE AND GROWING AND GREAT.

TOGETHER, ALL TOGETHER, THEY ARE THE INSTRUMENTS OF CHANGE.

—KERI HULME, *The Bone People*

CONTENTS

In which the author relates naïve and hubristic start-up stories of how she got into estro-charged globetrotting. Author also teases some of the saltier adventures and debacles to come—*headhunters! fugitives! emotional turmoil!*—yet tries not to give away too much of the story.

PARADOX FOUND

In which a film crew sneaks into Cuba to make the pilot for the *Adventure Divas* television series. A hurricane, a budding mother-daughter dynamic, and elusive interviewees all contribute to a far from seamless production. Nonetheless, a hip-hop group, an exile, and a Santería spiritual leader (among others) reveal divadom's unique elements in Castro's pinko outpost: Eros, Risk, and Machismo-Leninismo.

HEAD GAMES AND BOAR HUNTS

In which the author tells of a Malaysian gig that helped fund the Adventure Divas enterprise during one of many fiscal doldrums. Here, the author starts to sneak in larger geopolitical issues, such as globalization, environmental devastation, the obliteration of indigenous peoples, and the like—but after reading this chapter, you'll probably only remember the giant snake.

<u>4:45 A.M.</u> 98°, 94% humidity. Some Sumatran tree.

Mom— I am perched high in a tree awaiting a new day. To the north, over an archipelago, I see Borneo. A tinny call to prayer leaks in from the distant west; to the east lies the thick, wet Gunung Leuser rain forest, which just spat me out after a week in its digestive tract; down, directly south, a pile of Kleenex, damp and sickly yellow from blotting my weeping leech-bite pustules, is wedged between my crotch and the trunk. I am encrusted with a phylum's worth of bug corpses, and smeared with an Agent Orange-like repellent whose label falsely proclaimed it would deter them: The bug corpse-poison pastiche is sealed with an odd mildewy film that the rain forest silently sprays, like a cat in heat, on trespassers.

Yet here, straddling this limb, right now, I am having a perfect moment.

The heat, the release from duties, the magic of not knowing what's going to happen next and the funny mushrooms — somehow the whole thing has done away with my rigor mortis of the soul. Everything is changing when I get back, which is in a week — will call. Love, Hol

I am here.

V.S.A.

Seattle, Washington
98121

Jeannie Hoekis

PROLOGUE

"**M**y pod days are over, dammit," I thought to myself as I stood in my bedroom back in Seattle, looking at the wall. In my family, "pods"—the dispirited hulks from *Invasion of the Body Snatchers* who walked through life with eyes open but not really living—were the lowest form of being. I had stripped clean my walls, painted them white, and hung huge sheets of white paper and scrawled on them painfully self-conscious resolutions for the future: BODY, SOUL, WORK. All had subdivided categories. My gray backpack lay in the corner covered with Indonesian dust, and I was struggling to hold on to my hard-won modicum of actualization.

My mother, who was visiting, walked in. "What," she said, looking wide-eyed and askance, taking in the graffiti of self-help plastering the walls, "is this about?" I mumbled something about a headhunter and magic mushrooms in Sumatra, and tried to tell her how all this added up to something important. I rolled a new ethos around in my mouth, feeling for a name—a single word on which to hang the emerging philosophy that would mark a new phase in my life. The word needed to embody potential and individuality. Above all, it needed to be proactive, rather than reactive. Always a fan of four-letter words, I blurted out, "Diva."

"You want to be an opera singer?" Mom said. "Honey," she added delicately, "you're tone-deaf."

True, I could carry off neither the range of notes nor the plunging bustline of a traditional diva, and furthermore, I already had a job: I was a book editor.

When I left for that month in Sumatra I was the editorial director of a feminist publishing company, Seal Press, and weary with burnout. My work, on books covering everything from domestic violence to third-wave feminism to adventure travel, was gratifying, yet a part of my original spirit had atrophied after years behind a desk. I needed to move from theory to action, from the intellectual to the visceral. I had long believed that adventure was a way of life, not just a weekend theme; but I wasn't living it. Adventure is about hurling yourself at the unexpected; it's how you walk to the corner store, *and* how you walk the Australian Outback. Up in that Sumatran tree, I had determined that my next professional move would satisfy my hunger for politics *and* adventure. And over the next several months a plan took form.

In publishing and in life, I had started to see in divavision: to connect the dots, the acts, the scrappy charge toward ideals that characterized the people I admired. There were risk-taking, grassroots leaders—artists, activists, politicos—women who were making change on micro and macro levels around the world. I wanted to find them, expose their work, plumb their spirits—and add a new brand of iconography to the media landscape.

Tone-deaf? Pshaw. I embraced the first-person, power-injected moniker *diva,* and combined it with a philosophy of living I saw embodied in the women I respected. Together they formed the perfect name for the project: Adventure Divas.

I followed my feeling that there were unsung visionaries who might represent another way to wield power in this world that had become increasingly polarized between the dueling forces of imperialism and fundamentalism—between the profit-driven, culture-homogenizing multinationals that are turning the developing world into a "parts car" for the First World, and the tribal, regressive camps that advocate burkas, clitorectomies, anti-choice legislation, and, in general, a reactionary reliance on orthodoxy.

The ladies of divadom—adventure divas—I imagined, represented this alternative, third way. I wanted to hit the road and test my theory.

Could their leadership, vision, and habit of rewriting the rules represent a new empire simmering out there? Or at the very least, would there be value in creating a public testimony of global sistah-hood? (*Was* there a global sistah-hood?) In bringing these people to the attention of the world, would their ability to make change increase exponentially?

A truly global pilgrimage would provide a deeper understanding of how individuals live in, and change, the world. As a committed traveler, I knew that diving into other cultures and gathering the fruits of wanderlust enabled one to see the world with a wider, more original lens. "Travel," as Mark Twain put it, "is fatal to prejudice, bigotry, and narrow-mindedness." So while the principles of divadom certainly play out locally, I was committed to acting globally.

I would pull together a team of people who shared my belief in divas and the possibilities media held in leveraging them. I would quit my job, swallow my print pride, and turn to the medium with the largest global impact: television. After all, charting a coming paradigm was an ambition that required drastic measures, like tearing down the master's house with his own media tools. Why not use television to *change* people's minds, instead of deaden them?

So, the plan was to take divavision to television—and to the Web, and now this book, too—to storm the bully pulpit and launch a cross-media empire. The use of the word *empire* was quite deliberate. "Imperialism means thinking about, settling on, controlling land that you do not possess, that is distant, that is lived on and owned by others," wrote the late cultural critic Edward Said, which, metaphorically speaking, seemed an apt description of this bid for bandwidth. Of course, I was just talking about making a television series, not exactly taking over 30 Rock; making like Ted Turner, not occupying anyone's homeland. On one level I was just mucking around in the syntax of empowerment; on the other hand, I was serious: This was one destiny worth manifesting.

But book publishing had been my career of choice, and I was relatively clueless about TV. I didn't even have one.

What's a girl to do?

Call Mom.

My mom, Jeannie, had years of experience in local television news with CBS. She is five foot two, very energetic, and a born optimist. I shared exactly none of these traits with her, so I assumed we would make a complementary team. Because she had spent her career in corporate news media (mostly covering sports), I figured an independent venture just might appeal to her. And I knew the global adventure would be irresistible. When I was eight years old my mother had pulled my siblings and me out of school and dragged us and our father on a yearlong road trip through Eastern and Western Europe and the then Soviet Union. Putting her career on hold in the name of adventure proved her own divaliciousness (though for me, missing third grade means that to this day I can't write in cursive or do fractions). Jeannie had witnessed the graffiti in my bedroom, but when I actually told her The Plan, her response went something like this:

"Honey, TV is *very* expensive, especially good TV. TV thinks women just like to cry and portrays us as sexpots or victims. Television is about image, but executing this, well, it's gonna be all about *work*. A series can take years to get off the ground—and most never fly.

"Also," she said, "TV is run by myopic guys."

(Long pause.)

"Okay, I'm in," she said.

We filed the papers, slapped down ten thousand dollars each, and Adventure Divas was born. Take that, Rupert Murdoch.

Any Fortune 500 CEO will tell you that the first thing you have to do when you have an idea is get a focus group. So I called all my friends, pulled out a High-8 video camera, and asked, *What's a diva?*

"Eleanor Roosevelt. The fact that she made it through life with power *and* buck teeth always made me proud," said Kate.

"The New Freedom lady gone bad," responded Casey, with a flip of her skateboard.

"Well, it's like George Clinton's definition of funk," Evelyn said. "*Diva* is the awesome power of a fully operational mothership."

"She, against all cultural insistence, listens to the song in her heart," said my friend Inga, who was slated to write a travel advice column for the Adventure Divas website.

On the last day of our focus-group research, Inga came by and plopped a box on my lap.

"Look," she said, gently pulling from the box an eight-inch-tall plastic doll, with dark skin, a gauzy aqua tutu, and sturdy, sparkly wings.

Sky Dancer.

"She flies unfettered." Inga pulled the string on the doll's launcher-base, which jettisoned her, arms up, up, up, spinning into the air. "She's magic. She'll bring you gifts. And her tutu matches her hair."

"She'll always stay with me for good luck," I said, thanking Inga for the talisman.

Focus-group testing complete, Jeannie and I decided we needed a promotional video shot in "locations around the world" featuring international divas. Our personal funds were going fast (especially after, like any good garage band, the first thing we did was make T-shirts).

Right. So. We gathered up our frequent flier miles and got creative in a three-state radius.

> *Lara, I know you're an accountant, but here's a camera. Can you pretend to be a Japanese film director?*

> *Evelyn, can you just stand at this podium and shake your fist as if in front of an assembly in Cape Town? We'll use the George Clinton quote if you do.*

> *Stacy, there's a Russian freighter in port. Can you fling a seabag and make like a Russian sailor?*

> *Steve, we're going to interview a bush pilot in Alaska. Would you shoot it? We can pay you in T-shirts.*

"Deb," I said, on the phone to my sister who wrangled horses in Utah, "do you think you could help us out with our 'riding across the Mongolian steppes' shot?" "No problem," she replied, "and if you drive an hour south into the desert you could get a 'biking across the Sahara' shot."

We found a Buddhist monk in Tacoma and for a "contribution" he agreed to squat and counsel for the camera.

Our pitch tape went out to television executives and we received an impressive number of meetings. Jeannie and I developed a dog-and-pony show in which we tossed around words like *synergy, psychographic,* and *cross-media branding* with the strategic zeal of new MBAs. The meetings usually began with the executives saying "We love it!" yet, oddly, ended with them describing a version of the show that didn't even remotely resemble the vision we (thought we had) put forth. The collective response, after months of courtship with a handful of networks, was that they were intrigued, but confused. Encouraging, but noncommittal. Once, we got all the way to contract stage and they pulled out. Twice, we walked away from contracts because of the creative compromises being asked of us.

It seemed most networks were not prepared to take on a project that melded genres, tossed around terms such as *girl world pilgrimage* and had a whiff of a political agenda.

Either that, or our presentation sucked and the project was a dud.

We interpreted our situation not as an ominous warning to bow out, but as a sign that we needed to Go It Alone. That is, make the show without initial support from a broadcaster—colloquially known as the "If they don't get it, screw 'em" phase in every entrepreneur's career. We would rally investors to fund a pilot, on the strength of which we would then go sell the series.

I strapped on false confidence and gave speeches to organizations such as the Outdoor Industry Council. *"It is up to all of us to make our attitudes visible and desirable. In doing that, we will prove the market. Our media and our products should rejoice in our multiplicity, and send a message that fame, beauty, and wealth do not necessarily drive us, nor are they the criteria of our chosen icons . . ."*

"Do you really have to use 'creative *dominatrix*' on your business card?" Jeannie queried after one particularly unsuccessful meeting in a potential investor's office.

"It wasn't my card. There was no hope from the get-go. Did you see that picture hanging on his wall of him shaking hands with Reagan? And your comment is a perfect example of the generational thing this project is trying to move beyond," I pressed. "Your generation was promised a decent husband and maybe a job on the side. Mine," I said with some nostalgia and a hint of disappointment, "mine was promised *jet packs.*"

Even though I pretended I was not listening to my mother, I often was. And she was partly right. There was a fundamental conflict: defiance and idealism constantly butted heads with fiscal and marketplace realities. The diva wannabe in me demanded to have exactly what I wanted. But the broke neophyte TV producer was in no position to demand it. I learned over time not to use the word *feminism,* to stress the travel aspect of the show, and to downplay its bedrock social consciousness.

Still, we were already growing tired and had not even gotten out the door yet. "Jeannie," I said privately, hoping to drown my feelings of defeat in her optimism, "maybe it was a bad idea. I mean, how much blood can we let over this?" By this time we had both been working full-time for several months, without pay and with only one staff member, Stacy Lewis, as well as a half-dozen interns.

"I told you this would take a long time; but no—it was never a bad idea. Look at the press we're getting, and, my gosh, the e-mails. It will succeed." Right. I dusted myself off and went back to revising the business plan for a fourth time.

Our slow progress dismayed us, but we were encouraged by the many individuals who supported the idea, and by the press who, by covering a not-yet-realized concept, helped us articulate and promote its viability.

This period of time represented the first and only instance I drew anything of value from a Kevin Costner vehicle: If you build it, they will come.

The response to our newly minted website kept our spirits buoyed and convinced us that we were really on to something. The Web readers recommended divas from around the world, declared their like-mindedness, ordered T-shirts . . . and asked about our airdates. We used their suggestions and combined them with our hard-working interns' research to create an international list of women we could draw on during the series.

Throughout the year it took us to launch Adventure Divas, we stood firm in our belief that we could do good work, even be political, and still end up in the black. We distributed our business plan. We followed up every lead, and sniffed out who had idealism attached to their money, and who believed idealism could make money.

And we got results.

Step by step, common stock share by common stock share, we lined up the group of investors that would fund the pilot. Because we did not take any broadcaster or corporate money, we retained complete control of the project. We could pack our bags, hit the road, and start turning dream into reality . . .

Of course, I had no idea that embarking on this pilgrimage, and working with one's mother, could lead to a lot of blood and guts (not to mention lawsuits, fugitives, parasites, and the conundrum of what to do When Good Divas Go Bad). That said, through it all, the blood was mostly menstrual and the guts were only occasionally the gory entrails kind. I was naïve and idealistic. But, as Helen Keller said (in a phrase that became the footer of our business plan), "Life is a daring adventure, or nothing."

Sky Dancer

ADVENTURE DIVAS

PARADOX FOUND

—

We do not have the right, in the name of social justice,
to bore people to death.

—ASSATA SHAKUR,
BLACK PANTHER IN EXILE
IN CUBA

insert the latch into the metal buckle, pull the strap low and tight across my lap, and am scribbling notes on a slightly waxy barf bag when two white guys approach down the aisle. One is a collared priest and the other, big-bellied and teetering on the last rungs of middle age, carries a blue gym bag emblazoned with CIA in gold letters. They plunk themselves down on either side of me.

Flanked by paradox.

The Cubana Airlines Yak-42, a Soviet-built plane bound for Havana, looks as if it got left in for a few extra tumble cycles. The plane's interior is a chamber of chaos: broken seat belts and floppy chairs. Disconcerting smokelike vapors billow around my feet.

The threadbare burgundy fabric itches. I shift and try to look demure. Why would a priest be on a flight to one of the last communist (as in, aggressively secular) strongholds in this part of the world? And why would *anyone* sling a CIA gym bag?

The Spy turns to me and offers intelligence. "Don't worry. The vapor is normal. These old Russkie air conditioners aren't what they used to be."

"Oh . . . okay." I respond with a half-smile, leaving only an infinitesimal crack in the door of airplane social etiquette. The Spy slams his foot in the door and is off: "First time? Traveling without your husband?" The only thing I fear more than sitting next to the CIA when trying to sneak into a country and avoid getting busted for violating the Trading with the Enemy Act (which holds a penalty of up to ten years in prison) is sitting next to a lonely person on an airplane. I have no problem with loners. I just don't like being pinned between one of them and . . . God. Don't know whether I'd burn faster in Langley or Hell, but I've challenged their respective moral codes enough to ignite on contact.

"Reagan gave me this gym bag in 1985," the Spy rattles on, "and I've been to a cocktail party or two with Castro," he adds casually. Sounds like an oxymoronic social gathering to me.

Luckily, the Spy is mostly interested in hearing himself talk, so there is no pressure to explain my own presence on this flight. Just as well. With no visa and several thousand dollars strapped to my body, I might raise suspicion. My hand brushes over the important bulges: cash and passport. Ordinarily I list these as the only two essentials for a journey, but this time the list has lengthened considerably to include two cinematographers, a load of 16mm film, a sound person, and—my mother. A hurricane delayed us in Cancún but eventually we made it onto this flight, where we are now scattered about the plane in single seats. We are finally on our way to film the pilot episode for *Adventure Divas*. I wonder if my colleagues are as nervous as I am.

We tried to go legally. Really we did.

For months we begged and pleaded and touted our professional stripes, but no one would grant us the journalist credentials we were after. We had not foreseen the antipathy, or, in some cases, simple apathy, of the U.S. government and the Cuban Interests Section (Cuba's officiate in lieu of an embassy).

Fruitless pandering to bureaucrats left us desperate and defiant. "We've got to go guerrilla, through Mexico," I eventually concluded to Jeannie.

"Yep. No choice," she'd agreed.

Deciding to go on the sly raised a new set of anxieties. Would we piss off our hard-won investors? (Would we tell them?) Would we get sent upriver or fined into bankruptcy? Would our film get confiscated on our return to the United States?

A host of stressors have replaced the damn-the-torpedoes hubris that accompanied the early, blushing days of our endeavor. I jot *"Can adventure really be institutionalized?"* onto the barf bag.

Now and then, throughout the Spy's monologue and my internal mantra of worry, I turn to God, not as my savior, but because I cannot believe he has poured himself a tumbler of Johnnie Walker Red from his shoulder bag and is settling in to the latest issue of *Vanity Fair*.

Three aisles ahead are two men I recognize from the Cancún airport, where we waited out the hurricane. When I saw the long fishing rods wedged among their luggage at the airport, I began to eavesdrop: "Yeah, you won't believe it. They're plentiful and beautiful," the guy with the comb-over said to his friend in the Rangers cap. "A girl so hot she wouldn't look twice at you in the States is all over you like a fly on shit in Cuba."

Fly on shit, indeed. These guys are not going to Cuba to angle for fish, but for women who, for access to dollars and excitement, hook up with foreign men.

The in-flight purgatory thankfully ends when the Yak, rattling like a crate-ful of kindling, hits the tarmac at José Martí Airport. I walk down a rickety metal gangway that leads into the grays and blacks of night. The tinny taste of fear spreads through my mouth and catapults me behind several iron curtains, and four decades back in time. Outlines of soulless post-Stalinist buildings stretch out ahead. I feel like I just drank a whole pot of coffee.

I drift along a wave of muted, slurry Spanish, into a customs line. All five of us—the crew—are scattered about in different lines, warily making eye contact. My line moves and I shuffle forward, repeating to myself the six most important words of the shoot: *No estampa mi pasaporte por favor.* Three months of intensive Spanish back in Seattle and these are the only words that matter now. A Cuban stamp would raise the ire of U.S. customs officials on reentry to the United States, and the entire game might be up.

Scenes from *Midnight Express* flit through my consciousness as I step up to the counter. The forbidden is seductive from afar, but when you get right down to it, it's spooky.

"No estampa mi pasaporte por favor," I say, tentatively, to the customs official, whose downcast face is in the shadow of harsh fluorescent lights. He has dark hair and the moody, bored look hardwired into the DNA of customs guys the world over.

His brown eyes flick to meet mine, and he stifles a little laugh.

I can't tell if it's my bad Spanish or just a friendly *duh-you-have-an-American-passport-so-of-course-I won't-stamp-it* chuckle. Either way, I glide through customs unscathed and unstamped, and quickly pass my duffle through a boxy gray X-ray machine that looks old enough to have been used by Lenin himself.

I walk out of the José Martí terminal into the humid, windy evening, high on the razor-sharp awareness that there is no safety net. One by one my colleagues clear customs and meet me on the other side. Seasoned Cubaphile Pam Yates, later dubbed "Encyclopedia Pam" for her vast knowledge of this country, unshoulders her sound equipment bag and flips her long, dark hair into a ponytail. New York–based cinematographer Cheryl Dunn steps up wearing a smile and a charcoal-colored retro raincoat and has her hand-cranked Beaulieu camera tucked under her arm. Seattle-based cameraman Paul Mailman, low-key and talented, gently sets down a giant silver equipment box and runs his hand through a thick crop of what could be Latin hair. Jeannie comes through last, the thrill of having made it over this first hurdle evident in the bounce in her sneakered step. Excitement has won over fatigue and we revel in our success, and in that scary, wonderful state of no return. We are smoke jumpers behind the fire lines; Sally Ride breaching the atmosphere; a teenager who just got laid.

Just then a five-foot six-inch gringa with blue eyes, brownish-blond hair, and a personality I'd come to identify as Woodstock warmth and Harvard brains walks up to us. I know immediately that it is Catherine Murphy.

"Buenas, como están?" she says with the lilt of a *compañera.* "It's so nice to meet you in person."

Catherine is the rare American who has lived in Cuba for years, and is, as of this moment, our new best friend. We met her through Global Exchange, an organization that fosters cross-cultural communication and leads tours from the United States to other countries—especially those with whom the United States has "complicated" relationships. Catherine has provided a font of information throughout a series of crackling international calls routed through Mexico City (U.S. phone companies cannot do business with Cuba).

When making a TV show abroad, it is imperative to join forces with someone fluent in the language, as well as in the business of getting things done.

Negotiator. Point person. Translator. Person who knows what restaurant serves after midnight, what palms might need greasing, and how to find unfindable people. These are just some of the roles of this critical crew member called, in television's to-the-point vernacular, a "fixer." Catherine, our fixer, is relaxed and moves fluidly in her loose cotton pants and long-sleeved blue shirt. She was raised by her Cuban grandmother in Northern California, and has been living in Cuba for the past several years studying the country's world-renowned organic farming program.

"Over here," says Catherine, who has arranged for a rattling blue '58 Chevy to take us to our hotel. "We'll have to avoid certain streets because of the flooding," she says. The storm that grounded us in Cancún hit Havana with a vengeance. We drive down the Avenida de Rancho Boyeros, alive this warm blustery night with shadowy American autos from the forties and fifties, and with East German motorcycles, but mostly with bicycles. When the Soviet Union collapsed and Cuba lost its chief economic sponsor in 1989, gas became a rare commodity. With that, Castro led the Cuban people in a reverse technological revolution by importing 200,000 bicycles from China: thus, the "bicycle revolution."

"When the Special Period disappears we mustn't abandon this wonderful custom," Castro told his people, using the spin-doctored term for the post-Soviet era. The evaporation of the Soviets' annual six billion dollars of support and the continuing U.S. economic embargo has created a vicious economic double whammy for the people of Cuba.

There are few streetlights this late at night in Havana and vehicles appear as silhouettes, dodging into and out of recognition. We pass by the Plaza de la Revolución and a five-story metal image of Che Guevara—beret tipped, chin jutted—is ablaze on the side of the Ministry of the Interior building.

"Because of the energy crisis," Catherine says, nodding toward the monument, "it's only lit up on Saturday nights."

I look at Che, the Jack Kerouac of Marxists. "It's really important that we get the real story, not the party line," I say to Catherine, anticipating the interviews in the days to come and revealing my strange mix of compassion and wariness about Cuba.

For most of my life, Cuba has been an enigmatic pinko blip on my radar, and Fidel an aging revolutionary stuck in a fatigued fashion rut. But stories of a country with a spirit far from the dour lockstep reality one might expect from a communist outpost were seeping out, and captured my attention. The economic embargo had become a de facto information embargo and it seemed time to explore what lay behind one of the last tinfoil curtains. Witnessing revolution in action (and Cuba's—in theory, anyway—is still going on) spoke to the Adventure Divas ethos. A major goal of Castro's socialist revolution was to liberate the poor and uneducated from the dire conditions created by a U.S.-backed dictator. And to liberate the poor and uneducated is to transform women's lives. "Cuba's perfect. It's political and sexy—good for TV, right? And it's only ninety miles away, so flights will be cheap," I had said, lobbying Jeannie some months ago. "Yeah, ninety miles of political minefields," Jeannie had responded, correctly anticipating our battles to come.

The stakes had been raised, and a sense of urgency created, when we decided to make the pilot without the support of a broadcaster—all of whom had warned us away from Cuba. Now we have no choice but to get the story right, and my comments to Catherine reflect my slightly paranoid determination to do so.

"You know," Catherine responds calmly, gently setting me straight, the light of Che now just a dull flicker behind us, "some Americans think that if you come to Cuba and Cubans complain, that is the real story, and if Cubans don't complain, then that's the party line. Neither is fair. Life in Cuba is a very complex reality with hardship and with a lot of really beautiful, inspiring aspects as well."

Certainly the hardship is evident. Havana looks war-torn, but here it is decay, rather than violence, that is the nemesis. Much of Havana was built with armadas of money that flowed through the city from the Americas in the 1600s and 1700s. Havana's access to transient cash continued through the 1940s and '50s, often controlled by the American Mafia. At the time, Cuba was a playground for Americans with a penchant for dancing girls and casinos. Wealthy Cubans, along with their money, began to flee Cuba in 1959, when Castro's nationalist revolution prevailed, and the exodus quickened over the next handful of years as Castro began to show his communist colors.

I try to lean out the window of the car for my first, forbidden glimpses of Havana, but I'm jabbed by the dozen wads of twenty-dollar bills that are strapped with duct tape all over my body. We are officially *not here,* so we can't exactly write a traveler's check or whip out a Gold Card. I look arthritic and feel like a coke dealer.

Twenty minutes later we are at the front desk of a modest deco hotel in La Habana Vieja. I pull two twenty-dollar bills from our finite cache, and hand them to the concierge. "Doesn't feel like trading with the enemy," I whisper to Jeannie, as he smiles warmly at me and hands over three skeleton keys attached to pieces of chestnut wood bearing numbers.

"No going back now," she says. "This is it."

Paul yawns big, and we can all relate to his exhaustion.

A rooster's optimistic crow quickly followed by a belligerent truck muffler rouse me at seven the next morning. I am fully clothed, spread-eagled on the center of a concave bed, my open mouth pressed flush against the pilled, off-white cotton bedspread. My feet and five hundred dollars in cash are in my still-laced Georgia boots.

I slowly roll over, torso followed by reluctant limbs. I open my eyes and see Jeannie, who is sitting cross-legged on the other bed, glasses perched on the end of her small nose, writing on a yellow legal pad with a black felt-tip pen. This *has* been a drastic career change, I think, anticipating a first day on the road with my mother, and for the first time *truly* panicking. I have been going through a rebellious "my mother, myself" phase and lately when I look down at my thighs, I see *her* thighs, and thus my future, and the whole thing creeps me out. Could I really *work* with my mother? I shook off the dust of my suburban youth at seventeen and never looked back. Is this foolish? Will I live to regret it? Will we fail? Will she tell me to comb my hair?

I take off my boots and begin peeling apart fermented twenties and eating chocolate-covered coffee beans brought from Seattle, while she fastidiously makes lists.

We are both exhausted and our duffles have exploded on the black-and-white tiled floor of our plain but spacious room. We are all doubled up in hotel rooms for the night to accommodate our shoestring budget. Nobody wanted to room with me and Jeannie because we are "production"—the people who troubleshoot, grovel, manipulate, take calls at all hours, and generally don't sleep because if something goes wrong it's *our* asses on the line. But in our case, it is not only our asses, but our funding, professional reputations, and thirty-year mother-daughter relationship. (As the youngest of her four kids, I feel both responsible for her happiness and unable to resist piercing it once in a while.) Mutual respect has meant that we have worked well together in recent months, but moments of free-floating *fray* do occur and our handling of boundary issues is spotty. Occasionally, we spiral.

"I can't believe you let the film stock get X-rayed at the airport," I say, slightly huffy, flopping onto the bed.

"Look, I had no choice," she says. "At least it wasn't one of the Soviet machines. They're powerful, and we'd be in real trouble."

"And what about the ship's captain we want to interview in Santiago? We've got to confirm that. You were supposed to have confirmed that weeks ago," I say, unleashing my anxieties on her in an adolescent tone that would be absent if we were not genetically bound.

But—

Uh—you said—

Ohhh, I can't stand when you—

Hun-neee.

Mu-thurr!!

The conversation spins, down, down, down into a soupy X-chromosomal morass of guilt, confusion, blame—and ends with both of us in tears. Then, the final, devastating twist of the butter knife comes: "You may not realize this until I'm *dead*," my mother says *sotto voce*, "but I love you."

We both splash our faces with cold water. Mom hands me a towel. We leave our room to go meet the crew for breakfast. People often ask what it is like to work with one's mother. I think of this moment before simply answering, "Really great."

It is difficult to convey. The best thing about working with your mother is that you know, on a deep level, that someone always has your back. But you also feel, on an equally deep level, that someone is always *on* your back.

Cheryl and I take off after breakfast to explore the neighborhood around our hotel while the others prepare the gear and make production arrangements. On last night's drive to the hotel some "bad neighborhood" radar was going off, but in the light of a Caribbean morning Havana feels transformed. The crumbling Spanish colonial mansions are opulence in decay. We walk down narrow streets lined with stone buildings colored in a varied palette of chipped mustards, dusty corals, and chalky sea-foam green. My middle-class American brain thinks *Urban Outfitters wet dream* but knows the living conditions for most Cubans are anything but stylish. Music wafts out from behind clean, taut laundry that gently dances on drying lines strung between the wrought-iron balconies of La Habana Vieja.

Cheryl and I are the youngest of our crew, that is, the only ones who weren't alive to hide under school desks during the Cuban Missile Crisis. We met last year covering a Snowboarding for Breast Cancer event in Lake Tahoe. Cheryl's mission in Cuba is to capture "atmosphere," the spaces between the words that often tell the real story. I watch her swing her hand-cranked Beaulieu camera with athleticism and grace, her celluloid soaking up the gritty textures of Havana. She shoots from the hip, literally, and ends up dancing with her subjects as often as filming them.

"Lots of arches, but none of them golden," I say to Cheryl, noticing the Spanish architecture and the dearth of fast food. Seattle, with its social reserve and pandemic of Starbucks, feels like a stark contrast.

"Yeah, it's weird," she says. "Less than a hundred miles from the U.S. and no neon, no commercialism."

Decades into the revolution and the U.S. economic embargo, Cuba is one of the few countries in the world not drowned in consumer culture or subject to the whims of international capital. Certainly the Cuban people are suffering from economic deprivation, and the middle-aged revolution is in need of more than retooling, but there is something unique, if not honorable, about a country that has never been pushed around by the IMF or given a high school contract to Coca-Cola in exchange for a blackboard.

Cheryl and I have wandered far from our hotel, lured along like Hansel and Gretel by a photogenic trail of political propaganda that is splashed along sides of buildings and across billboards, which effectively replaces advertising: LA REVOLUCIÓN! CHE VIVE!

"Let's shoot that one," I say to Cheryl, pointing at a giant billboard with a cartoon figure of a wizened Uncle Sam, in an oversized red, white, and blue top hat, being yelled at by cartoon Cuban revolutionaries from across a body of water: MR. IMPERIALIST WE HAVE NO FEAR OF YOU! the rebels proclaim in giant red letters.

Images of the dashing Argentine revolutionary Che Guevara gaze intently over public squares and he is lionized on every peso. He was intelligent, sensitive, literary—or so the legend goes.

"In an easier time, Che would have definitely been a fly fisher," I say.

"Muy guapo," says Cheryl, panning slowly across a twelve-square-foot silhouette of his image painted on a cement wall. *Live* Che was pivotal in the revolution that freed Cuba from the grip of President Batista, "Mr. Imperialist's" Cuban puppet of the 1950s. *Dead* Che's martyr status (he was executed by U.S.-trained and -armed Bolivian counterinsurgency forces) has been leveraged for four decades by Fidel Castro in order to forward his own ideas, and to cement his power.

Fidel Castro's own image is not prominently displayed, yet *el Jefe* is omnipresent, like oxygen: all around, influencing everything, but invisible (except when delivering one of his epic speeches on state television).

Castro has done many unforgivable things. His ongoing persecution of artists and political dissidents, internment of gays and lesbians, and failure to make good on his promise of many years ago to hold free elections are just a few among them. But part of me has to tip my hat to this rare political leader who can elude the CIA's exploding cigars and poison pens (a couple of the Agency's more entertaining assassination attempts) and flip the birdie at Uncle Sam for forty years and running.

Cheryl has her lens trained on a strong, curvy woman who is striding by in a red, white, and blue Lycra jumpsuit. "Women really *own* their butts here," I observe as the woman turns down another street. Just then, a young man walks up to speak to us.

"De donde eres? Canadá? Inglaterra?" he inquires.

"Los Estados Unidos," Cheryl responds cautiously. He is only mildly surprised, and is very friendly. "The bar where Hemingway drank mojitos every afternoon is right around the corner," he says with a smile, switching to English.

Hemingway. Thus, the Fidel-Che-Ernest trio of Cuba's male cultural icons is complete. But just as Libya is not "one man in a desert," as the saying goes, Cuba is not three men and a cigar. We are more interested in finding our own brand of icon. "We want to interview women who are passionate, visionary, and independent—you know, *divas,*" I explain. The man backs away slowly, smiling kindly, and walks off.

On Day Three, dawn cracks hazy over Havana's Malecón waterfront and I no longer think I can see Florida.

"We've got to get something in the can," says Jeannie, sipping a coffee, ever sensitive to our abbreviated schedule. She's right: We have to make an hour-long documentary in nine days with a paltry ten hours of film (all we could afford). We lined up some interviews from the United States, but our production schedule isn't complete and we're prepared to lean on serendipity to fill in the gaps. That is why Cheryl and I hit the street and join in a local stickball game happening in a nearby vacant lot, where chunky remnants of a building from an era past mark the bases. Baseball is probably our respective countries' most profound common love, and the easy way these boys are playing confirms that the sport is not a new love to this culture. While Cheryl bats a double, I chat up twelve-year-old Oscar. "What's happening around Havana? *¿Hay música? ¿Fiestas?*" Oscar bunts at a rock with his bat, sending the stone zinging into what was once a load-bearing wall. He says his cousin said he knows someone who knows someone who said that there's a girl rap group called Instinto performing in a "basement" near Revolution Square in a little while. "Basement" doesn't sound promising but "girl" and "rap" and "revolution" do.

"Yeah, I know of Instinto," says Catherine, when I ask her. "Definitely worth checking out. They're one of only a few female rap groups in Cuba."

We grab our gear, pile into a '57 Bel Air hardtop taxi (or so says Paul, breathlessly), and are unloaded twenty minutes later near a massive statue of José Martí. Revolution Square is home to a slew of ministry buildings in all shades of gray, the requisite Che mural, the Comite Central of the Communist Party, and all the offices where Fidel and his ministers work. In short, we are inside the Beltway, madly running toward a basement full of rappers.

The basement is in fact an underground club (my bad translation) called Café Cantante, which is underneath the National Theatre. In the afternoons it opens to alternative youth bands. We pay our five pesos and descend into the darkness. We are immediately enveloped in a womb pulsing with teenagers and twentysomethings, showing considerable skin. The place is absolutely in blossom—pheromones zinging between people and off walls with an abandon that only takes place below the Tropic of Cancer. The fourteen-year-old girl in her first tube top, working the brand-new goods, epitomizes the high-pitched atmosphere. It is dark, which sucks for filming purposes and sends Paul into a funk. Yet when Instinto takes the stage they light up the dingy space. Talent. Voice. Belly. Booty. Confidence. In a word, divas.

Each member of the trio takes turns rapping front and center while the other two support. The skinny lead singer wears flowing loose cream pants and a snug-fitting halter top. The muscular girl with the black cap has on a brown silk collared shirt with a single critical button done under her strong, round breasts. The third performer, in tight jeans, a tan T-shirt, and sneakers, moves like magic under a jubilant cascade of long corn-rowed hair. But what they wear is quickly eclipsed by their more forceful elements of style.

> Come on, get closer
> I don't want to shock you
> I want to rap you close
> There is no wizard here
> What I do is art

(It works much better in Spanish, when it all rhymes and there's lots of body language involved.)

After ninety sweaty minutes, Instinto climbs off stage and Catherine and I walk up to their lead singer, Iramis. "We'd love to arrange an interview and performance somewhere with better light. Are you interested?"

"Sin problema. Estaremos encantados. Pues, ¿de donde son ustedes? Yo tengo un primo en Miami," Iramis responds, looking at me. ("No problem. We'd be delighted. Hey, where are you from? I have a cousin in Miami.")

Two hours later, Janet, Iramis, and Dori meet us at a cobblestone square and, with three unified claps of their hands, begin an a cappella street performance that would have MTV execs drooling.

Instinto creates its beat, covers ground, and conveys a message, with a groove so deep it looks accidental. They glide across the square, taking turns sidling up to the lens, delivering a booty politic, and backing one another up.

Mid-performance, a nearby grammar school lets out, and little girls and boys in red school outfits organically merge into the scene. We keep shooting. Instinto's *oomph* washes over the kids, who start doing their best to emulate them. Now, smooth, grown-up hips move in fluid rotation, next to tiny bodies that throw their whole selves into the effort.

Instinto performs three nearly flawless takes for us and in between each we talk about what fuels their music, and the effect they have. In broken Spanish, I ask the obvious. "*¿Hay instinto en su música?*" Is there instinct in your music?

"There is sooo much. Too much. Everything we do, we do with instinct. Everything comes out very fluent," says Iramis, "very, very spontaneously."

"We are like a vitamin for other young women," adds Janet (pronounced *yan-nay*).

"We are seen as a symbol of courage, because rap is a genre that is almost always about protest. So we are different from other women's groups in Cuba, which are mostly salsa, and they don't have the flexibility to say what we say in our music. We are proud of that," she concludes, chin up, smiling at her colleagues.

Wobbly antennas atop high-rises may have yielded the first sounds of hijacked rap from the shores of Miami, but Afro-Cuban rhythms, identity politics, and local realities were quickly infused to make a distinctly Cuban art form. Rap has become a vehicle to express frustration about poverty, racism, and the daily challenges of living in contemporary Cuba.

"We take the North American influences of hip-hop, soul, and rap and put it together with our roots, which are salsa, rubancora, rumba. Then we sing— we have these three beautiful voices, no?" She grins. "—and say what we want to say."

> Word is we're smooth as wine.
> We are instinct personified.
> Rap is my addiction,
> To deny the affliction of prejudice.
> Yes, this music has more Americana flavor,
> But it's made by my people and me.
> We mix and we conquer.
> We do it for you.

My rhythm is smooth.

My group is smooth.

My wine is red.

Instinto brings it all to you.

Satisfied with our footage, we sit with Instinto on a stone stoop, drinking flat soda, watching children of all shades play in their clean, worn clothes. A couple nuzzles in front of a brown building across the street. A smiling man sways his hips as he perches his baby on the hood of his old blue De Soto. He is holding her arms in the air, and teaching her to dance. Relaxed couples bike by us—girls on handlebars, boys peddling—and the light turns from rich yellow to rose to hazy burgundy, a muted rainbow that works in sync with the colors of the buildings. A man and woman lock eyes ever so briefly as they pass each other on the street. Both look back.

At the risk of trading on certain Latin stereotypes, I'll say that sensuality is a food group here. Cuba feels intrinsically *sexy,* in the best sense of the word. There is a particular self-possession that shows itself in everything from a glance during a salsa move, to the deliberate stir of a mojito, to the steady gait of a cane cutter making toward the fields.

From what I've witnessed, checking one another out is normal, and it goes both ways between men and women. The streets are filled with lingering, un-self-conscious head-to-toe-to-head-again appreciations that begin and end with eye contact. This is a bit of a shock to my system, as Seattle is the home of loose-layered fleece and Nordic reserve. A Cuban "appreciation" in Seattle would probably result in a restraining order.

Two women, both in tight red pants, are walking toward us. One wears a tight lime-green halter top, the other a white sleeveless blouse. I am starting to discern a certain dignity, a two-thousand-calorie richness with which Cuban women move through space. Both have a magic, invisible string connecting their well-postured shoulders and fully possessed, proud, round buttocks. I wonder if booty consciousness suggests an alternative seat of power here in Cuba and, if less impacted by the shame and insults imparted by consumer cultures that employ the female body primarily as a marketing tool, women here experience a healthier delight in the sensuality of life—in other words, are better set up to "own it." As the two women pass by I see they are carrying a white sheet cake on a piece of cardboard.

As we pack up, Janet tells us they will create a rap for us to use in the show, and Catherine agrees to mail the song to us after our departure. We will use their rap to mimic a classic device in Cuban films in which an omniscient singing narrator tells the stories of the characters in the film. Rap has the ability to tell many stories, and theirs will help create the TV parable of our cross-island road trip. "Great job," I say to Paul, who has had to maneuver almost as deftly as Instinto (and do so backward) in order to film them. I turn to wave as we are about to leave and see Iramis snapping her fingers, teaching a little girl in a white cotton shirt and red skirt a particular hip-born move.

We speed across town to see Lizette Vila. Paul is getting whiplash admiring the old cars that weave through the potholed streets. *"Qué bonita,"* he muses as we idle next to a fifties-era black Chevy at a stop sign. These old cars are painstakingly preserved and have been maintained through decades of extremely limited resources. They're very valuable to their owners as taxis, which provide access to tourist dollars.

We arrive in Vedado, a beautiful neighborhood filled with mansions built in the teens and the twenties, and now the center of Havana. We pull up in front of a magnificent Spanish colonial mansion—once a rich guy's house but now the headquarters of the Federation of Cuban Women (FMC). The rich guy is probably in Miami with his bag packed, ready to return to this grandeur the moment Castro dies. That will be an interesting knock at the door.

Catherine hands the driver a dollar. *"Muchisimas gracias,"* she says.

Having sat in a fair share of dismal basement offices with putty-colored carpet and pressboard furniture usually missing a leg—that is, the typical "women's organization" office in the United States—I find the marble and swank of the Federation of Cuban Women refreshing. The federation, a nongovernmental organization to which most women in the country belong, was created by Castro right after the revolution to defend Cuban women legally, socially, economically, and culturally. Castro officially criticized the macho ideal (which saw women at home and inferior) because it was at odds with the society he was trying to create—a socialist society in which all people work to-gether to create political and economic quality. It's ironic that in the most deadlocked years between the United States and Cuba, the seventies, both countries endeavored to make significant feminist strides. Cuba worked from the top down, implementing policies and laws to institutionalize equality. The United States, working from the bottom up, was abuzz with consciousness-raising groups but failed to pass the Equal Rights Amendment.

Lizette Vila shares the values of the FMC and has created what seems to be the Cuban version of Adventure Divas. We have landed an interview under the guise of covering her show and getting some interview leads, but Lizette her-self has a reputation as a *pistola,* whose frankness sears through rhetoric, polit-ical or otherwise. She is a honcho in the government-controlled television association and represents Cuba on the international stage. In a nation where no women worked in television and film before 1960, Lizette has now made her mark as the president of the Cuban Association of Cine, Radio, and Television; a prolific producer; and the creator of *Te Cuentan las Estrellas* ("The Stars Will Tell You"). Despite its soap-opera title, the show is about the achievements of take-no-crap Cuban women from all walks of life who, by ex-ample, inspire others.

Lizette arrives solo yet enters the room with the g-force of a person with an entourage. A blur of energy in a bright pink silk shirt and scarf, she plants a kiss on each of my cheeks. *"Bienvenido mi amor, mi amor,"* she says dramati-cally, her short brown hair perfectly framing her face.

I give her the calcium pills we brought from the States at her request. The embargo and the country's general economic disarray have left medicines and vitamins in short supply. *"Gracias, mi amor,"* she says.

We sit in the windy, sun-dappled courtyard of the mansion. In Spanish, with Catherine translating, she explains her TV show.

"A housewife—a star; a scientist—a star; an athlete—a star. But the con-cept of 'star' is about the light she radiates, the space she fills. How can I tell you . . . the environment she illuminates," she emphasizes with a smile, as a thick band of sunlight washes across her face in uncanny timing. "It is with this vision that the program was created," she says.

"How does that go down with men?"

"I have received criticism from men, even from intellectuals who work in my field. They don't understand. Some people think that feminism is 'anti-men,' but that simply isn't true. Cuban machismo is special. I call it 'Machismo-Leninismo,' " she declares with a laugh, playing off Cuba's Marxism-Leninism, an equally powerful institution.

While she's speaking, Lizette's arms and hands move in front of her face, as if molding the ideas in front of her.

"I think it's terrible," she adds, jutting a shoulder forward and raising her eyebrows, "because you can say that feminism has a philosophical current—it is full of ideas, aspirations, tendencies. But machismo, *es nada!*" she says with a wave of her hand, as if swatting away empty ideas.

"Machismo has never hurt me. I have prepared for that story, you know what I mean? Machismo is just an awful thing, absurd, uncultured, indecent—I mean, who can defend such an idea? But those are things that culturally take many years to change, and are sociocultural, historical phenomena."

Castro's revolution allowed women, even poor women, access to education and health care and routes besides prostitution out of poverty. That is the upside. The downside is that while the ladies may have equal rights on the books, and now comprise 50 percent of professionals (and might even have mansions for offices), that equality often does not translate into day-to-day reality. There are socks to be washed (by hand, in the developing world) and children to care for, and it's women who get saddled with the entire domestic burden. In short, cultural traditions, such as machismo, often trump official edicts.

"Do you ever feel embattled? Tired?" I ask Lizette.

"We Cubans live in terms of comedy or, rather, in those elements of laughter and sadness which are magnified by the current situation," she says, referring to the Special Period. "Humor is central to the Cuban sense of resistance. My god! The way we laugh about things. If you are able to resolve things with a certain sense of humor, *chica!*" she says with a Latina flourish of the hand, "that is the most important thing in life. Yes?"

Lizette articulates something I've been sensing but couldn't put my finger on: a sort of Cuban duality. There is real struggle, but a joie de vivre appears to win out. And enlisting humor and love as allies seems to be part of the recipe. Bus drivers hug their passengers regularly. Couples nudge and smooch in public like puppies at play. Music and cake are as much staples of the Cuban diet as rice and beans.

"Life in this country is very intense and people have a strong desire to live and accomplish many things," Lizette continues. "Maybe I am exaggerating, but this is what I feel happening. I feel so happy. I feel . . ."

Her eyes get glassy; she looks up and composes her thought.

"I don't know, like a missionary."

She wipes a tear of pure, unadulterated emotion.

I am agog. And hoping like hell our film roll doesn't run out. This is a coup—to have your subject actually cry on camera is akin to getting to the scene of the crime when there is still blood on the street. ("If she cries, it flies" and "If it bleeds, it leads.") But mostly I am surprised because she is among the most powerful people in Cuba, a player in the government, and she has the self-assuredness to cry on camera.

"I am very passionate. I enjoy emotions very much. The good ones and sometimes the bad ones too," she continues, brushing away a tear without stopping her train of thought. "But what I say to you, I say from my soul. Truly."

Unapologetically passionate, Lizette is revolutionizing Cuban television and changing the system from within. I leave the headquarters of the Federation of Cuban Women with fewer calcium pills, a satchel full of diva leads, and a reminder that emotion is an undervalued source of power.

We spend the first half of the following day in the countryside outside Havana shooting b-roll. *B-roll* is a term for a collection of pretty or illustrative pictures used to glue together the storyline in a film or television show; visual support for a described action or idea. Plus, whenever someone coughs or swears or says something uninteresting in an interview we can simply "cut to b-roll" to cover up the edit of the offensive or dull moment. B-roll is another thing, like Instinto's rap, that we are collecting in our bag of tricks that will enable us to take big, messy, wonderful meandering epics (a.k.a., life) and reduce them all to a snazzy little story: TV.

Afterward we speed back to Havana on the country's biggest highway in a white rental van, running late to meet with filmmaker Gloria Rolando. She has been on our list ever since we read on the Web a speech she gave at a black women writer's conference.

*Many of our ancestors shed their tears, but many others never shed
theirs because they converted those tears into rage, into rebellion and
history. . . . Oral literature, the personal histories of our people,
are the obligatory reference to penetrate into this universe of the
collective memory.*

I respect this independent filmmaker's commitment to leveraging personal histories for political change, and I am particularly interested in that she explicitly explores race in her work. The party line is that racism doesn't exist in Castro's Cuba, and certainly Cuba has less racism than a generation ago, but the realities of race and racism here are complex. As Instinto singer Dori said when talking with the writer Margo Olavarria, "I am Cuban. I am black, very black, but my grandmother was Filipina and my grandfather was Catalan. I have a whole world in me."

By the time we find Gloria's building in the Chinatown district of Havana, we are three hours late. We stuff ourselves into an elevator the size of an airplane lavatory, punch 3, and ascend in pitch black to the filmmaker's apartment. The lift grinds to a halt and with a flip from the other side, a diamond-shaped window appears, revealing a living space, some sort of schnauzer mix yapping furiously, and a smiling Gloria Rolando.

"¡Hola, bienvenidos!" She ushers us in, and we move from the dark into the small, tidy apartment. A shaft of fast-fading natural light pours over her tiny balcony and illuminates a rocking chair. Gloria is wearing a bright floral do-rag, a deep-gold cotton sweater, and dangling African earrings that dance with every welcoming kiss bestowed on our group.

Gloria wants to show me the house where she grew up, so after the greetings we clamber back into Havana's old stone streets for a "walk and talk." We dodge carts and playing children on a narrow street in Chinatown. When interviewing Cubans all you have to say is *"¿Como estás?"* and the floodgates open. Gloria is no exception. Speaking in English, with the slurred charm of the Cuban accent, she tours me around her childhood neighborhood. "I love Cuba very much. I grew up in Chinatown. In Havana we had a big community of Chinese people. I grew up between black people and Spanish, and Chinese, and Jews. This is Cuba: many people and only one people," she says, guiding us to the right, down a narrow street. Gloria points to a dilapidated façade of what must once have been a spectacular building, with high rectangular windows topped by arched portals. Only now there is no glass, just spaces roughly filled by plywood. Gloria nods toward the first floor. "That was our home. My sister and I were right there when a huge explosion shattered the glass above us."

That blast was Gloria's first taste of the revolution that would eventually reshape her homeland, and her life. With the forced end of the Batista regime, and the social and educational reforms that emerged under Castro, Gloria was able to accomplish what was previously unthinkable for an impoverished black Cuban. She earned a graduate degree from the University of Havana, and became a working filmmaker.

Unlike Lizette Vila, who works within state-sponsored TV, Gloria is an independent filmmaker. In her work she explicitly explores race through preserving the images and heritage of the African diaspora—the loose community of people throughout the Americas whose ancestors were brought here as slaves.

Several of Gloria's best-known documentaries have explored the religion of Santería, a faith that emerged from the collision of the West African Yoruba religion with the Catholicism that slaves encountered in the New World. Forced to convert by their masters, Yoruban slaves continued to worship the guardian spirits, or orishas, of their native religion, but hid them behind the façade of Catholic saints. A similar process took place throughout the Caribbean, giving rise, for example, to the Haitian practice of voodoo.

"When you grow up living in this kind of neighborhood, you see images of Santería. It was normal for me to listen to the language of the drums; to see altars with many flowers—with Catholic images but also special devotion to orishas like Ochún, Changó, and Obatala." I figure this religious activity must have been somewhat clandestine, because when Gloria was a kid the government's ban on religion was strictly enforced. These days, things have loosened up.

Back in her apartment, Gloria pops one of her films into an old video player and shows me an excerpt. In it a possessed, sweaty, shirtless man is circled by dancing worshippers and repeatedly beats a broad machete into the stony ground. Edited into the scene are shots of an actor playing the part of Oggun, the god of iron, war, and labor, doing pretty much the same thing. She shows me another, more ethereal scene, in which a drop-dead-gorgeous woman in a flowing yellow dress moves sensuously through a swamp.

"Ochún," Gloria says, as if this explains it all.

At this point, my head is chock-full of new information. I have no way to process these unfamiliar words and images. Clearly I must learn more about Santería if I plan to properly reflect Cuba in this show.

Gloria gets up to stop the VCR and tells me that she recently founded an organization called Imagenes del Caribe (Images of the Caribbean) in order to "do things her way" and pursue topics that most compel her, whether or not she has institutional support. Sounds familiar.

"Since I took the decision to direct my own documentaries, my own films, I didn't stop because I don't have resources. I can't wait; I don't have the *right* to wait. I don't *want* to wait," she says with loads of conviction in her round chestnut eyes. "And for that reason, the struggle is part of my life."

Cuba's shattered economy creates a difficult climate in which to make films. Plus, artistic freedom under Castro, a topic Gloria declines to discuss with me, complicates matters even further. While the revolution helped Gloria get an education, I can only guess that it's also responsible for restricting her expression.

As media makers in the United States, I suppose we do not risk being charged as political dissidents, but the fact that all our major media outlets are owned by a handful of corporations (PBS being an exception) acts as its own unique form of censorship. An independent filmmaker might be able to scrape together the money to create a film, but if she or he is iced out of distribution outlets due to a topic that challenges the agenda of the corporate parent company—or simply because the topic is not commercial enough—isn't this too a kind of cultural censorship?

"Are there ways in which struggle has actually helped you?" I ask Gloria, noting that the word *struggle* has come up frequently in my short time here.

"Struggle is everything for me," she responds. "Everything. You need to *attack* the realities; you need to, you know, to be strong. Of course I cry—I am a human being also—and I have to sacrifice many things in my personal life. But I think that is a way I could express my love," she says.

Pfffft.

Shit. The interview comes to an abrupt halt. Our only lightbulb has burned out on cue (and it's not like we can hustle down to Wal-Mart for another). The orishas are telling us something. But I am frustrated. It is nine o'clock at night and Gloria is leaving town in the morning, so there is no way to continue our interview. We are left with love.

The love *thing* still lingers the next morning, when we set out on a cross-country road trip to do more interviews. I don't completely understand the largesse in Gloria's use of the word. I assume love, as Gloria expressed it, means love of her people and her heritage. Her work celebrates and memorializes a culture ravaged by slavery. Capturing Afro-Cuban art and achievements, and reflecting it back to the people and to the larger culture, is how she expresses her love.

James Baldwin said, "Love takes off the masks that we fear we cannot live without and know we cannot live within. I use the word not merely in the personal sense but as a state of being or a state of grace—not in the infantile American sense of being made happy but in the tough and universal sense of quest and daring and growth."

But this kind of love still feels remote to me. My understanding is more in keeping with *Life After God* author Douglas Coupland's musing on suburban youth: "I think the price we paid for our golden life was an inability to fully believe in love; instead we gained an irony that scorched everything it touched and I wonder if this irony is the price we paid for the loss of God."

I look out the window at sugarcane fields zipping by, wondering how—*if*—one can muddle together irony, politics, and love, and end up with something like a refreshing mojito (and not blue Kool-Aid).

I'm intrigued by some of the tools the people we've met so far wield in their struggle to realize their passions and politics: emotion, booty, love. Unusual for a place usually defined by its identity as a pinko outpost and a revolutionary state. Perhaps there is a new kind of pink think brewing.

Poets, of course, are the natural peddlers of love. Poets are the ones who distill life's giant je ne sais quoi down to a pot of sweet nectar. So, it is a poet who we are on our way to see. Early on, Catherine tipped us off to Carilda Oliver

Labra, and since then we have noticed her poetry in the country's ubiquitous bookstalls. (As an editor on the lam, I appreciate this reflection of one of the revolution's successes: Cuba's 98 percent literacy rate.) Labra is the author of many volumes of award-winning poetry. Her first collection, *Preludo lírico* ("Lyric Prelude"), launched her career. In 1950, she won the National Prize of Poetry for her book *Al sur de mi garganta* ("To the South of My Throat"). She took considerable flak in the forties and fifties for the steamy content of some of her work. Her collection *Memoria de la fiebre* ("Memory of Fever") sealed her reputation as an "erotic" writer, and for a time her work was banned. But now, with age and increased government tolerance, she has morphed from scandalous hellion into Cuban national treasure.

Three hours after leaving Havana we arrive at the town of Matanzas, a port city filled with faded austerity that feels relatively provincial after five days in the hustle of Havana. In the early 1800s, booming with wealth from the slave and sugar trades, Matanzas became a cultural Mecca, and it remains so today. The town is often called "the Athens of Cuba," as it is, and has been, home to many artists, poets, and writers. Labra's house, small and elegant, oozes intellectual richness and sturdy supple-leather good taste. We walk in and the living room buzzes with a small group of women who seem like handlers and serve us slices of yellow sponge cake with sugary white frosting. The women are fawning and doting and, well, handling. (I later find out they are representatives of the Federation of Cuban Women and are here to help host us.)

Carilda is wearing a white linen blazer and has big red hair. She is as creased and sparkly and attractive as her home, but the most striking thing about her is that she is in a hurry.

She is the first person I've met in Cuba who is *actually* in a hurry.

Carilda is on her way to give a reading in a nearby town but still has us in for a quick visit. Her forty-year-old husband breezes through, evidence that Carilda must still have the erotic spark that created so many poems. She is eighty-one.

Despite her standing in Cuba, Carilda is little known in the United States and only one of her volumes has been translated into English. A by-product of the economic embargo has been a forty-year constipation in the exchange of art between our countries. Most of the books available in the United States are by Cubans who left with the revolution, or their offspring, the first-generation

Cuban Americans. When it comes to music—rap, say—illegal satellite dishes and bootleg tapes spread that Americana through Cuba. Black-market poetry has yet to become in vogue, even though many organizations, such as Global Exchange, have worked hard over the years to encourage a steady trickle of cultural to-and-fro. There is also the challenge of being published in her own country, not for lack of popularity but, rather, for lack of paper on which to print the books.

The Cuban Missile Crisis of 1962 inspired Carilda to write "Declaration of Love."

I ask if I'm wise
when I awaken
the danger between his thighs
or if I'm wrong
when my kisses prepare only a trench
in his throat

I know that war is probable
especially today
because a red geranium has blossomed open.

Please don't point your weapons
at the sky:
the sparrows are terrorized,
and it's springtime,
it's raining,
the meadows are ruminating.
Please, you'll melt the moon, only night-light of the poor.

It's not that I'm afraid,
or a coward.
I'd do everything for my homeland;
but don't argue so much over your nuclear missiles,
because something horrible is happening
and I haven't had time enough to love.

"My best poetry," she has said, "is that which expresses erotic love, but also the love between a man and a woman integrated with universal love. For me, poetry does many things: tells truth, creates and praises beauty, contributes to the intellectual pleasure, allows us to unite with all humankind as it denounces injustice and captures the essence of life."

"What are you going to read us?" I ask Carilda, as we set up our cameras to film her recitation of something I hope will be erotic. I despise how older women are always depicted as asexual, and this could be an opportunity to transmit a new image. Carilda slowly leans back into her antique wooden chair, crosses one bare calf over the other, and tells me, in a voice that galavants between lilt and husk, "When my grandmother came from Spain, married with her three little children, one of which was my mother, she brought a little bit of Spanish soil in a bag. Once in a while, I would see my grandmother taking the little bag that contained the soil and smelling it, thinking 'Ay, my Spanish land, I will never go back to Spain,' with such nostalgia and sadness. Then, when my mother went into exile, I remember that she searched for a little bag and filled it with Cuban soil. When I visited her for the first time in the United States, she said to me, 'Didn't you bring a little bit of soil?' I said, 'But you already have a little bit of soil.' She said, 'Yes, but it has lost the scent of Cuba.'

"My mother never could come back to Cuba and that is why this poem was born," she tells me as she settles even farther into the leather and begins to recite.

> when my grandmother came she brought a bit of spanish soil
> when my mother left, she took a bit of cuban soil
> i will carry no bit of homeland
> i want it all above my grave.

So it is love of homeland, rather than love of the loins, that she chooses to share with us. But I'm beginning to think, in this place of wide-ranging eros, they're not so far apart.

That night I'm lying on a bed blotting my forehead with a wet hand towel. The weather delays that left us waiting in Cancún ended up shaving three days off our shoot, resulting in frustratingly brief visits with the divas. "It's like McDiva Nuggets! The storm just killed us," I say to Jeannie privately in our Matanzas hotel room. My complaint elicits an apology; and thus, I have prodded Jeannie into violating one of the ten commandments of second-wave feminism: Thou shalt not apologize for the weather.

The exigencies of making television (tight budgets, head-spinning schedules, neurotic behavior, and finicky equipment) seem at direct odds with creating heady, well-simmered storytelling. What I'd initially hoped would be in-depth biographies are more likely to end up being snapshots of women whose lives allegorically represent their country. I silently vow that future shoots will be at least three weeks long, rather than nine days.

"Maybe this is why television is so often banal—no time for depth?" I ask Jeannie.

"It's all about getting the nutgrab," she says while logging film cans.

"The nutgrab?" I ask, assuming it's a term left over from her days reporting from the locker room.

"Yeah, the important core of the story, succinctly put."

"Nutgrab," I repeat, liking it. Strange. But Mom must know what she's talking about.

The phrase, which I would immediately latch onto for the duration, reminds me of my grandmother. Some years ago when I told my grandmother about a struggle to hammer a meandering college essay into shape, she responded with a parable.

"Hol, did you ever hear the one about the fifth-grade teacher who was tired and wanted some quiet time so she assigned her students to write a story she thought was impossible?"

"No," I said, wondering what this had to do with the significance of windows in Willa Cather's *My Ántonia*.

"She sent them all back to their desks with the admonishment that all good stories must have Religion, Royalty, Sex, and Mystery. She figured she'd have a good two hours to read her Harlequin," said my grandmother. "Well, little Suzy walked up to her desk one minute later, said she was finished, and handed her the paper.

" 'That's impossible,' " said the teacher, who looked down and read the story:

" *'My god, said the Princess, I'm pregnant, whodunit?'* "

Somehow, remembering my dead grandmother's joke gives me hope about our show, and perhaps even about television. The "biggest ideas" can be delivered in the smallest packages. Poetry is one case in point. Maybe TV is another. My new-medium learning curve continues. I look over at my hardworking colleague. Jeannie. My mother. It occurs to me how much easier it has always been for me to take lessons from my grandmother, rather than from her. Taking a cue from Santería, I wonder if ancestor worship can start before the ancestor's death.

Jeannie and I sit together, compiling our notes, making plans, and her thighs don't even cross my mind.

Leaving Matanzas, heading into the countryside, we discover that people needing rides stand about on corners to flag down vehicles. Or, for a peso or two, they pack into the beds of old Russian trucks belching black smoke. Our white van pulls out into the fray, pointing toward Santiago de Cuba. For the next several hours we join a light, varied trickle of tractors, scooters, pedestrians, and buses that make their way through the quiet Cuban countryside. Scrubby grass fields give way to endless lush cane farms, which give way to the occasional small town, always friendly seeming in their washed-out pastels and the Caribbean light. Then finally we close in on the place where we'll stay for the night, Lake Zaza. From what I've read, Zaza will provide a bit of respite. I want to shore up morale in the group and rejuvenate my creative brain cells for the final few days of the shoot. And—

"Take a right here," I say, directing us off the main highway. Jeannie looks at me suspiciously; I'm usually wholly uninvested in where we stay.

I pump my arm in a casting motion. She nods knowingly.

We pull up in front of a duck-hunting lodge that abuts the lake, and proves charming, in a Stephen King–ish kind of way. Grand. Empty. Currently not a hot destination point. But the prospect of fishing isn't quite the same without my own rod, which I had mistakenly left at home.

"It's like if you didn't have your trusty Zeiss wide angle," I say to Cheryl, trying to make her understand.

"Whatever," the Manhattanite responds, her eyes wandering off toward the deserted lobby, which has an empty, thatched-roof open-air bar attached to it.

As a child, I chased trout in the soggy Northwest with my grandmother, who, in a single gesture, could teach me how to thread worms on hooks *and* view the world with political precision. Balancing *The New York Times* on her knees, she would soak up the latest minutiae of the Watergate scandal while awaiting her prey.

"Take that, Tricky Dick!" she'd suddenly bellow, rocking boats a mile away as she reeled in her hapless catch.

Cuba is surrounded by water, but I'd noticed that, strangely, fish was never on the menu in restaurants there. Another paradox. Encyclopedia Pam filled in the gaps over dinner at the duck lodge.

"When the Soviets crumbled and famine became a real threat here, Fidel tried to offset the cultural bias against fish eating by handing out fish recipes on slips of paper wherever he went. Didn't work," she said, forking the last bit of chicken on her plate.

If Cubans don't eat much fish, and don't fish for sport, then Cuba's fish have been growing fat for the past three decades! This is an interesting and providential side effect of Cuba's political isolation.

I read aloud a quote from a copy of the *Cuba Handbook:* " 'Cuba is a sleeper with freshwater lakes and lagoons that almost *boil* with tarpon, bone-fish, snook and bass.' "

Cheryl doesn't get it. "What exactly is the attraction? The five A.M. call time? The icy waters? The slime?"

I try to explain rhythm and meter, and angling's strangely satisfying intel-lectual depths. Boldly, I wax poetic about the scrumptious pandemonium of the take, the sloughing away of worldly troubles, the high of tangoing with a primeval creature from another world.

"I respect your passion, but I don't get it," she says with a touch of pity. "And what," she adds, "is a snook?"

After dinner I lobby Cheryl hard. She is behind the bar learning how to make mojitos from the bartender, José. ("The art is in the muddling," he tells her.) Every other crew member has flatly refused to go fishing with me, opting instead for our first, and as it would turn out, only, chance at a seven-hour night of sleep.

"Listen to this," I say, again quoting from the *Cuba Handbook.* " 'Americans fishing home waters apparently catch, on average, only one bass every two days

Snook

of fishing. During those same two days a bass fisherman at Lake Zaza might expect to catch a hundred bass of incredible quality. *There's a good chance that a world-record bass exists in Cuba'* " (emphasis mine).

"Okay," she agrees, tossing a final sprig of mint into the tall, thin glass. "I'll go fishing with you, but I'm just going to watch, and maybe film."

At four-thirty the following morning I knock on her door. I have few reservations about stealing these few hours from the shoot, while the others rest up. Fishing is never the wrong thing to do. On a tip from last night's bartender, we go in search of a man named Cheo.

Cheo is old and weatherworn, and his gait transmits a blend of resignation and dignity. The romantic in me calls up the image of Hemingway's Santiago in *The Old Man and the Sea,* even though it turns out Cheo has a boat with a motor (not a skiff with a sail), works with a rod (not a long line), and, most notably, is fishing for a living (not living for a fish). But, like Santiago, Cheo speaks not a word of English.

As dawn breaks we motor out for the morning bite. Apricot skies. Calm waters. Mimed promises of *bigguns.* I steel myself for the massive lure that will replace my usual tiny nymph, and signal a fall from grace. Cheo pulls a six-inch-long, obscenely pink, and very barbed rubber worm out of the pocket of his windbreaker and dangles it in front of our faces. Cheryl blanches.

The effete fly fisher in me is horrified—but my inner angler, bred on midwestern bass and candy-striped Mepps, screams out in carnal joy: *These fish must be enormous!*

I start casting.

Cheryl finesses her cameras like a musician before the big performance, then stops, as if she's received a signal from some cosmic maestro.

The sun breaches the horizon and the water gently laps against the boat. Time is metered by the reel's muted clicks. We do not comment, or joke. For at least twelve minutes not a note of irony passes between us. It is one thing to know you can work together, another to know you can be silent together, and, perhaps most profoundly, to know you can fish together.

Strangely, I feel as if the entire shoot—the nerve-wracking entry into the country, the inspiring but frustratingly brief interviews, the ubiquitous cakes, and the crew camaraderie—have led up to this moment. Cheryl, and this time-worn ritual, remind me that work and play *can* be one and the same, and the global pilgrimage regains focus.

But sincerity hits the floorboards as my forearm plunges toward the bottom of the boat, and the moment collapses in on itself. A tank of a fish, but a fighter nonetheless, the *pez* I've hooked has me waltzing around the tiny boat, Cheo following my lead, net in hand. As the battle rages, Cheo manages to light a cigar, and a boatful of loud Italians motors over to our honey hole. Cheryl bobs and weaves, filming and giggling. "Yee haw," she yells from behind her Beaulieu. Cheo puffs calmly, but my endorphins surge with each and every centimeter of line the fish takes. *Chica* against fish. A beating sun. The mighty swordfish (well, I mean bass). A duel of passion, nobility, and, increasingly, ego. And then, to put it in spare Hemingwayesque prose—

I win.

My forearm bows as I haul in the glistening large-mouthed bass and I am breathless at the size. The fish tops twelve pounds, dwarfing the measly bass of my youth. *"¡Buena pescadora!"* Cheo yells out from one corner of the boat; and Cheryl just keeps repeating with city-girl awe, "Oh my god. Oh my god. Oh my god."

On the way back to the lodge, just as the last traces of morning light's magic veil burn off, Cheryl says, "It's not about the fish . . . is it?"

I smile and respond, "Whatever."

The piercing blue sky is crystal clear the next day when we make a pit stop in Camagüey. A young, green-clad Cuban militiaman gives a friendly nod and shifts his big Kalashnikov to the other hip. I've seen less "military presence" in Cuba than I expected. Years of ingesting media images of revolutionaries in fatigues must have colored my expectations. On my first day here, this guy with a gun may have raised my fear hackles. But the warmth and openness we've experienced from Cubans makes it difficult to be intimidated. I nod back to the soldier and climb past him to the top of the pyramid-shaped Che Guevara memorial. A giant bronze statue of Che (also with oversized weaponry) stands on top of the structure. I have been reading Che's *Motorcycle Diaries* and may have to rethink my earlier theory that he would have become a fly fisher. The privileged cult would have surely chafed at his Marxist tendencies. After all, fly fishers spend hours watching bugs, tying flies, wandering in the poetic bliss of nature, all in an effort to catch a fish and then *let it go*. In short, we have *time* and we *don't need to eat it*. A perfectly acceptable definition of privilege.

Born into a (slightly on the wane) bourgeois family, Dr. Ernesto "Che" Guevara hopped on the back of a motorcycle in 1953 and became an original "doctors without borders" type, with Karl Marx in his hip pocket. While he would go on to lead an important social revolution, those youthful South American road trips seemed as much loaded with machismo as with budding revolutionary altruism.

Catherine knows a more contemporary revolutionary whom I find at least as compelling: Assata Shakur. Since deciding on Cuba as our first location, we have been trying to connect with Shakur, a former Black Panther who has been a fugitive in exile in Cuba since the late 1980s. Catherine had said over the phone that meeting Assata was a very delicate matter, and later, on the ground in Cuba, no doubt tired of my pestering, she had asked me to stop agitating. "I've passed several messages but haven't heard back. You need to know that when dealing with Cuba it's best to never expect and never push. And then it will happen."

But I have been anxious for the show to depict another sort of revolutionary. I did stop pushing, but I never stopped expecting, and Jeannie and I were thrilled yesterday when Catherine told us she had received word that Shakur had agreed to an interview.

Formerly JoAnne Chesimard, Assata Shakur was among the Black Panthers who were hunted down by J. Edgar Hoover's illegal COINTELPRO organization in the 1960s and '70s. The Panthers, once a symbol of the 1960s

Black Power, are now a scattered group, some dead, many in prison, others holding political office, and a few, apparently, living in Cuba. Assata Shakur was convicted of being an accomplice to murder and imprisoned in 1973 for her involvement in a New Jersey highway shootout that left a state patrolman and one of Shakur's companions dead. The trial was highly controversial, with physical evidence supporting Assata's claim of innocence. She escaped from prison in 1979, went underground, and then turned up in Cuba in 1984.

Castro has given asylum to Shakur and a handful of other Black Panther and Black Liberation Army members over the years. In a country refreshingly devoid of the culture of celebrity, except for the aura that cropped up around a few baseball players and heavily branded revolutionaries, Shakur has managed to become a star.

A high-ranking Panther, Assata was an activist for the rights of prisoners and welfare recipients. Since her arrest, she has become an icon, as highly regarded in certain circles as Malcolm X or Nelson Mandela.

I mull over whether fugitive status runs counter to diva status, but remain focused on Shakur's long-documented humane approach to politics and social justice that initially drew me to her story. She wrote: "I believe that there needs to be a constant campaign to educate people, sensitize people and analyze racism. The fight against racism always has two levels: the level of politics and policy, but also the level of individual consciousness."

Developing an inclusive awareness of the international community—thinking globally—is a key part of Assata's revolution. "It was clear to me that without a truly internationalist component nationalism was reactionary. . . . To me, it was extremely important for all the descendants of Africans everywhere on this planet to reverse the political, economic, psychological, and social patterns created by slavery and imperialism."

I nervously flip through my notebook while we wait, surrounded by lush tropical scenery, at an out-of-the-way, dollars-only black-market eatery called a *paladar*. Assata Shakur walks in, alone. She is striking. She is wearing a gold-patterned tunic over solid-gold-colored pants. An orange, black, and white African cloth rests across her shoulder. Long dreads and low dangly earrings frame a face not nearly revealing her fifty-plus years. She shakes all of our hands stiffly and says, "Hello, nice to meet you." She sets down her purse and seems on edge. She agreed to meet us on Catherine's endorsement, and because of my track record in socially conscious book publishing, but clearly she is ambivalent about exposure. Shakur has been deep underground and almost never grants interviews. We're keenly aware of what a coup this is.

Of course the tabloid reader in me wants to ask what kind of divine Houdini-ism enabled her to bust out of the maximum-security wing of a New Jersey prison. But I'm resigned to the fact that she won't rehash her political past with me.

Once I've explained the diva mission to her, Assata recalls for me her first impressions of Cuba. She seems to loosen up, now that she is sure that we are not here to attack.

"Everything was so green and alive," she says of her initial days in Cuba, then goes on to laughingly admit, "And, before I came, I thought everyone in Cuba would look just like Fidel Castro. I was expecting a magic-wand revolution—a perfect society—and it wasn't that. Women have made a lot of progress in Cuba and a lot of things that exist in the U.S.—battering and vicious attacks—you don't see in Cuba. You don't see that kind of violence and pain. But it's still very much a macho society and I've come to understand that it's a process. It's going to be a long struggle to get rid of that baggage."

I remember Lizette Vila talking about her struggle with machismo in the male-dominated TV industry. She used humor as an ally.

"How do you approach the struggle?" I ask.

"One of the things that has been especially good for me has been to broaden the idea of struggle. In the sixties there was this idea that we were supposed to be revolutionary—very serious," she says, making a mock grimace. "You were supposed to just talk *at* people, not *to* people. You know, so many people that I met in the sixties who were locked into that style of struggle are looking and saying, first of all, it was *boring*. You know? And we do not have a right, in the name of social justice, to bore people to death."

She pauses for a moment of consideration, then continues. "It's not fair to ignore people and say that you're struggling for people. We have a duty to make what we are doing a people activity, which means acting like people, which means being concerned about people, which means including children. I think that's one of the more important lessons that I've learned in my life."

I take from this that she means the Panthers' extremist language alienated many of the people they were attempting to liberate. The fight for social justice in the post–civil rights era meant working to solve the problems caused by a system of racist oppression: poverty, violence, lack of access to education, and hunger, among other issues. There was a disconnect between the needs of the many thousands of African Americans who were suffering due to oppression, and the Panthers' pumped-up rhetoric of radical nationalism and aggressive takeover.

"I'd come to see revolution as a process," she states near the end of her book *Assata*. Writing about herself as a newly minted revolutionary in the late 1960s, she says, "Back then, people used the word 'revolution' just because it sounded hep. Half the time what they were really talking about was change or some kind of vague progress. But the reality of achieving it seemed a long way off."

I ask Assata about fear. "I've only been here a week," I say, "and fears, or shadowy commie stereotypes I didn't even know I had, have completely fallen away."

"I had fears too, at first. But with time I learned about the Cuban character, and fear," Assata says. "In the United States there is a kind of reserve. People are isolated, separated, alienated. At first, I thought the Cubans were nosy—always asking if they could help and inviting me to this meal or that party. But then I realized they're simply not afraid to talk to each other. I always believed in a 'people society,' but my imagination never conceived that a society could produce people so unafraid of other people."

Fear keeps people in place, afraid of one another and afraid to connect. We all have fears but perhaps the trick is in what we (individuals, nations) *do* with that fear. Maybe the United States' imperialist tendencies grow out of fear— fear of "other" and fear of losing what Americans have. In Cuba, where people have very little, they are not so afraid. Is this a coincidence?

I am pelted by a strong vibe from Catherine that says that our audience is up.

I throw out one more question.

"What happened with the Pope thing?" I ask tentatively, knowing that New Jersey officials had written to the Pope before his late-nineties visit to Cuba and urged him to press Castro for Shakur's extradition. His Holiness declined.

"I guess he decided that God was not on the side of the New Jersey State Police."

There was speculation that the Pope's visit might have led to a thawing of U.S.-Cuba relations (making Cuba to Clinton what China was to Nixon).

However, on the Pope's first day in Cuba, all cameras and laptops fled north to D.C. as the story of our former president and his intern Ms. Lewinsky broke— trumping both God and Castro and featuring one naughty—and, ironically enough, Cuban—cigar.

No press coverage, no change.

Cheryl shoots a single still photo of Assata standing, looking straight down the lens, her earrings swaying ever so slightly in the Caribbean wind. After a gracious set of good-byes, she disappears around the corner of the stone fence that surrounds the *paladar.*

"This is gonna be like no travel show I've ever seen," Pam says, coiling up a power cord. She understands the political hurdles we may face if we include Assata in the show. To many Shakur is a visionary; to others, she's a fugitive cop killer. The latter identity might rankle television executives.

"What do you think will happen to Shakur when Castro dies, or the embargo comes down?" I ask Pam, knowing those are the only two things that protect Shakur.

"I don't know, but Castro will never give her up, embargo or not."

Back on the road, on our last leg to Santiago de Cuba, I can't stop thinking about something Assata said to me right before she disappeared around that corner. She told me that although she has lived in Cuba for nearly twenty years, she still never feels completely at home. As she said to Christian Parenti in an interview in *Z Magazine,* "Adjusting to exile is coming to grips with the fact that you may never go back to where you come from. The way I dealt with that, psychologically, was thinking about slavery. You know, a slave had to come to grips with the fact that 'I may never see Africa again . . . I'll be separated from people I love.' "

I suppose that is the lot of the exile. The notion of exile must loom large for Assata, and for Cuba itself. There are Cuban exiles in the United States (such as Carilda Oliver's family), and American exiles in Cuba (such as the Panthers). The ongoing repercussions of the slave trade and revolution- induced diasporas leave huge numbers of Cubans with the constant sense of being uprooted.

I can feel a new transitoriness growing within my own wandering soul, but my pilgrimage isn't *exile*. It's a choice. And therein lies the significant differ-ence: A pilgrim travels by choice, with a specific quest for meaning, and an ex-ile is pushed into motion by chance, disaster, crime, political upheaval, or the like. The voluntary voyage is about self-discovery and getting the prescription right on one's glasses. But as Erik Leed says in *Mind of the Traveler*, "The forced departure initiates a journey that is suffering or penance rather than a campaign or a voyage. Often one-way or endless journeys, they muddle rather than define the persona of the traveler."

In short, travelers can go home; exiles can't.

Only two precious days of shooting remain, so we bear down on Santiago de Cuba at seventy miles an hour—past sputtering scooters with live pigs strapped on back, past Soviet-built trucks loaded with canefield workers, and through the famous Sierra Maestra mountains, where Che and Fidel hid out and cultivated their revolution. We've been stopping periodically to hunt down phones to try to reach Cecelia Gomez, a ship's captain and potential diva who is said to base in the harbor of Santiago de Cuba. Only feet fill my boots now, and we are down to two slim wads of cash, one in my hip pocket, one in Jeannie's. Jeannie is chewing her nails. (Jeannie never chews her nails.) We're short on material and desperately need one more interview—and so far the captain is eluding us. We'll have to go down to the harbor and look for her in the morning. This late in the day, the docks would be deserted.

"Don't worry," Catherine says, as we're slowed, nearly to a halt, by a herd of goats crossing the street. Catherine repeats her "never push, never care, and then it will happen" advice, which I've come to believe contradicts 98 percent of television production behavior, but I try to make like a Cuban and give des-tiny some breathing room.

As has happened so many times in Cuba, we hear our destination before we see it. We drive into Santiago on an audible red carpet of jubilance and drumming and follow our ears down a tree-lined cobblestone street to cruise into the main square in town, Parque Céspedes (where Castro officially de-clared the revolution won). We chase the wafting sound through the fancy lobby of the whitewashed Hotel Casa Grande and up a dark staircase onto the hotel's rooftop. A half dozen shirtless men line one side of the rooftop, thumping the taut animal skin that stretches across the top of the three-foot-high *bata* drums. Women and men, in a series of advancing lines, their shoulders and bottoms moving in circles to the beat of the drums, are performing traditional Afro-Cuban dance in the balmy glow of a Caribbean dusk.

It turns out this is a rehearsal of Santiago's leading folkloric dance troupe, Katumba, and they are exercising the traditions of this province, whose people have the highest percentage of African blood anywhere in the country, largely due to agricultural sugar workers who came here in the thirties from Haiti and Jamaica.

I get nearer to the line of drummers and am amazed at how one man, using a drumstick in his right hand and only his bare left hand, can create such intense sound. In the Afro-Cuban religion of Santería, *bata* drums and the accumulated power of the spoken word are believed to play a key role in communicating with the pantheon of orishas who represent, and rule, every force of nature and humanity. Song, rhythm, ritual, repeated verse, and trance possession are ways in which to tap into what is said to be a very interactive and reciprocal relationship between people and deities.

Gloria Rolando's films featured the feverish dancing of possessed Santeros and Santeras, who are akin to priests and priestesses. But this performance makes me *feel* the presence of Santería in this culture, and lulls me into the incantatory power of drums and repeated verse. The sky over the roof deck is purple now, and the dancing slows along with the drumming. One by one, the women begin to fall out of line, and pull their sweats over their shorts. The men put on their shirts and the rehearsal is over.

We head downstairs for mojitos in the Casa Grande's lobby. As in so many developing countries, catering to First World tourists is a growing component of the economy in Cuba. Tourism brings hard currency as well as painful new developments. Hotel lobbies are filled with young Cuban women and men looking for foreigner dates. They are called *jiniteras* or *jiniteros;* the colloquial, all-purpose word is usually translated as "hustler," but literally means "jockey"—that is to say, a paid mount.

In the pre-revolutionary era, prostitution and domestic servitude were the only options for poor women. After Batista and the U.S. interests—including the Mafia—were gone, Cuba largely did away with prostitution. But with the rise in (and government encouragement of) tourism, and its attendant much-needed hard currency, the world's oldest profession is on the rise again. This hustling isn't *exactly* prostitution, but there is a clear quid pro quo at work. Hustling here is not about paying rent or scoring drugs, neither of which are huge factors in Cuba, but about procuring a big meal or a pair of shoes—things that require dollars, not pesos. The "tricking" may not be institutionalized in the way it is in, say, Asia and the United States, where women are peddled by pimps and/or traffickers. Here, children aren't for sale and the women are free agents, answering to and providing kickbacks to no one. Nonetheless, these are teenagers selling their bodies in part because of a disastrous economic climate; and these are grown-up, wealthy First World men happily taking advantage of the situation. The guys in this bar are on the same make as the "sportsmen" I first saw when we were en route to Cuba. Perhaps this is a negative aspect of Cuba's booty-owning sexiness. Foreigners come here and, with their pocketbooks and hypersexual voyeuristic lens, engage in the worst sort of objectification.

In addition to the *jinitera* scene (and sometimes integral to it), there are a dozen Hemingway look-alike wannabes. Pooch-bellied, gray-haired, mojito-swilling men sprinkle the bar.

We order a round, and try to film the *jinitera* activity. With each round of mojitos, Cheryl and I get bolder with our shooting; I shoot her doing a cartwheel or speaking to the camera and surreptitiously shift ten degrees right to capture a fifty-year-old German guy with his fourteen-year-old Afro-Cuban date. The girl is amused by our antics; the man, no doubt, hopes our "home video" does not show up in his hometown. "Does our insurance cover an angry john, busted?" I say to Jeannie facetiously, while changing tapes.

Yerba Buena and Havana Club go down like pure potential, and the carefree tune of "Guantanamera" dissolves all worries in the roomful of disturbing sexual politics. The evening devolves into a mojito fest, and the wee hours find us in a dance club, trying to salsa, digging deep for the booty liberation we first saw in Instinto, giving nary a thought to our cameras stacked in the corner like dead, forgotten fish.

Dawn brings a pounding head, my period, and a dissipated crew. We hail Mary and head for the dock where Captain Cecelia Gomez keeps her boat. We don't have an appointment but I am hoping we can just show up and find her. When we arrive at the harbor, the crew begins tinkering with their equipment and Jeannie and Catherine go to look for *café cubano*.

I shuffle off, heavy with post-party shame, to ask, ask, ask in hangover Spanish. A couple of grizzled boatmen are playing chess on the edge of the dock.

"*¿Conocen a la Capitana Cecelia Gomez?*" I ask. A fellow with a green cap points over his shoulder, out over the roiling Caribbean Sea, and says in Spanish, "Sorry honey, she's out for at least a week."

"*Gracias,*" I say, deflated, and walk over to sit on a cement seawall. I stare out at the ocean and attempt to pull myself together. I am panicked. I have no plan. I am worried that I'm losing the tenuous respect of the crew, who might smell a neophyte director and be wondering what the hell our next move is.

I'm cranky.

We missed our diva.

I have cramps, and it feels like the revolution has moved to my uterus.

I *hate* everybody.

I take three deep breaths, kick a chunk of mud out of the waffled sole of my boot, slide off the seawall, and walk slowly back toward the crew, lamenting the loss of Zen clarity I got from fishing that's now gone down the hormonal drain. What would a diva do? Where does a "creative" turn in the dark, stymied moments when the meter is ticking?

"We're going to church," I announce.

I first read about the nearby town of El Cobre in Hemingway's *Old Man and the Sea,* in which Santiago swears he'll make a pilgrimage to La Virgen de la Caridad del Cobre if he can just land the damn fish. Hemingway donated the Nobel Prize for Literature he won for that book to that very shrine.

We can see El Cobre's triple-domed church for the last three winding kilometers of the drive up to it. The church is nestled in the foothills of the Sierra Maestra, and pilgrims travel from all over Cuba, sometimes crawling for the final miles, to pay homage to the Virgin.

We walk into the dark, stone narthex. Every horizontal surface is filled with flickering votives, crinkled sepia photos of loved ones, military medals, and an extraordinary number of tiny boats. All are offerings, left with a prayer.

Talismans of spiritual grounding. The room is positively thick with the hopes, dreams, sadness, and potential of the Cuban people.

I sit on a stone bench to watch the pilgrims and lean my back against a cool wall. I send up a little prayer for us to meet another diva to complete the show, since we will not have the ship's captain we were counting on. I immediately flog myself for spiritual dilettantism (which probably nullifies the prayer before it's even reached the ozone layer). Then I mentally flog myself again for hijacking the prayer because there is, after all, the slight chance it would have worked. The self-flagellating tail chase comes to a halt when a gorgeous dark-haired girl in a white dress enters the church.

"She looks pretty young to be a bride," I whisper.

"It's her *quinceaños*—a fifteenth-birthday rite of passage that all girls in Latin America go through," Pam replies, characteristically informed. This ritual announces that the young ladies are on the market to be married. More social than religious, a *quinceaños* could be likened to a debutante ball in the United States—except that this Latin American tradition is much more widespread and culturally significant.

I'm not fond of dogma, be it religious or political, but I do yearn for ritual, which seems to be the common language of all spiritual quests. Jeannie sees me write down that last thought in my notebook, the contents of which will eventually be used to write a script for the documentary.

"Jeez, Holly, the only ritual you have is your morning coffee jag," she says with a laugh.

"And who's responsible for the fact that I was raised in a spiritual vacuum?" I whisper in retort.

"We wanted you to choose for yourself," she responds, which totally surprises me. My parents were both sportscasters and my dad is an ex–Chicago Bears football player. So Sundays were holy days in my family, but for NFL reasons. I assumed my parents just forgot about the God thing.

I continue to sweat rum in the corner of a rural Cuban church, wracked with cramps, arms loaded with film stock, whispering inappropriate personal baggage to my mother.

"Here they come," says Jeannie excitedly, "shhhh."

The girl is led by her mother up to the altar, and is presented to La Virgen de la Caridad del Cobre, Cuba's most sacred icon, also known as the Black Madonna. The icon is tiny. We are talking a nine-inch deity. But she's nothing short of the protectress of Cuba.

The Black Madonna is housed in a fittingly tiny glass cage and swathed in a glittery gold embroidered robe. A sparkly gold halo and crown, ten times the size of her head, top her off. My experience with Catholic iconography is mostly limited to giant suburban churches with giant crucified Jesuses (a suffering presence I've often felt steals from the joyous wedding ritual at hand). I like this better.

The church is dark and there is an entire *quinceañera* procession between the tiny Virgin and us. Paul has a challenge on his hands. "I cannot zoom in any closer," he says, a bit too loudly, when I nudge him to move in.

Legend has it that three young fishermen found the Black Madonna floating off Cuba's northeast coast in the Bay of Nipe around 1612. The Madonna apparently had a sign around her neck that said Yo soy la Virgen de la

Black Madonna

CARIDAD ("I am the Virgin of Charity"). There was a storm, the young men were about to capsize, they grabbed on to her (she was made of wood), and the rest is history.

The Black Madonna represents the melding of Catholicism and Santería. She is Catholic Cuba's patron saint of charity, and she parallels Santería's deity Ochún, that vibrant goddess of sensuality I first saw represented in Gloria's film. My eyes and mind linger on the small sparkling gold burst of energy that commands the room. This icon of faith, who is a draw and a comfort to so many, is complex and real: She is a vortex that represents the melding of Europe and Africa, lover and mother, saint and warrior. A powerful, biracial diva.

Back outside, Cheryl and I buy a Black Madonna tchotchke made out of scrap metal from a group of young entrepreneurs, and sit down across the street from a nearby schoolyard. The solace of church and a few ibuprofen have lifted my spirits considerably.

I reach in my canvas shoulder bag and take out Sky Dancer, our own lucky, nine-inch deity given to me by my friend Inga. The doll is quickly becoming the show's mascot and we hope to give her a cameo in every episode. Sky Dancer's tutu is a bit wrinkled but her blue wings and blue hair and brown skin sparkle with vitality. Cheryl and I walk across the street to launch her with some girls playing hopscotch in the schoolyard. I demonstrate how to pull the string out of her base and send her shooting into the air, arm-wings a-twirl. Cheryl manages the difficult task of capturing on film the doll flying through the air, as well as the laughter of the girls who are setting her off into the bright blue equatorial sky.

That evening, back in Santiago, we walk into a dollars-only *paladar.* We find a family of four half-watching a tiny black-and-white TV flickering one of *el Jefe*'s fist-waving speeches. The mother, in green housedress, stands and takes us to a windowless back room with two tiny wooden tables covered with red-checkered tablecloths. Over six plates of crispy fried chicken, fluffy white rice, and what might be a kilo of beans, we bat around ideas about how the show, in theory, might end now that we don't have the captain to sail off into the sunset.

The magic and challenge of both travel and documentary is that neither can be scripted. The story is built from the nuggets—or, nutgrabs, as Jeannie would say—that are revealed along the way.

I pass on the dessert of farm cheese and guava paste, excuse myself, and step outside to mull. I lean against a powder-blue cement wall. But an American can't loiter around urban Cuba very long without getting chatted up, and within two minutes a man named Pablo has introduced himself, in near-perfect English.

"We're a film crew, with nobody to film," I say, after the usual pleasantries. I tell him that our last contact has fallen through and that we're scrambling. We need one more woman, I tell him, to help bring Cuba's story to life. I jabber on about our visit to El Cobre, and he simply nods, not interrupting me. Then I pause. I hate it when people pour confessional minutiae onto strangers, and now I am doing it to this guy.

Then he turns to me and says, "Why don't you go see my godmother in Cardenas? She's a Santera."

A Yoruban high priestess! That's exactly *who we need to bring this show home.* I don't know who to thank. The Black Madonna? Sky Dancer? Or Pablo? I cover my bases and run back to the *paladar.* We drive all night, most of the way back to Havana, and reach Cardenas at dawn, just in time to be comforted by the roosters' first crows.

Cardenas is a town where horse-drawn carriages share the streets with Edsels. We wend our way through cobblestone labyrinths, and despite the all-nighter, I am tingling with the knowledge that this is where the show is supposed to end. Soon we find the Santera's home. Catherine and I bang on the giant, weather-worn wooden doors. On one a single rusty nail dangles a piece of paper with EMILIA 312 handwritten in black ink. The door opens slowly. Emilia Machado is very tall, and thin, and wears a purple floral dress and red and white dangly earrings. She has big, black, stiff hair with a few shocks of gray pulsing through it. We sent word asking if we could see her, so she is not surprised. We take in her simple home in a single glance: tile floors and stark white walls, a single bulb hanging from the ceiling. In the corner, an altar with only one identifiable item: a gun encrusted in some sort of molasses and twig recipe.

Note to self: Investigate priestess's handgun.

Emilia Machado was a Communist Party official for many years. "When I was twenty-five, I became very sick. Through that I discovered Santería," Emilia tells me of her change of life.

Illness, and a divine cure, led Emilia to leave her job as a party official to follow a life of devotion during an era when religion was banned. We have heard she was persecuted during that time, but this is not something she acknowledges.

"I have no contradiction between being a Santera and being a revolutionary," is all she says on the matter, and I steal a glance at the gun. Eight days ago I would have considered that a party line. But I'm developing a deeper understanding of how things live together here, and I remind myself that paradoxes seemingly contradict, but in reality express a truth.

Emilia walks toward an altar. Not the one with the gun, but a different one that features a red and white drum, a red crown with a line of seashells decorating its perimeter, and a red baseball bat. Of the baseball bat, she says: "Changó is a warrior who goes to battle. Instead of me going to battle, I give him the attribute—in the form of a bat—and let him do it for me."

Makes sense.

Every Santería worshipper has a guardian orisha. Emilia's is Changó. Changó's colors are red and white.

"I am the daughter of Changó. My religious name is Obbadele," she says.

"Changó was born with a crown. He is the only saint born with a crown and that is why they call him *Obba*—King," Emilia says, explaining the altar to me.

Emilia picks up an *ache,* a red and white gourd filled with seeds, and begins to shake it vigorously.

"You must call him with the *ache.* Everything you say to him, you say with the maraca, so that he will hear," she says as she shakes the maraca. "Changó gives his initiates the power of divination. Some people say this in jest, but it happens. His initiates are divine by nature."

"Do you have a goat?" Emilia asks me as she puts down the maraca.

"Uh, a goat? No, we don't have a goat," I say, looking at Catherine quizzically. Catherine explains that we have been invited to participate in a very secretive several-day-long ceremony that would include dancing, music, and trance possession. The ceremony would culminate in the sacrificial slaughter of the goat. Blood sacrifice is de rigueur for the more complex rituals and is the seminal act toward tapping into an individual's personal spiritual power, or *asé*.

We are once again bound by our schedule. I explain that we have a flight out of Havana in twenty-four hours. I don't explain that we are down to the lone crumpled Jackson in my pocket, with no way to get more cash. We could afford the goat—it's only a few dollars—but we cannot afford the time.

"Do you want me to call Changó?" Emilia asks.

I nod. Even though the Communist Party stopped peddling atheism in 1992 (and thus, ceasing to persecute religious practitioners), Santerían beliefs are well-kept secrets among the faithful. Cameras and recording devices are often forbidden during rituals, so I'm relieved she's willing to do this for us.

Emilia leads me by the hand over to the altar that sits in the corner of her front room (the one with the gun), which is now ringed by burning candles, wax seeping free-form onto her tile floors. Emilia begins a complicated ritual by blowing cigar smoke onto gourds with creaturelike faces. She salutes the ancestors and orishas and asks their permission to perform the divination. Ancestor worship is a way to connect with the wisdom and knowledge of the collective past via the power of our dead relatives. She tosses coconut rinds, and begins to divine.

"Lucumi, imbaye . . . bayen tunu, guabami gua . . . imbaye, bayen unig guabami gua."

Okay, here's what I know. This complex system of divination, *ifa,* is said to be a sort of cosmic Google search to provide a way into humankind's answers to fundamental questions. Put another way, through divination the will of the ancestors (wisdom, power) and the orishas (energy) is discerned. With the Santera (or Santero) as a go-between, a devotee asks questions and receives impartial answers, which lead the devotee to informed decisions and appropriate action. Fate is not set. Santería strikes me as an interactive faith, in which an individual wields a significant amount of power in destiny.

"Each of us is born with a path," Emilia says. "The goal is to travel it. Divination provides the roadmap to our potential."

"The Santera is the interpreter of the roadmap," whispers Catherine, who is translating.

Emilia is a "godmother" to dozens, like Pablo, who sent us to her. She has an essential role in the community as a sanctioned third party who protects the interests of the orisha, the community, and the devotee. (In this case, me.)

"Ay Eleggua! Here I am, I am your daughter to ask you five one three . . . in this day, what for? Imbaye, baye tuni five one six . . . happier than Lucumi, in-baye, bayen, oudule, Machado, to my father, to my brother, guabami gua, bayen, five three two."

Emilia is tossing coconut rinds and chanting and interpreting their omens and, apparently, receiving from them answers to yes-no questions. Despite the yes-no dichotomy, there is no concept of good versus evil in Santería; everything is seen in terms of fluctuating polarity. Shades of dark and light. All things are said to possess opposing yet complementary powers.

The scene is mesmerizing but wholly confusing. I feel like I'm being handed the funny underwear in the secret ceremonies of the Mormon Tabernacle without having even gotten the lesson about Joe and the Tablets. I feel slightly disingenuous dabbling in another's spirit world, but I'm completely drawn in.

What I *do* understand is that Emilia's beliefs combine divine direction and individual empowerment in a way that is refreshing, especially when set next to the lightning-bolt edicts of most orthodox religion. And her gutsy decision to deny the secular powers that be (in her case, the Communist Party) and devote herself to Santería, which led the way for a community to reclaim its original faith, defines courage. I admire anyone who lives in that squishy ether of faith; anyone who gives it up for the intangible.

Somewhere in all that divination is a conclusion. Emilia tells me, in sum, that I am on the right track, but that I've got a *looong* way to go. I choose to take that as both an affirmation and a warning about what lies ahead on the Adventure Divas path.

"Next time, the goat," she says quietly, and kisses me on the cheeks as we are leaving. I vaguely wonder what destiny could require blood sacrifice.

We pass a billboard of José Martí when we enter the airport that bears his name. Martí, a poet, nationalist, and martyr, wrote the "Fundamental and Secret Guidelines of the Cuban Revolutionary Party," although most of his prose was decidedly more flowery than that. His poetry speaks of the zeal of a free human spirit and the redemptive powers of love. Is the billboard an homage to Martí the nationalist or Martí the poet? Either way, it's an apt final image in this country where music, love, and magic sit right alongside ration cards and dark irony.

Caribbean energy and communist rigidity are certainly odd bedfellows, but Emilia Machado, and many of the people we met, seem to soften this giant paradox through spiritual grounding. And Gloria Rolando, the filmmaker back in Havana, crystalized this sentiment when I asked her what a diva was: "For me, a diva is not something that lives in the sky. It is a woman who lives on the earth. It is a woman who suffers, is a woman who dreams, is a woman who wants to struggle. If you ask me if I am a diva, I don't know; but I am a warrior. And the main quality of the diva-warrior is not to be scared of life. Not to be scared of the difficulties. Whether you have support or not, whether you have money or not, you need to have a spirit."

Sky Dancer is in my brown Filson shoulder bag as we approach the customs agent in Dallas International Airport, our entry point back into the United States. We push the seven carts of equipment and shot film up to him. I will myself to *not care*. The agent rolls his slightly bored eyes. I know without looking, but with mymothermyself sureness, that Jeannie is also holding her breath. The agent does not even ask where we have been, or what is in the massive pile of shiny metal boxes. He simply waves us through.

2

HEAD GAMES AND BOAR HUNTS

—

*Psychiatrists, politicians, tyrants are forever assuring us
that the wandering life is an aberrant form of behaviour;
a neurosis; a form of unfulfilled sexual longing;
a sickness which, in the interests of civilisation, must be
suppressed. . . . Yet, in the East, they still preserve the
once universal concept: that wandering re-establishes
the original harmony which once existed between man
and the universe.*

—BRUCE CHATWIN,
THE SONGLINES

am a voodoo doll for a sadistic nurse who is probably suffering from
Seasonal Affective Disorder (SAD), an affliction endemic to the United States'
Northwest and to certain Scandinavian countries. Forty degrees. A cold, re-
lentless drizzle has fallen for two months straight; the gray ceiling of the
Northwest is closing in like a dreaded inevitability. I am in the travel inocula-
tion ward of Group Health Cooperative and it is a dark February day in
Seattle. As the sixth silver needle plunges into my already throbbing arm, I
think, *Why am I doing this?*

Questions like this usually don't arise until I am two days from anywhere,
one Snickers bar left, trying to suction thick-as-syrup muddy river water
through a filter that falsely claims to remove all scents, tastes, protozoa, and

bacteria. But this time, the reservations have hit me in the jab lab. I've become a junkie, weak in the face of my drug: adventure.

Peg, the nurse, tosses her modified Dorothy Hamill haircut slightly before saying, with a titch of admonishment, "You've come in too late to be protected for dengue fever and Japanese encephalitis. Here are the malaria pills. They'll kill all your natural flora and fauna—"

"Um, *fauna?*" I gently interject, to no response.

"—so start taking acidophilus now. A small number of people get psychotic episodes from them, but I think you'll be fine."

"Most importantly," says Peg, unwrapping the final syringe, "if something goes very wrong, and things *break* or *tear* or get *severely punctured*"—she pauses and looks me in the eye—"beg for an air-evac with an IV. *Don't* get a transfusion."

"Have fun," she concludes cheerfully, throwing the used needle into a bin that somehow hermetically seals itself, combining *Andromeda Strain* style with HIV reality.

I tell myself it is Peg's job to overreact. She is, after all, wearing incredibly sensible shoes.

It all started with a phone call.

"'Allo there, Holly. Ian Cross from Pilot Productions 'ere," boomed a congenial Australian voice over the phone from London. "How'd you like to go talk to some headhunters for us, in Borneo? Yaaaaaeh."

Several months ago, Ian had read about *Adventure Divas* in *Blue: The Adventure Lifestyle* magazine, asked to see some tape, and then offered me work hosting some of the Lonely Planet and Globe Trekkers travel and trekking documentaries. In the cracks of time we weren't doing postproduction on the Cuba show (that frenetic phase of writing, editing, and penny-pinching that takes place after shoots), I'd crisscrossed the United States and done a dozen programs for Ian. On these shoots I'd received a vital crash course on how to make television *and* how to lasso charging cattle, evade a posse of pregnant tiger sharks, rapel down cliffs, sweat through a sundance, run class-five rapids, and milk everything from emotional moments to smelly goats to interviews. I'd been bit on, shit on, and hit on—all the while paying attention, and learning as much as possible about this new business. I'd asked for adventure and I'd gotten it; some days the new lifestyle teased out the fetal stirrings of my own inner diva; other days I just happily collected the paychecks that helped support my primary passion: Adventure Divas. On the Pilot programs, unlike the *Adventure Divas* series, my creative role was limited to being the on-air "talent," a role I had mixed feelings about. In any case, my publishing days were a quickly fading memory and I was now headlong into this new medium.

"This is the first episode in our new *Treks in a Wild World* series—all international," said Ian. "So it must be good; you gotta let it all hang out." He explained that the program would culminate in a hunt for a wild boar with the indigenous Penan people who lived in the deep interior of the jungle, and he asked about my aim with a poison blow dart. In addition to the Penan, he said, we would film at a longhouse with a river-dwelling Dayak tribe (former headhunters), and also report on the lives of the island's endangered orangutan population.

"Sure, I'll do it, Ian," I said confidently, though I wasn't so sure about my facility with a blow dart.

I was keen to continue to widen my global perspective, and had become nearly inured to my dog's lack of eye contact once the backpack got pulled out. My boyfriend's justifiable grumblings were hardly registering on my domestic Richter scale. All this made it a good time to leave, especially since the wait to find out the future of Adventure Divas had become excruciating.

"Taking off again?" asked Jeannie after I hung up the phone.

"Yep," I responded.

Jeannie and I were recently back from Alexandria, Virginia, where we'd met with Mary Jane McKinven, head of Science and Exploration at PBS. We'd sent her our Cuba pilot, and she had invited us to national headquarters. We were nervous and arrived one torturous hour early to the meeting, so as not to be late. We sat in the building's coffee shop, picking lint off of each other's blazers, trying to anticipate questions, and dreaming of the empire to come. At two minutes to two o'clock, we went upstairs and were admitted to a big, empty conference room. Mary Jane walked in, introduced herself, and sat down.

"Well," she said warmly, smiling from Jeannie to me, "this is one of the best presentations I've seen in my years at PBS. Tell me more."

Jeannie looked at me, her optimism now spliced with a bit of "I told you so."

We launched into our talking points and told Mary Jane of our ambitions—prime-time series commitment, Web real estate on pbs.org, marketing dollars—forgetting, in our zeal, that most groups requesting this kind of cash and commitment were large production companies with long track records, not a linty mother-daughter team.

We left encouraged but not greenlit.

Now, back in Seattle, we were in the waiting game. Would they buy the pilot? Would they commission the series?

At 4:30 A.M. I wrap Sky Dancer in a cheesy I CLIMBED THE GREAT WALL! T-shirt and wedge her in the side pocket of my gray backpack next to a dog-eared paperback edition of *The Year of Living Dangerously*. All-night bill-paying and packing sessions have become de rigeur on departure eve of these shoots. I wake up the Boyfriend: "Do you still want to come? Jeannie will be here in ten minutes. You don't have to," I offer.

"Is there coffee made?" he responds groggily.

Mom and the Boyfriend drive me to Sea-Tac Airport as pink takes hold of the Olympic Mountain range.

"Honey," she says, her voice concerned as she hugs me good-bye, "I know you found some sort of, of . . . deliverance in all that blood loss last time you were in the jungle, but please be extra careful this time. I'm worried. . . . And we don't have 'key man,' " she adds bluntly, switching from Mom back to Jeannie, and referencing our production insurance policy that doesn't cover loss of a critical employee.

The Boyfriend gives me a kiss and "that look," which says I-can't-believe-you-are-leaving-me-again-and-won't-nest-with-me-but-because-I-am-an-evolved-nineties-guy-I-will-support-you (at-least-when-other-people-are-around).

Now, dear reader, I know what you are thinking: "Two people drove you to the airport at five in the morning! You are loved! You are lucky!"

Point taken.

I am.

Truth is, I do feel slightly guilty about leaving Jeannie holding down the Diva enterprise, and the Boyfriend with the dog. But I also resent that guilt. Why is it that when Robert Redford–cum–Denys Finch Hatton flies away in the golden glow out in Africa, he is pursuing his destiny? And when I walk away I'm just a chick who's scared of commitment and on the run, who's weird for ignoring *Glamour* magazine's prediction of her eggs drying up?

Leaving is an underrated form of liberation.

Rarely in the books and movies of popular culture, much less in life, do we ladies get to go on a genuine non-male-identified adventure—and avoid punishment. Thelma and Louise, long touted as feminist adventurers—sheesh, well, they got theirs. The nutgrab: You have to be dead to be liberated. Part of the Adventure Divas' mission is to put new *real live* icons on the screen. Women who face challenge, gaze beyond their (possibly pierced) navels and white picket fences—and make it to the other side of the canyon. Xena, Warrior Princess, is an exception, if a fictional one. She travels the world with her best friend while slaying injustice. She doesn't even bother to have a home. It figures that one of TV's most divalicious characters also has superhuman powers and D-cups.

So despite my fear of becoming talent, of the twenty kinds of invertebrates that infest the jungles of Borneo, and of the Boyfriend, who is none too pleased that I am once again leaving, I am committed to this adventurous lifestyle. "It's in my job description," I now say with legitimacy, embracing the nomada growing within me.

The good-byes leave me feeling guilty, irritated, and thrilled to be escaping, even though, according to my understanding of the globe, I am being sent the wrong way. (Seattle to Borneo via London?) Details aside, my excitement ramps, and the tray table bows, when I plop down the research that the producer has sent. I HEAR YOU LIKE TO READ UP, says the hurriedly scrawled note attached to a six-inch-thick stack of paper.

I start highlighting: *The Malaysian jungles are some of the oldest undisturbed areas of rain forest in the world . . . existed for about 100 million years. . . . Orangutans are one of man's closest relatives and have proved highly intelligent. . . . Sarawak is one of the great battlefields between conservationists and timber merchants. . . . Ensure that you have a bag of tobacco leaf to rub on yourself to prevent leeches.*

I also learn that Borneo is the third largest island in the world (right behind New Guinea and Greenland) and is divvied up between Indonesia and Malaysia. The split is just one result of a long history of vying—by white rajahs and the British Empire, among others—for this island's rich natural resources, primarily oil, timber, pepper, and rubber. Sarawak and Sabah, the states where we are going, became part of the then-new country of Malaysia in 1963.

Ten hours after leaving Seattle, the plane noses down in Heathrow and my crew meets me on board. "How's my favorite Yank?" Georgie Burrell greets me with a thump on the back, and heaves her camera bag into the overhead. Georgie is a lanky, long-haired blond Londoner most often found in a T-shirt with a cig hanging out of the side of her mouth. For Pilot Productions and in the name of television, she and I have lashed together a survival lean-to and spent a long stranded night staving off a flash flood with our prayers, and hypothermia with the bubble wrap that protected her camera. We have rappelled down cliffs into raging rivers in the pitch black, and known the blue-green glare of more than one emergency room. Georgie is a tough girl whose only high-maintenance tic is her oft-stated declaration, "I don't do cold, *dahhllling*." Meaning, Georgie will only take international film shoots in locations between the latitudes of thirty-five degrees north and thirty-five degrees south. Cold will not be our nemesis on this shoot. We are headed for 115 degrees longitude, zero degrees latitude. Equatorial Borneo: red, hot, and wet. "Should be a piece of cake, this one," says Georgie. "What's a wee walk through the jungle?"

"Yeah," says red-haired, pale, and understated Scottish soundman John Burns, "and we've brought enough cigarettes to burn off every leech in the country." He holds up a carton of Silk Cut.

Eleven overpackaged meals, thirty-seven wet-naps, one flip-flopped magnetic field, and a day and a half after leaving Seattle, I've entered that jittery netherland in which the body's hardwiring goes color-blind; the red wires are wrapped up with the green, and the black one just dangles. The brain is completely flummoxed about what that black one is for. Hunger is a vague, tinny presence that cannot be sated. I look around at my fellow passengers and feel like my entire person is an appendix: irrelevant, useless, taking up space amid much more worthy organs.

We are on the sixth and last leg of the journey, closing in on Borneo—still in the air, mind you—and clearly I already have *circadian desynchronosis,* as my aerospace engineer brother Dan, the oldest of my siblings, explained it: jet lag. "Increase pressure in the nasopharynx by performing a Valsalva maneuver [read: hold your nose and blow]," he advised. "And don't worry about the gamma radiation on those international flights; the only place you really get zapped is over the poles, where there's less geomagnetic field to protect you. Equatorial area, you're fine—the field's pretty thick there," he said, earnestly.

The jungle appears fast and definitively, like spilled ink from a well. From up here it looks like a petri dish of mold. Dusty dark green, bumpy, with tiny creases and valleys and shadows. A patternless pattern of crumpled anarchy. Definitely alive.

Once we land at the tiny, humid airport, we look for the two people who will round out our team: Dutch producer Vanessa Boeye and British director Rik Lander, both of whom have been on the ground in Borneo for a week doing reconnaissance. Vanessa, blond, blue-eyed, tall, and willowy thin (and posh, I suspect, in spite of her casual travel attire), walks up as our pile of twelve aluminum boxes and backpacks appears on the back of a tractor. As the producer, part of Vanessa's job is to feed "the talent's" ego. In short, it is her place to tell me I look fabulous even when we are two weeks in the bush, *sans* shower, grimy with bat guano.

"Nice to meet you. You look like hell," she says cheerfully, with a British accent.

We're going to get along just fine.

We take over every socket in the lobby of our hotel in the small town of Limbang before setting off for the interior jungle. While the batteries charge, I wander outside the hotel and spot an Internet café, or more accurately, a tiny cinder-block room located behind two cows tied to a metal fence post leaning at forty-five degrees. WIDE WIRLD WEB RM1 TEA 2, reads the handwritten sign. I scuttle around the cows and log on to see if there's any word from Diva HQ.

TO: HOLLY
FROM: JEANNIE
SUBJECT: AIRDATE!

Hol—MJ called and PBS is buying the show! We did it. Looks like they are going to schedule Cuba to broadcast on a Monday night in prime time. They've asked us to take out your reference to menstruation in the narration "the revolution has moved to my uterus"; and they want you to add a reference to yourself as a "journalist" (more credibility, I guess). But those are the only changes—which MJ says is remarkable for a first submission. Unfortunately, they won't commit to the entire series until seeing how the pilot rates. She signs all her e-mails, "Onward!" I love that.

Jeannie/Mom

p.s. I was looking at your itinerary—why did you go through London? Isn't that the wrong way?

I return to the hotel, recharged by the exciting news from home. Our team gathers in the hotel lobby and we set out for the interior jungle of Sarawak. Our guide, Martin, is in his early twenties and has chestnut skin and jet-black hair. He is Dayak (the indigenous people of Borneo) and of the Iban tribe. Though he has taken ecotourists into the jungle before, I wonder if he understands the constant demands and challenges of a film crew.

The network of chunky, easy-moving, tea-colored rivers is the closest thing to infrastructure in this part of Borneo. Our young, barefoot boatman is poised at the front of our hip-wide longboat, ready to pole when shallows, still water, or rapids threaten our progress. A beefy old outboard motor dangles from the back of the boat like a very important, yet untended to, participle. Vanessa and I stare suspiciously at the sputtering two-stroke.

On the river, the jaggy mold I saw from the sky has become a dark green, menacing mass that lines the river. The jungle seems aggressive, as if the vines and trees are taking back the water's edge, instead of cohabiting with it in pastoral bliss, as a forest might meet a babbling brook. I imagine the density beyond our sight as unreasonable and unforgiving. A vicious chaos. I notice Vanessa noticing me recoil.

"Sorta feral looking," I say to Vanessa, explaining my discomfort.

"Rhoyyt then," says Georgie, with a game smile. "How much longer 'til the lodge?"

Periodically the jungle breaks and gives way to waterside communities. Longhouses with roofs of corrugated steel (rather than the traditional wood and rattan) pepper the river highway. People work together on the long porches and nod when we quietly chug by. "Dayak do not like to be alone," says Martin, and I think of Assata Shakur's saying that, in Cuba, she'd never met people so unafraid of other people.

The dwellings appear fewer and farther between as hours drift by and we sink deeper into the anarchy I first identified from above, from outside. I've come to crave these rare places that are off the grid; they can thrust one into the epiphany zone. Ironically, it is TV, that most "on-the-grid" medium, that now brings me to this state.

Urban Borneo thrives with the cultural and spiritual diversity of all of Southeast Asia, but the upriver longhouses, though no longer offering the display of bare breasts and bloodletting a broadcaster might hope for, can be a reservoir of traditional spiritual beliefs—a reservoir spiced with baseball caps, T-shirts, and, not so infrequently, film crews.

Malaysia's official religion is Islam, but zealous missionaries and North Borneo's status as a former British colony make Christianity widespread. Yet here in the interior of Sarawak, the rules of the West and the rules of the East are handily trumped by the rules of the Jungle—and animism is operative. Unlike Judaism, Hinduism, Islam, Christianity, and other doctrines of the world, Kaharinga—Iban animism—does not distinguish between this life and the hereafter, between the religious and the secular. Religion is everyday life. Animism, quite sensibly, is more interested in the here and now and the supremacy of nature. Natural phenomena, as well as things animate and inanimate, are all said to possess a soul.

To the upriver Iban's traditional eye, the steamy, humid atmosphere is thick with *antu* (spirits) and *petara* (gods). The spirits and the people work in concert. (A quid pro quo of sorts: We give you offerings, you help the rice crops grow.) The spirits hold the upper hand, to be sure, and their behavior can run the range from benevolent to capricious.

Our small procession of overloaded canoes sputters up toward the traditional Rumah Bala Lasong longhouse, where Vanessa and Martin have arranged for us to spend the night with Iban tribal members.

Martin grew up in a longhouse and, partly due to his excellent English, has landed a coveted job in the world of tourism. I am quizzing him about the surrounding area.

"What are the biggest hazards?" I ask.

"A few leeches, sometimes a snake. Only drink the bottled water," he responds casually, offering a whitewashed version of reality. In fact, I know there are tens of thousands of species in this national "park" (a misleading term that implies the jungle is somehow under the control of humans) and some of them, particularly the cold-blooded ones, could be a problem.

Put a frothing rabid dog in my path, and I respond with the calm of Atticus Finch. Bring on a mama grizzly, and I am as sharp as her claws slicing through the flesh of a wild king salmon. But show me a cold-blooded, slithering critter and I turn into an irrational, mute, quivering . . . appendix.

Indulging a strange habit of dashing toward what I fear, I press Martin on the snake issue. Vanessa has told me there are twenty-five kinds of snakes in this part of Borneo, many of them poisonous.

"Yes," Martin admits, "there's the *Python reticulatus;* the Javanese reed snake, *Calamaria borneensis;* the red-headed krait, *Bungarus flaviceps;* the banded Malayan coral snake, *Maticora intestinalis;* the cobra, *Naja naja;* and the—"

I hold up my hand to stop the recitation.

"You had me at *python,*" I say.

My phobic (that's phobic, *not* phallic) response to snakes irks me. I can't stand having an irrational fear that plays right into the hands of Freudian pundits.

We move through the hours at double the river's slow pace: outboard time. The rhythm is in marked contrast to my time in Cuba, when we were constantly racing from one diva to the next. Here, we tinker with equipment, apply sunscreen, and get to know one another with banal small talk, as if it were the first day at camp. *What tribe are you in? How many languages do you speak? How much tape stock do we have? Where do we pee?*

After hours of collective ruminating, we round a bend and, out of nowhere, Martin says, "They are expecting us." When, thirty seconds later, we hear the distant sounds of a welcoming party, I look over at Martin and think of Spock, his deep Vulcan wisdom, always right and always three steps ahead of his earthly comrades. Then again, I know the ring of a telemarketer a mile off, so it makes sense that Martin is tuned in to the greeting rituals of his home turf. As we close in on our destination, a collaboration of gongs and drums begins to overtake the jungle's cacophony of cicadas.

We round a gentle curve on the snaking river highway and see a headman, or *tuai rumah,* walking down a planked pier followed by a dozen boys, women with babies on their hips, and excited children. The headman is small and must be seventy; lithe and bent, but not at all decrepit. On his shoulders are swirling floral and reptile tattoos. He is wearing a flamboyant arching warrior headdress decorated with enormous black and white feathers of the locally revered hornbill, a species no longer found in these rain forests. We have heard of this sacred welcome ritual, called a *bedora,* but didn't expect we'd earned such a greeting—which is clearly camera-worthy.

Unfortunately, to be dignified and move fast at the same time is the rare province of Bolshoi ballerinas, successful NASA liftoffs, and, occasionally, Nelson Mandela, but hardly ever film crews in boats.

CANOE #1

I stand too quickly and Martin lunges for my ankles to keep the canoe from tipping over. I will the headman's eye contact to me so he does not notice the frantic fumbling about that is emanating from Canoe #2.

CANOE #2

"Goddammit, start filming."

"Bugger, the battery just died. Get another, quick."

"We don't know how long this will laaaast." The obvious is stated with friendly Brit urgency.

"Martin," Vanessa queries with a nervous smile toward Canoe #1, "do you think the headman would do it again for us?"

He looks at her blankly.

We clamber out of the canoes and follow the welcoming procession up the walkway to the longhouse, which stretches into the distance like an army barrack, but is much more inviting—especially as it rests on wooden stilts. Stilts, meant to protect the house from floods and animals, are surely the friendliest of architectural elements.

The longhouse is the traditional communal living structure, home to approximately fifteen families and up to a hundred people. We climb a wooden ladder to reach the first of three primary areas: a "porch" that stretches the length of the structure and is exposed to the outdoors. This is the area where clothes hang to dry, visitors arrive, and muddy shoes are removed. The second is a screened avenue, or gallery, that also runs along the length of the building, and has a bamboo floor. The gallery seems to be where life happens: One woman is in a distant corner mending a fishing net while another is weaving an intricate cloth with a wood loom; children romp around, excited by the prospect of visitors.

The third area, which we have yet to see, is beyond a rattan wall, and is the families' individual cooking and sleeping quarters. Under the structure reside, according to my keen olfactory and auditory sleuthing skills, pigs and chickens.

I say good afternoon to an older woman who is sitting on the floor with a red and yellow sarong knotted above her breasts, husking rice. *"Salamat tongah-hari."*

"Rindu amat betemu enggau nuan," she responds in kind with a blood-red smile, and then spits between the slats in the floorboards, adding betel-nut juice to the menagerie below.

"You are our honored guests and the festivities will begin soon," says the headman, with Martin translating.

Our ungraceful arrival was hardly honorable, but clearly Vanessa and

Martin had done their groundwork. My expectations for the evening are high after having read *Rajahs and Rebels* by a guy named Robert Pringle, who wrote in 1970, "A vigorous tradition of hospitality has come to be a hallmark of longhouse life. . . . Longhouse dwellers are typically open and gregarious with foreigners, eager for news of the outside world, and extremely fond of entertaining. There is often dancing and more often drink, and the fun may go on for most of the night." The Iban are also known for their confidence and pluck.

I ask a young girl about a toilet. *"Dini endor kitai mandi?"* She takes me back through her family's private space beyond the rattan wall. Our sleeping bags are already piled in an area where we will sleep with our host family. In the rear of the space, the floor slopes down into a short passage that leads to a dark room with a blazing open hearth. Giant black pots sizzle with the impending feast, and an older woman crouches next to the fire tending to an eviscerated critter twirling on a spit, flames dancing off its charred hide. The girl shows me to a door off to the left of the cooking room. At this point, with Seattle three sleepless nights in my rearview mirror, my exhaustion has graduated to the daze phase, and my synapses sputter instead of fire. I go into the dark and tiny room with a cement floor and corrugated metal walls. I look down and barely make out a squatter toilet. That is, a hole in the ground with imprints for footpads to aid in your balance and aim-taking. There is no flushing or toilet paper involved—merely a saucepan of water to move things along.

A tiny stream of light slices through a crack in the wall. I have not slept since Tuesday and we have been traveling in ninety-five-degree heat (and just about as much humidity) all day, yet the London series producer's pleading that I "spruce up" ("Just a bit of color would be grand") is what echoes in my mind. I want to please the broadcaster, but I don't want to appear vain to the crew—or ridiculous to our Iban hosts—and thus I find myself bent over in a wet, slightly putrid, cement-floored room, trying to catch the single shaft of light in my two-inch drugstore pocket mirror and apply Bobbi Brown's Brillant à Lèvres Raspberry Shimmer #8 lipstick.

Ker-plunk.

Oh god.

I have dropped the mirror into the hole.

Oh *ghaaad.*

I stand in the dark room, panicking, trying to figure out what to do.

The mirror is expendable, but the consequences of a drop and dash—i.e., clogging the rudimentary plumbing system of one hundred people—would qualify as bad manners, if not septic suicide. I want to weep with fatigue and disgust, but this is no time for a talent hissy fit.

I've got to *Go In.*

I roll up my sleeve, turn my head, hold my breath, and squint. I plunge my hand four inches down the pipe, and feel a potpourri of chunky spindly oozy stuff, but no mirror.

God please.

I sink two more inches and my fingertips graze the mirror's plastic edge.

Don't barf, don't barf.

One more thrust into the muck and, oh, oh—I've got it!

I wet-nap down, and join the party, Bobbi Brown intact.

When I return, the *tuak*—rice wine—is flowing heartily and the cameras are rolling. Georgie is filming a young Iban women who is dancing. "She took off her sarong and AC/DC T-shirt and put on some traditional kit," confides Georgie. "I guess both outfits are authentic. I didn't ask her to change," Georgie adds, with a hint of defensiveness.

We are all sensitive about barging into an indigenous culture and, worse yet, misrepresenting reality. The execs might prefer the Iban of one hundred years ago, but in fact this is a tribe that has been exposed to "visitors" since the fifteenth century (the Portuguese, the Dutch, the Brits, the Japanese), as well as to missionary influence. There is little chance our bumbling would cause any cosmic shift; but there is a fair chance, if we are not careful, that we will cross the line that marks disrespect and display unacceptably bad manners.

Growing up in the Midwest, manners consisted mainly of never discussing sex, always bringing the Jell-O salad, and remembering to say, "Thanks for coming!" or "Thanks for having me!" after sleepovers. (Come to think of it, that's the closest we got to discussing sex.) But I've learned that being a mannerly guest in a global context requires more; it requires one to drink, eat, smoke, snort, and chew a wide variety of animal, vegetable, and, occasionally, synthetic materials. I try to avoid anything concocted in suburban basements and derived from cleaning agents, but short of that, good manners usually involve *intake*—regardless of a few dead brain cells or a wide-eyed night.

So I sip my fourth glass of fermented rice booze that tastes like sake resin, and settle in for the evening's events.

Twenty of us, our crew and other invited inhabitants of the longhouse, sit on mats on the floor in a large circle and the women serve us a feast of steamed rice in bamboo cylinders, leafy green vegetables, and dried fish. The girls and women dress in heavily embroidered cloth with many bangles and wear skirts made of interwoven coins. The headman says a blessing and his lithe, tattooed arm swings a stunning black and orange rooster, with its darting eyes and poised-to-snap white beak, over the food. He deftly plucks two grand tail feathers from the bird's behind as an offering to the gods.

"I thought you said it would be sacrificed. You know, a *blood* offering," Rik whispers to Vanessa, disappointed.

"This isn't a wealthy longhouse. They can't afford to kill a valuable cock for an offering," she responds.

The offering has been made and it is time to eat—and drink. Destroying social harmony is a major transgression in a longhouse, and as *our* "host" I am expected to imbibe, drink for drink, with *the* hosts. *Tuak* is passed in bowls and jugs and swilled with exhortations of *"Ngirop, ngirop!"* For the first hour, I feel confident that I can go head to head, as long as nobody breaks out the Jägermeister shots. The *tuak* is not terribly strong, though the copious amounts are worrying. The rest of the crew appear to be in their element.

Events become fuzzy after hour two as my fatigue progresses from daze to death rattle. Interviews are derailed because I am unable to retain answers for more than six seconds, dashing any hope of a decent follow-up question. *"Ngirop!"* I hear as another sloppy *tuak* is thrust under my nose, and I sway with fatigue as much as anything else. By hour three, complete exhaustion taking hold, I am barely tracking conversations, including those in English. My last memory is an image of young Iban men in the middle of a circle kicking high and wild, full of athleticism and punch. "Some combination of traditional Iban dance and frat party gone bad," I mutter to camera. And then, me and my Brillant à Lèvres #8 lips fall asleep, upright.

"Royyt, cut, we've lost our presenter," is the last thing I hear Rik say, and I am half-carried, half-rolled through a doorway adorned with a carving of a crocodile swathed in a snake.

That night, dreams come fitfully. Snakes are slithering all over me and out of my hands, and I am unable to move. The auguries could be saying any number of things.

1.   I am in touch with the ancient power of the serpent who embodies the female principle; I may be pregnant; I may be poised to transform or evolve; I am definitely in touch with my libido; I am dangerous to the foolishly unwary (this, according to the historical mythology of most ancient cultures).

2.   Patriarchy has subsumed all matriarchal realms; thus, I am scared of the all-powerful penis and my own sexuality. I have issues (this, according to Freud et al.).

3.   Animals and dreams are the vehicle for messages sent from the parallel universe, which is with us at all times. The female god who rules that parallel universe is represented by the serpent dragon. The upshot: Someone important is trying to send me a message (this, according to Iban cosmology).

4.   The holey mosquito net, which binds twelve of us (our crew and the host family) in a row like corpses, has pinned me in place and I underwent a nocturnal panic attack that manifested itself in my sleep as snakes (this, according to my logic).

The still-alive cock—*caakkaaa cooo, caakkaaa cooo*—brings an end to sleep. I rouse to a symphony of snores. A four-legged animal of some sort snuffles below the slatted wooden floor. The surrounding jungle is warming up its diurnal chorus; birds and trees and fish all stretch for the day ahead.

I keep my eyes shut and try to wring a bit more sleep from the short night, but the sounds and smells of jungle life won't allow it. I reluctantly open my eyes and see two giant dogs at the far end of the gallery scratching their hindquarters, their beefy back legs slapping on the wood floor. *Thump. Thump. Thump.*

Scratching hindquarters sounds appealing, as the mosquitoes have left no flesh unturned, but first I must unwind the net from my neck and ankles. I notice Vanessa scratch, and raise my right eyebrow to say *Join me for some caffeine?*

The kitchen is not yet operational but there is a fire crackling outside. We climb down the ladder and join a woman who I noticed spent all yesterday afternoon at the loom. Today she is making tea; *"Salamat pagi, ngirop,"* she says, the last word sending a wave of nausea through my gut as she hands me a cup to drink. We nod and sip.

Vanessa, ever the on-task producer, even at six A.M., says something in Iban to the woman.

"What did you ask?"

"If this longhouse had heads."

Vanessa's practiced competence in Iban tells me that Martin coached her, and that she considers the headhunting story key—in other words, a *nutgrab.* If this were an *Adventure Divas* shoot we might be asking about the intricate cultural storytelling that is embedded in the patterns of the weaving that the women create with their loom work, but on this shoot, dusty human skulls are the sexier angle we're chasing down.

Poor Borneo.

The rain forest is a natural wonder, filled with thousands of species, only a fraction of them named, much less understood. Both sanctioned and renegade logging decimates the environment. The island is one of only two remaining habitats of the mighty orangutan. All this, yet the only word that comes to many people's minds when they think about Borneo is *headhunter.*

The woman points up toward a corner of the gallery. Vanessa and I trade looks, and gulp down our tea. We climb back up the ladder and walk slowly toward the far corner, protected from direct light. Hanging in a net, strung between a wooden beam and the ceiling, are a half-dozen eerie, rough-hewn, grayish, charbroiled, seven-inch-diameter orbs: human heads.

They look like a bunch of giant, calcified, rotten grapes.

"Dear. I guess that's one way to resolve neighborly disputes," says Vanessa with a nervous laugh.

The headman, a title that suddenly takes on new meaning, walks up behind us, with Martin, Rik, and Georgie in tow.

I am stymied as to how to start the interview.

"Um, what is the significance of the heads and how old are they?"

"These heads were taken seventy years ago, by my great-grandfather," he tells me. "There was a raid on another longhouse."

Martin adds that headhunting largely came to an end in the forties (the white rajahs found the practice unsavory and discouraged it—often by sending others to take the heads of those who took heads), but there were a few cases of Japanese heads being taken during World War II.

"They are powerful. They bring good fortune and a strong harvest to the longhouse," says the headman, with Martin continuing to translate.

For the Iban, heads were (and still are) associated with the fertility of both their women and their rice fields. Historically, heads were also taken to mark the end of a mourning period. The head possesses a strong spirit, and when a head was taken, it was thought that its spirit then belonged to the new owner. In many ancient cultures, the head and spine are said to contain a person's essence (Polynesians call it mana). To the Iban, heads are chock-full of essence that serves to replenish the family or village when hung inside the longhouse.

"Even now, a longhouse without heads is not a lucky place," says Martin.

"Do you want me to take one down?" the headman asks.

"I, uh, well," I say, stumbling. I'm all for good television but am conflicted about holding a human head—a powerful orb of fertility. "Will we have to replace it if we drop it?"

Even now, if you read the Bornean news carefully, you'll find that amid the run-of-the-mill murders that all societies have, there are still a fair number of decapitations. But lest we judge, every country seems to have a preferred, culturally based method of suicide and murder. Decapitation is to Borneo as immolation is to India, as gunplay is to the United States, as hanging from a construction crane is to Iran.

"We all have our fatal traditions," I say to Vanessa, after we've gleaned all we could from the headhunter story, and begin to load up the canoes for our return trip.

I've heard the locals say "upriver is a state of mind." Perhaps this is why the jungle seems different this time as we navigate its waterways. What seemed just a day ago to be a nefarious Rorschach test begins to reveal enchanting patterns and wildlife whimsy. Chains of orchids (of which there are some three thousand species in Borneo, which boasts 10 percent of the world's total orchid population) outline the trunks of sixty-foot-tall trees; chaotic assemblies of vines become launchpads for kingfishers and starlings. Rhododendrons, their red blossoms bursting, push branches closer to the water. The regular crashing and crackling in the forest adds dimension, rather than warning. Even the rapids, which on the way in sent soundman John leaping to keep his equipment dry, are being welcomed as a good rollick and an opportunity to admire spectacular boatmanship attuned to the uneven depths and eddies the river put in our path.

Halfway back to hot water and Internet, we stop at a riverside community. Three old ladies, two in floral sarongs and one in a man's work shirt, are sitting on mats in the shade, under a crop of jutting jungle flora that protects them from a blazing midday sun. The woman on the left waves me over and hands me the makings of a betel-nut chew. Martin joins us. I fold together the areca nut, betel leaf, and limey paste, then wedge the bundle between my cheek and gums.

"Spit," she says when she sees me struggling with profuse red saliva. "Ladies don't swallow." I swear I see a wave of giggles subtly pass over the old women's faces. We all squat and spit and enjoy a little communal buzz. The heavy, steady song of the cicadas skips and lilts down its endless trail; and I wonder at the thousands of species that are listening to the very same tune.

A mere two days in the jungle have made my dreams ripe with the place and its creatures. That night, at the Shangri-La Hotel in Kota Kinabalu, I dream that thousands of orangutans are boarding the luxury liner *Queen Elizabeth II*. There are far too many wanting entrance and many are falling off the edges, off the gangplank, dropping into the water and dying. *Splash. Plunk. Collapse. Bang.* Bang Bang BANG on my door. I wake with a snap, jolted and sad, and late for our flight to Sabah, where we're going to do a story on the endangered orangutans.

We arrive in the town of Sandakan to visit a sanctuary for the animal that shares nearly 98 percent of DNA with us humans and is referred to by conservationists as the world's most "charismatic megafauna," that is, mega-useful for conservation campaigns. (Think whales, seals, wolves, pandas.)

The street leading to the Sepilok Orang Utan Rehabilitation Centre teems with the skinny, long-limbed monkeys known as gibbons. One chucks a stick at the van and it pings off the hood.

We walk by two nubile European interns who are holding baby orangutans. "What is it with chicks and chimps?" I ask.

"Tits, mate," replies Georgie. "All these babies lose their mums and crave surrogates—emotionally, anyway."

Orangutans, whose name comes from the Malay word meaning "person of the forest," have been brachiating (moving hand over hand) through the forests for an estimated two million years. They once covered all of Southeast Asia and numbered in the hundreds of thousands; now they only exist in small, protected areas of tropical rain forest on the islands of Sumatra and Borneo. The orangutan population is down to under twenty thousand, and dropping.

In Sumatra, I saw wild orangutans in the tropical rain forest. *Snap! Crash! Crackle!* we'd hear, and look up to see an orange flash in the jungle canopy overhead. Our hearts raced and for a minute we forgot about the oppressive, perpetual damp. But that was before the fires of the late 1990s, a devastation that left many orangutans orphaned, injured, and hungry. The fires were partially caused by global climate change: Traditionally, the farmers and loggers set fire to their land every year, and the fires are extinguished by the monsoons. However, one year, the monsoons never came, and the fires raged uncontrolled through hundreds of thousands of acres of one of the richest forests in the world.

In both Sumatra and Borneo, mechanized logging and palm-oil plantations are destroying orangutan habitat. In addition to land conversion (which fosters fires), poachers shoot the mother orangutans (who eat from the palm trees when faced with diminishing habitats), peel the babies off of the corpses, and sell them into a black market that peddles baby orangs as pets–cum–status symbols. Some live in captivity for years, well into adolescence and adulthood; many die of disease (or some say depression); others make their way to rehab centers with the aid of people who are sensitive to, and informed about, their plight. Sepilok is one such center, a halfway house of sorts. Whatever their respective histories, each orangutan at this center is learning how to be an orangutan, and, it is hoped, will eventually return to the rain forest. The youngest, and those not in captivity long, have the best chance of returning to their native habitat.

The government-run spread consists of a collection of small cinder-block buildings, including a medical facility, and some some ropey jungle-gym-type structures for the animals. On the grounds are a number of roofed edifices under which dozens of small cages are stacked atop one another. The cages are teeming with baby orangutans. Red balls of fire, leaping and squeaking, back and forth, up and down.

The cages send me into a Sally Struthers–style tizzy but I quickly strap on my congenial persona when a man named Melvin introduces himself to show me around the center. As infants, Melvin tells me, orangutans are fed and held and taken care of much like human babies. From three to five years old, they are taught the use of their limbs and how to climb (strangely, orangutans do not know how to do this instinctively).

"After year five, the center works on 'survival training,' that is, reducing the orangutans' dependence on people, teaching them to fend for themselves and to mate," says Melvin. He hands me a young orangutan to hold while he fixes rope for the animal to play on.

Before I can follow up on that last, evocative bit of information, a warm liquid slowly courses down my belly and continues on down my leg. My charge quietly, and without fanfare, has begun to piss all over me. His hot urine drenches my chest and pants and I feel the strange combination of feelings I have when I pee in my wetsuit: naughty and gleeful and comforted, all at the same time. Nonetheless, I thrust the young orangutan in front of me, trying in vain to avoid his seemingly endless trajectory.

"Sounds as if the organization is *mama*," I comment to Melvin, sopping up the piss, which has become much less pleasant now that the actual moment of being pissed on is over.

"Yes, and that is a very big job," confirms Melvin.

Mama. Gives milk, teaches you to use your body, eventually gives you the sex talk, and then boots you off to college with fingers crossed that you do not come back. The process of rehabituation takes years of teaching, nurturing, and patience. Now I understand the cages. These little fellas are here for a long stretch, and they need structure for a while in order to survive.

We walk out to a feeding station where recently rehabituated orangutans can return from the forest for a fix should the dorm food be insufficient or not plentiful enough; a twice-daily supplement of bananas and rice is available to them in case they are having a hard time finding the vegetation they need. Each orangutan in the wild needs 1,200 acres of forest to survive.

A wiry-haired, brownish-orange female orangutan, about three feet tall and two feet wide, with a baby clutched to her side, swings down hand over hand from a tall tree, like a trapeze performer, and gracefully lands on the platform. Some consider this feeding part of the rehabituation process cheating. Biruté Galdikas defends the practice in her book *Reflections of Eden,* writing, "I cannot understand this purism in the face of habitat destruction, slaughter and imminent extinction. Human beings cheated the ex-captives of a normal upbringing by an orangutan mother in the forest canopy. Human beings are also consuming the orangutans' natural habitat at an alarming rate. At the very least, we owe them some rice and bananas."

I read a lot about Dr. Galdikas because she was on our original diva list. She arrived in the jungles of Borneo thirty years ago from Lithuania, via UCLA. Twenty-five and driven, she tackled leeches, disease, and poachers to eventually earn the respect of the local Indonesian community and the trust of hundreds of orangutans.

I also read in her book that orangutans do not, instinctually, know how to build nests like birds do. Adolescents practice and learn from their mothers and eventually get the hang of it. And even when they do make a nest, they move and rebuild every few days. Wild orangutans, especially the adult males, are nomadic. Although we as humans are separated from the orangutan by fourteen million years of evolution, I find myself relating to the often-solitary, on-the-move life of the orangutan, who has no instinct for nesting. Transitory nesting. I figure a long-term nest can get really stinky unless you're committed to frequent cleaning. Duffle bags and hotel rooms, that's the answer.

Melvin asks me to help him with a tiny infant orang named Cha whose mother, Luwa, was killed by a poacher. We do her weekly weigh-in (2.2 kilos). "She has gained weight," Melvin says, pleased, and scribbles down some numbers.

He leaves me with Cha, knowing that these babies crave and need loving attention, especially from mammals with mammaries. Cha attaches to me, with vigor, immediately, proving Galdikas's point: "Wild orangutan infants spend all their time with their mother. The mother-infant relationship is extremely intense. Only the mother orangutan carries the infant. The mother is the infant's primary playmate. . . . Infant orangutans are genetically programmed to cling to their mothers."

Cha gently touches my cheek with the pink, supple skin on the palms of her baby hands. Goofy orange puffs of hair sprout out of her precious bald head and tickle my chin. Her very warm chest huddles to my breast, arms around my neck now; her dewy chocolate eyes are full of need and love. A strange, deep, almost instinctual wave begins in my gut and spreads upward, over my heart, and a thought washes over me:

God . . . what a *sycophant.*

Having a kid, even one that knows how to clutch on during the skip from nest to nest, must really slow you down. (Okay, I know my mom and plenty of other women managed kids and active careers, but I'm afraid I didn't inherit that spunky martyr gene.)

I put down the boiling hot, clingy critter, suddenly glad I didn't touch those fertility heads at the longhouse.

My own maternal shortcomings aside, it is true that the orangutan population is in dire straits, and that the ladies are good with the primates. I mean, there *is* something about chicks and chimps: Jane Goodall and her African chimpanzees; Dian Fossey and her mountain gorillas; and Biruté Galdikas, who created the Orangutan Foundation International and has been a leader in the fight to protect orangutans and their habitats for the past thirty years.

What do these three pioneering scientists have in common? A man: Louis Leakey. Seems the late Anglo-Kenyan paleontologist felt that women were better suited for research because they tend to be more observant, less aggressive, and more empathetic toward the animals than do their male counterparts. Goodall, Fossey, and Galdikas were often called "Leakey's Angels," but in fact, it was Leakey who was the angel as he spearheaded financial support for the vital work of these three divas of primatology.

For decades, Galdikas was a hero in the worlds of conservation and primate research. But alas, heroism is a tricky thing. In the late 1990s, she was ousted from her Garden of Eden by a barrage of objections to her methods of acquiring and caring for orangutans, among other accusations. Writer Linda

Spalding went looking for her hero, and, 269 pages later, she had charted and solidified Galdikas's alleged downfall in her book *A Dark Place in the Jungle,* published in 1999. If Galdikas had died early, like Dian Fossey, who was murdered in 1985 and became a martyr to environmentalists, she might have gone down as an environmental revolutionary. But she lived long enough to see her reputation tumble. What happens when good divas go bad? For now, I only had to face the question theoretically.

As we walk out of the rehabilitation center, livid, deep, miserable shrieks charge across the compound and stop me dead. I look across the grounds and see a huge adult orangutan, yanking at the bars, violently heaving his body against the cage. "We didn't get him in time," Melvin says quietly. His spirit defiled, this orangutan can only be caged for the rest of his days. Or else die.

What happens when free-range instincts are squashed by forces greater than the individual? This consumes me as we leave the sanctuary and set off for the heart of Mulu National Park for a look into the lives of the Penan, the only true nomads in Sarawak.

The Penan hunter-gatherers inhabit the deep jungles of the central and northern parts of the state. An estimated three hundred Penan hunt, gather, run, roam, live, and die under the jungle canopy of the park; another seven thousand or so Penan have been jettisoned from their lands by the logging industry and put into "settlements" with promises of health care and education—promises that have largely gone unkept.

We travel by river out to one of these government-induced settlements, which is a line of clapboard dwellings accented with the odd bit of cloth swinging in the wet wind to dry. I sense depression. Unlike the upriver longhouse, which felt emboldened by tradition, pride, and humor—not at odds with modernity, but rather choosing what they would incorporate—this settlement reeks of defeat.

Whatever its hardships, the nomadic lifestyle holds some romance for me, a newly professional wanderer. Forced settlement of nomadic people seems particularly cruel, as it cuts them off from their way of life, cultures, and traditions. Just as exile (forced movement) was a theme that hovered over our Cuba trip, the notion of mandatory settlement (forced *non*-movement) haunts me now.

Moments after we arrive, a downpour begins, and we run for one of the shelters and sit among some wet hay to drink tea, and wait for the heavy rain to subside. "The Malaysian government backs the logging industry and the Penan, to put it bluntly, have been in the way," Vanessa confirms.

When the rain stops, we gather near the water's edge. A middle-aged woman plays a nose flute that sounds to me full of sadness and hope and maybe epic tales. The men work on their hunting implements. The ancient and inspiring parts of the Penan culture begin to shine through the trappings of the settlement as the rain stops and daily activity resumes.

The Penan hunt and trap gibbons, macaws, civet cats, squirrels, and reptiles. I'm shown the poison-dart blowpipe, which has a 150-foot range and is used for killing small game, including monkeys. A Penan hunter blows a dart (whose tip has been dipped in poison) through the barrel of the blowpipe using strong breath from the chest and stomach, rather than the mouth. The blowpipe is lighter than a gun, makes no sound, and can be shot with deadly precision. The poison, the blowpipe, and the darts, essential items of the Penan existence, are all handmade with materials found in the rain forest.

"Tomorrow you'll be going on a hunt for wild bearded boar," Vanessa tells me. "So brush up on your blowpipe skills," she says with a mischievous smile. (Producers secretly love to torture talent.)

Day folds into night and we camp near the settlement. Artificial light plunges up into the sky in the east, the direction in which we have heard the din of chain saws all day. I lobby to go, to film the devastation that is destroying the Penan way of life. "It's part of the story," I say, trying to convince myself, and Rik, that Westerners with cameras can become part of the solution, not the problem.

"I heard a film crew was here last year and said they were doing a cultural story. Instead they went in and filmed the logging. The crew went missing," says Rik. Gone. Poof. Never to be found. Yet another rule of the jungle.

"You must only do what you are permitted to do," reinforces the humorless middle-aged fixer who we hired to help us set up this story. I concede the battle but decide to sneak off from camp that evening to have a look.

For years the Penan have been fighting for the preservation of their native territories, which have been defiled by logging companies that (in addition to logging) dump oil and chemicals into the water, causing acute stomach pain and skin diseases among the Penan people. The Penan staged an uprising in

1987 in which they blockaded bulldozers and logging areas. As the plight of the Penan became world famous, Penan rain-forest preservation became a hip celebrity cause and gained popular attention in the early nineties. Support eventually began to wane, however, amid sharp criticism from the Malaysian government. For a time, Mulu National Park was a global environmental battle-field, with the East telling the West to mind its own business and address the issues of its own destructive policies and stolen indigenous homelands. The Penan continue to fight for their right to the land that they have lived on for centuries, but the crisis of rain-forest destruction is more acute than ever.

Just after dusk I lace up my hiking boots and head for the floodlights, which look to be about half a mile away. I get to the perimeter of the action and stand in the shadows, looking into a void that is being created. A vast swatch of the dense, dark, mysterious forest has been exterminated and replaced with bright, artificial nothingness. A few giant arboreal corpses lie around, waiting to be hauled off. This Armageddon-like scene feels downright pornographic. It reminds me of the opening scene in *Terminator,* in which huge machines are steamrollering life out of existence. Helmeted men with chain saws quickly fil-let the kill. The smell and sound of the thick, fecund forest is replaced by the stink of wet, flat death.

Not a single cicada sings.

I am overcome with—not rage, not righteousness, not curiosity—but gut-socked sadness and a dose of guilt. I eat soy. I use chopsticks. I use palm oil and too much toilet paper. I am complicit in this, one of globalization's dirty little secrets.

I brush seven swollen mosquitoes off my forearm, take one last glance at the void, and turn to leave. Now I understand why activists in the Pacific Northwest try to get politicians up in planes to see the logging carnage in Washington's Cascades. One can justify or jury-rig the political landscape from behind a hardwood desk, but it is difficult to deny the visceral horror of such ravaged natural landscape.

Manners. Remember your manners, I think as I sit deep in the rain forest with a family of Penan hunter-gatherers trying to swallow a third glop of wild sago.

How I wish the glop were Jell-O salad, or matzoh ball soup, or anything but what it is. The mother twirls more gluey *na'oh* around a stick and hands it to me, and my gag muscle twitches as if contemplating a chunky (and not meant to be chunky) dairy product. Sago is wild palm, which the Penan depend upon for their housing, baskets, and food. It is 90 percent pure carbohydrate, and it used to be mixed with animal blood to form a mineral-rich source of nutrients. But Christian missionaries, reacting to the gore, convinced the Penan to stop eating blood. The nutritionally unbalanced staple that resulted keeps the Penan malnourished. To my Western palate, *na'oh* tastes like warmed Silly Putty. The plenitude of sago determines how long a nomadic Penan family stays in one place (it goes, they go).

At dawn this morning we shoved off in our canoes and traveled several hours to arrive here, deep in a protected forest area in which a group of nomadic Penan are still able to practice their traditional way of life. To keep away from the incessant drizzle, we are huddled under a lean-to made of giant pandanus leaves and branches, built by the mother of the family. Berti, the father, dips the head of a just-sharpened dart into a dark liquid. The poison.

I down the third glop of sago, hyper-aware that I have no choice, as the greatest transgression in Penan culture is *see hun,* or, "failure to share." The prospect of another meal of sago is motivation enough to succeed in today's wild boar hunt. Give me the other white meat any day (even if it has a beard).

Having wheedled our way into this boar hunt, a rare "pure" remaining aspect of Penan life, I am feeling more than ever as if we are nefarious culture skaters. We really should not be here. But my time to protest has long since passed. This is television and we have set up "an experience," and—by god—it is my job to have it.

Only one gringa is allowed per hunt, so Georgie sets me up with the small Canon video camera and shoves a couple of extra tapes in my pocket. "Okay mate, if you get one make sure to get plenty of cutaways. And careful not to let the blood splatter on the lens" is Georgie's final advice.

Martin translates for the three men whom I will join for the hunt. The leader is Berti, the father of the family who shared their sago with me. As he issues instructions, Martin says, "Berti says to stay close, but never move in front of the group. When they catch one beware of its teeth."

———

"Woouh, woouh, woouh," goes the high-pitched Penan chant as we trot along, and then quickly turn up the pace a notch to a steady run.

The men are wearing smallish skins that cover their loins. I am wearing thick cross-trainers, long, thin wicking pants with eight pockets (four of which I have yet to find), and a microlight long-sleeve shirt with mesh ventilation under the armpits. I am Ex Officio. My shoes crunch clumsily on the forest floor; the men travel in near silence, as if they are human hovercrafts.

After about five minutes I stop Berti and the guys and ask them to run around me in circles so I can get full frontal footage of them. I fear I will only see their backsides from here on out given their increasing pace. No translator is on site, so "asking them" means me running around in a circle miming the hunt of a wild bearded boar (as if I have some idea what that entails). They laugh at the foolish tall white lady, and gamely comply. Before we take off again I get a close-up of Berti's feet. They are small and have an intriguing network of roundish muscle landscapes. Given the speed and gallantry with which they deliver him through a forest floor of logs, prickly sticks, and vines, it seems Berti's feet have a range of talents wholly incomprehensible to the average pampered First World foot.

"The Penan are so profoundly different," wrote Canadian linguist Ian Mackenzie. "They have no writing so their total vocabulary at any one time is the knowledge of the best storyteller. There is one word for he, she, and it, but six for we. There are at least eight words for sago, because it is the plant that allows them to survive. Sharing is an obligation, so there is no word for 'thank you.' They can name hundreds of trees but there is no word for 'forest.' Their universe is divided between the land of shade, the land of abundance, and the land that has been destroyed."

The hunt begins in earnest. Berti and the two other men are ripping through the dense tangles of vines, trees, and kooky jungle growth at high speed with six-foot-long blowpipes and spears in their hands. The speed and agility with which they traverse the terrain is uncanny and I wonder if they are doing *mal cun uk* ("follow our feelings"), a Penan way to navigate an unknown part of the jungle. I put the camera on autofocus, lock it on record, and pull out every last one of my stops in order to keep up. *I will not fail, goddammit,* I think as I flail with gusto through the dense underbrush, willing my bad ankle not to snap.

Last year CNN put me through their war-zone training for journalists in the swamps of Georgia, where I learned that camera operators have a misguided sense of security. That is, the irrational belief that they are invincible, that somehow looking through a lens protects your body as bullets fly by, grenades are lobbed, or, in the current case, as you hurl yourself through lethal jungle, full speed and sans peripheral vision, on the tail of Penan warriors who are wielding poison blow darts in hopes of skewering a wild, bearded boar. The adrenaline is pumping. *I am keeping up!* I can see the nutgrab now: HE BLEW THE POISON DART WITH THE ACUMEN OF A THOUSAND YEARS OF HISTORY, AND DOWNED THE SQUEALING SWINE IN A SINGLE SHOT.

Ah-ha! The story is mine!

Just as I am about to delude myself that I am both a journalist and a hunter, I go ass over tit into a felled log and a sticky, prongy vine becomes the new look in choker collars. My head is thrust back into a giant mossy divot in a hundred-million-year-old tree; another scratchy vine has bound my torso and I am firmly lodged in some twisted B-movie S-and-M jungle position. I look up at the thick canopy above, pant, and think of Peg the nurse's final admonition and wonder if anything is *broken, torn,* or *severely punctured,* or if the term "air-evac" has ever even crossed the lips of a human being within a thousand-mile radius.

The Penan's hunting chants fade into the distance.

I am instantly miserable.

My head itches. I hurt. My wrists are sweating. In the back of my mind anxiety simmers because I know this is the exact kind of moment I will be required to write about or describe to camera, and I think, *Can't I just have the fucking experience?* I enter a moment of schizophrenic self-pitying delirium: What would others write?

ERNEST HEMINGWAY: I am hot. I will just shoot the pig.

ANNE LAMOTT: I'm feeling hot and my Birks were not the best choice but what I really want is to have a stiff drink but Sam wouldn't like it because he doesn't have a father.

Paul Theroux: I'm very hot. I feel as if I'm in the furnace of an old 1926 steam engine.

As I try to untangle myself, the punishing humidity fuels a steady stream of sweat into my eyes, which makes the wall of electric-green foliage that incarcerates me jitter like the preamble to an acid trip.

The spongy, fetid jungle floor is alive, a constant microorganismic frenzy. It is sending out an endless, deafening, gurgly hum that tells me that billions and billions of small creatures are surrounding me and are very hard at work and I am just lying there like a dead animal, soon to be decomposed.

Mosquitoes (malarial, I'm sure) swarm mercilessly. I become convinced that a slimy overwhelming power is morphing me into something else, and I will end up a moth—and not in that comforting reincarnation way.

I would just be a moth.

It's when I hear myself nearly whimper that I ask myself what a diva would do. *Take action.* I scramble to my feet and turn the camera on myself in a desperate *Blair Witch* moment. This is as good a time as any to deliver some "top tips" and "emotional diary entries," both of which were mandated by the series producer, who is currently sitting in a posh office back in London's Notting Hill.

"Whenever you're hunting for wild boar in the jungles of Borneo, wear a long-sleeve shirt," I say to camera and pan down my arm, which is dripping blood from the hostile vine. Of course, only one in a million viewers will ever hunt wild boar in this godforsaken hell.

Seems Berti and the others are long gone, and rightly so. My stealthless presence made their chances of sticking a boar about as likely as my chances of finding my way out of this jungle unaided.

I just hope they'll come back for me.

I hang my sweaty overshirt (now ripped for additional ventilation) on a branch of a tree that I notice has been *molong*ed. The Penan tradition of *molong*ing trees consists of marking the trunk with a machete to signify it as a fruiting tree, rather than a lumber tree. If a tree has been *molong*ed, other Penan will not cut it down, but only pick fruit from it. This example of ecological stewardship stands in ironic contrast to the mowing for profit I witnessed last night.

I wander about twenty yards and position myself in what passes for a clearing. Like any good Chicagoan, I try to face the virtual door so that when a threatening mobster character comes in to take me out, I will be prepared. Unfortunately, the jungle is all doors. Pity the editor who has to go through the footage I burn during the next ten minutes as I deliver my "diary moments," which rumble closer to a pitch of pure panic with each minute that the Penan hunters do not come back for me.

"Excuse me, but I do *not* think Julia Roberts was put through this when she did a show in Borneo. Please, they just wheeled her out of the trailer, stuck baby orangutans on her ample breast, and rolled film." And finally . . .

"My brother gets my record collection; my sister the dog; sign the 100k death-and-dismemberment insurance over to Adventure Divas."

Does wretchedly slow decomposition count as dismemberment? I turn off the camera and watch the blood weep down my leg from the latest leech incursion. I sop the ooze from another ulcer, an older bite. Leeches have three jaws, each of which contains a hundred teeth. They use one end of their body for attaching to their host while the other end feeds. Their saliva contains an anticoagulating agent and a mild anesthetic, so that they can suck you dry, unnoticed. In a half hour a leech can consume up to five times its body weight—that is, half a shot glass of blood. They can balloon from two centimeters to two inches fat, depending how much blood they suck. I flick off a small leech that is beginning to dig in at my ankle.

And then it becomes painfully clear that one tampon was not enough for today's excursion.

The army of jungle bugs turns up the volume a notch in unison. At this moment, in the belly of the beast, Borneo's tropical rain forest seems endless and all-consuming. Hard to conceive that it could all be destroyed. Yet, if all systems remain go—that is, the logging continues 24/7 under floodlights, and the Penan who are staging protests do not prevail—it will be gone in five to ten years. Forever. Poof. Like the film crew that tried to record it happening. But my compassion for the rain forest atrophies with each moment the environment keeps me trapped and fearful. No Stockholm Syndrome for this panicking pig hunter.

I slide into what my friend Kate calls the "secret happy place." That is, the place where you go in your mind when your heaving face has been planted over the toilet in a third-class Indian train for six hours straight; that place you go when your sister has had one too many cocktails at Christmas dinner and you can see her wind up to chuck a hardball at the dysfunctional house of mirrors that tenuously holds the gathering together; that place you go when you have intestinal parasites and shit your pants on a Guatemalan Bluebird bus (and that place you go after you clean yourself up and it happens again five minutes later); and finally, that place you go when you've been abandoned by Penan tribesmen in the jungles of Borneo and find yourself seeping from five different holes—some natural, some not.

My secret happy place is under a piece of heavy oak furniture where I mouth to myself, "You're all alone in this world and the sooner you realize that the better; you're all alone in this world and the sooner you realize it the better." My decades-old ritual response to pain (secret, but come to think of it, not very happy) has adapted, in this case to: "You're all alone in this world—*except for the goddamn crew, who'd better come find me*—and the sooner you realize that—*one dumb gringa life is nothing compared to the genocide*—the better—*I'll miss the broadcast of the Cuba show! I'll never know if the project comes to fruition.* You're all alone—*calm down calm down . . . oh god. Jesus. I'm not cut out for this nomad life*—and the sooner you realize it . . ."

To calm myself, I try to buy into the Penan belief in the interconnectedness of all things material and spiritual, a belief that puts a more palatable spin on death. After all, when you're in the tropics with very limited access to medical facilities, death can strike at any moment and, in the cosmos of the local people, fate can never be avoided. Without a conceptual distinction between this life and the hereafter, one cultivates an easy acceptance of death. This, in turn, it is said, leads people to live joyously.

I am so *not* there.

Another ten minutes pass, and I begin to wonder if this is all one of those malaria pill–induced psychotic moments Peg mentioned.

And then, it happens. Eight feet to my right, at about two o'clock on the cosmic clock, a five-foot-long black and green snake with orange stripes slithers into a patch of sun that managed to defy the thick jungle canopy and beam onto the forest floor.

The snake stops.

I stop.

The world stops.

The snake does not recoil to strike, nor does it coil to sunbathe. The snake simply lifts its head three inches off the ground and stares. At me.

Oddly, instead of heightened panic, I feel utter calm. No itching. No fear. A strange union.

It sticks its tongue out at me.

I stick my tongue out at it.

Everything has disappeared—the jungle cacophony, the weeping leech sores, television. This staring contest lasts a full two minutes. Biruté Galdikas says looking into the eyes of an adult orangutan is like looking at a hundred million years of history. Calming and frightening at the same time. I avert my eyes, in submission. The snake slithers away and I am left to interpret its message.

A half hour later Berti finds me sitting on a log. I don't tell Berti or anybody about the snake. The visit was like a strange gift from Boo Radley, hidden in the trunk of a tree. Nobody's business, really. Especially not the cable-viewing public's. There was no kill today, but somehow I think I got the nutgrab.

"Tell us what it was like," Georgie asks, sticking the hulking DigiBeta camera in my face. "I already did, to camera, in there," I say, pointing into the arboreal abyss, and handing her the Canon. "Let's be done for the day," I say.

On the way back I think about Berti's feet and the snake's eyes, and the twirling sago and the disappearing magic. All the secrets that are being felled.

3.

HOLY COW

—

diva, from Italian diva, goddess, lady-love, "fine lady":
Latin diva, goddess, female divinity, fem. of divus,
divine, god, deity.
deva, from Sanskrit deva, a god, a bright or shining one.

—OXFORD ENGLISH
DICTIONARY

Mount Rainier, its jagged edges buffed by a thick blanket of snow, was looming presidential and sparkling as it took up what seemed half of the clear, blue horizon on the day Mary Jane called from PBS: The Cuba show had aired to good ratings and great reviews, and the top brass was greenlighting an entire *Adventure Divas* series.

We bought martinis for our soon-to-be-paid interns. "To the empire!" *Clink, clink.* For a pink, potential-filled moment, it looked as if our dream might actually come true. The energy wafting around felt like that pregnant pause when "The Star Spangled Banner" ends, just before the hockey crowd goes wild. A slice of unbridled possibility. Of course, in our private moments, Jeannie and I felt like the characters at the end of *The Candidate,* when the idealistic darkhorse candidate, Bill McKay (Robert Redford), who never thought he would get elected, does just that. McKay looks at his equally shocked campaign manager and simply says, "What do we do now?"

Teamwork, Jeannie and I agreed, rolling from the heels to the balls of our feet in preparation for what was to come. We had to deliver eight programs, on

four countries, in six months, and we were determined not to become formu-
laic. After all the months of idling, we suddenly slammed the rig into overdrive.
Unfortunately, we had no chassis to speak of.

We needed headquarters, pronto, so I confidently plunked down a check
for $2,312 to our new lefty landlord, Knoll Lowney. If you stood on a chair and
pointed your tippy-toes southeast, you could make out the top of Rainier from
the window of our storefront office. Our neighbor to the west was called
Outlaw, a barber whose chair had been the seat of neighborhood information
and ten-dollar haircuts for thirty years. To the east was Philadelphia Fevre, a
cheesesteak joint, a rare bastion of meat and grease, for which we were grateful
in vegan-leaning Seattle. Upstairs, there was a firm of environmental lawyers
who also owned the building (threatened salmon were frequent clients). Our
office's last retail incarnation was as a pager store, but more recently, and more
importantly in terms of juju, the space was the crash pad for the leaders of the
protesters who stymied the World Trade Organization talks, and got the attention of the world, in 2001. The protesters slept like litters of puppies on the
floor of this office when they were not dodging tear gas or putting HISTORY
WILL NEVER FORGIVE YOU stickers on the walls. I figured the anti-globalization
smudge would be good for our small business that hoped to promote a different brand of World Organization.

We began to staff up and, in order to enhance our modest PBS-lined cof-
fers, Jeannie and I took our pitch to the outdoor retail industry for additional
underwriting, and to venture capitalists for cash investment.

Meanwhile, an excellent core group of colleagues came together. Jill
Hodges on editorial and Kate Thompson on design began expanding www.
adventuredivas.com, managing our growing online community and preparing
for pbs.org deliverables. Michael Gross, who was the lead editor on the Cuba
show, and so critical to its success, climbed on board full-time. Heather Reilly,
Rena Bussinger, and Susannah Guttowsky hammered away on research and
preproduction for our next shoots. This represents only a few of the many individuals who contributed to the enterprise.

Two weeks after we moved into the office, we were laboriously rearranging
our heavy, gray metal desks bought for five dollars apiece at Boeing surplus. I
noticed Jeannie staring ominously at the calendar; her face stiffened. "We need

to settle on producers *now*," she said—her way of telling me to *quit interviewing and start making decisions.*

After the Cuba shoot, Jeannie and I had decided that a divide-and-conquer approach would be best for business (not to mention family Christmases for the next thirty years). She would manage the office stateside, and I would take the shows on the road.

The Cuba show received significant attention and excited freelance producers out of the woodwork. Among them was seasoned feature-film producer Julie Costanzo, whose career was forged in the Coppola crucible in the Bay Area. The day she arrived she had to leap, in her two-inch heels and pure silk chemise, over a stream of raw sewage to reach the door of the new Diva world headquarters. Her long dark hair and smashingly sophisticated Italian good looks immediately lent our office new credibility.

Experienced, smart, and willing to work for a modest sum, Julie seemed perfect. But I was worried about her high fashion sense, a forte that would surely wilt under 110-degree heat. Plus, could she work effectively with a stomach full of amoebas?

"What is your next destination?" asked Julie.

"India," I replied, scanning her reaction for any sign of quiver. "Look, Julie, I have some concerns. I don't know if you've done shoots exactly like this. We're talking difficult conditions . . . high ideals, but low budget . . . and . . . and . . ."

"I know what you think," she said, assertively uncrossing her Manolos. "Don't worry, I can go days without sleeping, have a constitution of iron, and a stash of Cipro that could keep a crew of twenty working for a month."

And, she hadn't flinched at the sewage-line break.

Hired.

We wanted to go to India because our research had identified Indian women who were making massive change, activism on the scale of the huge challenges the country faced. And the "nominate a diva" section of our website was regularly turning up people from the subcontinent.

But I had other reasons, too. Spirituality was a floater in the corner of my vision and perhaps it was time to coax the little irritant away from the periphery and into the center. *Diva* means "deity," says the OED, and according to the *Lonely Planet* guidebook, India is chock-full of them. "Some estimates put the total number of deities at 330 million," the guidebook says of the Hindu pantheon. Certainly a country with a three-to-one human-to-deity ratio must have an inside line on the big question: how to find the divine in the everyday.

"Delhi has ten million people," says our taxi driver, Rajbir, as a way to explain our lurching progress down New Delhi's Pusa Road on our first day of a three-week stay in India. I'd learned from Cuba about the shortcomings of too brief a shoot.

"Yeah, but," I say to Rajbir, noting the unusual traffic jam we found ourselves in, "it's the ox carts, buses, rickshaws, scooters, and—"

Rajbir suddenly slams on the brakes: *eeeeeerrreescrrrrrrrrruchhh!!!*

I plunge forward and my head snaps to a stop, eye to eye with a statue of the goddess Kali on the dashboard altar. A displaced shaft of incense smoke juts sideways in slow motion, and the garland of orange carnations slung over the goddess swings like a slow, heavy pendulum.

"—the cows that make it tricky," I finish, picking my chin off the back of the front seat.

A large white cow with a heaving udder and a fuchsia smudge across its neck languidly saunters across the road in front of us. Julie bends over to collect the rolls of 16mm film that have tumbled onto the floor. "How's it going with Phoolan Devi?" I ask her about India's well-known bandit-turned-member-of-Parliament. Julie has been in India for a week scouting, and Devi is one of the people she's been trying to connect with.

"Raghu has been calling every day but no luck yet," says Julie, "and just so you know, Raghu is a great fixer."

"And the fishing," I ask expectantly. "Found a place yet?"

"Not yet," she responds, not looking up.

"Mostly Hindu, some Muslim, all mayhem," is the sophisticated theological analysis I am able to eke out for a first standup later in the day before my foot is run over by a young man in a Ted Nugent T-shirt pulling a wooden cart full of

greens. We are filming at a memorial to Mohandas Gandhi as part of a brief rundown on Indian history.

"I can see we are going to have some logistical challenges," says San Francisco–based DigiBeta cameraman John Chater to Julie, nodding toward the thirty-five boys and men who have crowded around the camera and are looking straight down the lens. Good-natured, strong, and tall enough to shoot over the crowds, John will be a huge asset on this shoot, as will his quiet, mustached soundman, Doug Dunderdale. Sound technicians, not surprisingly, are almost always quiet.

"See you back at the hotel," says Cheryl, as she sinks, undaunted, into a mass of pedestrians with her small Beaulieu camera. Cheryl's freewheeling footage added a unique element to the Cuba show, and I'm glad she was available to join us in India. Ideally, we intend to keep crew consistent from one show to the next, but prior commitments and the contingencies of production have meant that, this time, Cheryl and I are the only returning crew members.

Of all of India's iconic leaders, it is Mohandas K. (Mahatma) Gandhi, with his combination of spiritual practice and political action, who most intrigues me. A leader during the country's long struggle for independence from British rule, Gandhi began his civil disobedience as a young lawyer in South Africa by burning the identity cards that were required of nonwhites. After returning to India, he was a participant in the Indian National Congress and later used civil disobedience, fasting, and marches as political tools in his work. Known throughout the world for his dedication to nonviolence (*ahimsa*) and truth (*satya*), Gandhi was nominated five times in an eleven-year period for the Nobel Peace Prize, but never received it. As with many of India's leaders, a cult of personality surrounds Gandhi, almost deifying him.

India's reputation as a place of truth and nonviolence, popularly embodied in Mahatma ("great soul") Gandhi, stands in contrast to another rap: a place of widespread corruption. Today's headline in the *Times of India* blares out: TOP GUNS TO SLUG IT OUT IN BATTLE ROYAL and goes on to say that money, muscle power, and the mafia play an unhealthy role in elections.

Politicians with criminal backgrounds are not uncommon in India. Phoolan Devi, the Bandit Queen who we're trying to track down, is a case in point. On the one hand it seems shocking that a renowned bandit can be elected to office, but on the other, if white-collar crime were prosecuted as aggressively as drug-related crimes in the United States, our country would have its share of convicts-cum-politicians.

To explore how widespread corruption thrives in this birthplace of truth, nonviolence, and pacifism, we have arranged to meet one of Delhi's top cops, Kiran Bedi, at a police training center an hour outside of the city. She said in a speech, "I do firmly believe that police in any country can be the greatest protector of human rights and the rule of law—as it could as well be the greatest violator of both."

Bedi became India's first lady beat cop when she joined the service in 1972, and she has since climbed the ranks despite her habit of stepping on toes of the higher-ups. She is a former tennis champ, the author of several books, the founder of many social service organizations; she has a slew of degrees; and she won the Asian version of the Nobel Peace Prize—the Ramon Magsaysay Award—in 1994. Her résumé sounded right-on when I first heard about her. But it was almost *too* good, and I was a little suspicious. Was she just a Brahmin with a foolproof infrastructure of support? (In American-speak: a Kennedy?)

"Plus," I had said to Julie back in Seattle when I expressed my initial reservations about Bedi, "she's a celebrity, and we're trying to avoid that." The show's mission is to seek out "unsung" folks whose work is driven by personal passion, not "achievement" status. I was concerned that Bedi was more of a high-profile celeb.

"Trust me," assured Julie, who had read much more than me, "this woman *is* a diva. She's constantly going at it with the establishment. That's why she got banished to prison duty. Nobody thought she could succeed, but she did." She handed me Bedi's 1999 book, *It's Always Possible: Transforming One of the Largest Prisons in the World*.

Bedi was sent to run the infamous Tijar Jail, a maximum-security prison and the largest in South Asia. It was an infamously brutal place where 12,000 prisoners were crammed in a space with a stated capacity of 4,000. By all accounts, rather than flinching, or dodging the posting, she ran straight at the challenge. Her most striking innovation was to introduce Vipassana, a meditation program that includes a ten-day silent retreat, as a part of prisoner reform. She also instituted a "petition box" where prisoners could post anonymous complaints, make requests, and expose corruption and abuse; invited non-profit organizations into the prison to provide child care, medicine, literacy, and advocacy; and instituted gardening programs. In short, she started treating prisoners like human beings.

The London *Times* stated: "In seven months . . . she has made a hellish institution humane." The "hellish" institution is now colloquially referred to as the Ashram, and the humanity and dignity she brought to India's prison system has created a reform model that is being adopted all over the world. Bedi's achievements in reforming the prison system are even more impressive given the male-dominated, set-up-for-failure environment in which she was operating.

Since her success at Tijar Jail, Bedi had moved on to a new role training and reforming the Delhi police force, an institution often associated with corruption. She wrote of policing: "It pains me to see the extent of hypocrisy prevailing in the police and in the administration as a whole. . . . The leadership is undemocratic. It encourages subjugation, fear and short-term results. There is no visible vision. . . . There is only one shared anxiety: protection of one's own position by degrading the others. . . . The entire system appears to be based on money, power, influence and conspiracy of silence."

Such brash truth-telling has gotten Bedi in trouble, but the magnitude of her successes, such as the prison reform, has made it impossible for any corrupt higher-ups to get rid of her. She's considered by some a bone in the gullet that "can be neither spat out nor swallowed," wrote her biographer Parmesh Dangwal. "Many attempts have been made to subdue her, but phoenix-like she has risen to greater and greater heights."

We drive out to the sweeping, walled police training grounds an hour outside New Delhi. Within the red-brick walls I witness order unlike I've yet seen in India. Across the manicured acres, groups of people are practicing martial arts, women in bright white are climbing ropes, men with rifles turn at attention and practice their formations. I catch up with Bedi in a classroom, at the end of a talk she is giving to a group of managers, most of whom are looking at her with palpable awe. She has short, cropped dark hair and is small, maybe five foot five. Her khaki uniform has attached to it a name tag, several colorful bars that must mean something important, and a number of shiny stars and shapes affixed to the stiff shoulders. Atop her head sits a heavy, high-brimmed officer's hat, like the one my veteran grandfather wore, which always represented to me some mysterious remote power.

"Hello, hello, have you been well taken care of?" she asks me, without coming to a full stop. Her second-in-command has toured us around the facilities for the last half hour. She's clearly efficient, and her smile and eyes dance like those stars on her shoulders. "Let's go to the range," she says. No delicate chat over four cups of Darjeeling with Bedi. She grabs my arm and we head out to shoot guns.

Bedi, just like the hundreds of male and female trainees in her charge, must pass target practice on a regular basis. On our way to the range we slowly thread our way through a field of young women in pure-white saris, with loose-fitting white pants underneath, practicing karate moves in unison. "Haaa! Hurrr! Heee!" they yell, thrusting their arms and legs.

"They must be confident to defend themselves before they can defend others," explains Bedi. Then, we wend our way around a hundred men of varying age, sitting cross-legged in perfect rows, wearing white T-shirts and khaki pants, exhaling in unison—"ha, ha, ha, ha, ha"—as part of their daily yoga practice. This morning, as every morning, all the officers meditated for an hour.

"Tell me more about your training philosophy and management style. What are these officers getting?" I ask.

"They're getting equipped to be police officers, which means physical fitness, physical courage, knowledge of law, skills in handling difficult situations, but also a human *heart*—a human heart which is sensitive and says 'I came to this profession to defend and protect, and not to kill.' "

Prioritizing a human heart in law-enforcement training is revolutionary, and I'd imagine it's extremely difficult to institute.

"What was the initial reception to the meditation idea? Was there resistance?"

"No, to the meditation, no," Bedi responds. "Because these meditation programs are not conversional programs, they're not sectarian; it's introspective meditation, which means you are trained to bring out the emotions within you and then observe them, through your breath. Whether it's your addictions, your anger, your revenge, whether it's your lust, whatever it is, it surfaces through these techniques," she explains.

"So it's not religious in the dogmatic sense," she continues. "You can be Muslim, Hindu, or a nonbeliever and do this. The intellect is the wisdom which judges between one right thought and one wrong thought."

"I love this training," she says, nodding toward fifty men working in formations with rifles, their khaki berets all tipped alike. "But without the introspective technique, this training would be a burden of knowledge."

"A burden?" I ask, not getting it.

"A burden because if you are a human being with a lot of knowledge and do not know how to use it, I think you are a liability. It's very important to recognize that police training equips you with all the power."

We arrive at the firing range. Two women officers and three men are firing off revolvers and 9mm pistols at the red and white bull's-eye standing a hundred yards in the distance. The crew and I trot after Bedi as she surveys the range, unconscious of the camera.

"We can equip people to fire perfectly. But fire to defend or fire to kill?" she says emphatically, as much with her hands as her words. "Fire to protect or fire to murder? Which?" Bedi excitedly conveys her philosophy. "That's his hand," she says, pointing toward an officer, "and the hand is linked by thought to the mind." She runs her own hand from her wrist to her head. "The mind has to be developed. This training is not just to make them good police officers, this training is to make them good human beings, because finally it's the humanity in you which is going to be projected in your legal work."

"Very nice work, very nice," Bedi commends the officers, and then she fires off a few cracking, loud rounds herself. I flinch. Satisfied with her accuracy, Bedi holsters her sidearm and we walk back across the field. She smiles and nods at everyone we pass along the way. They seem to regard her with respect, but not fear. We find some shade under a tree, and continue talking.

"Why do you think people respond to you in the way they do, almost magnetically?" I ask. I, too, am beginning to feel the tractor beam.

"Because I don't wait for them to come to me, I go to them. And I go to them because that's my duty to do, but it's also a source of joy to me. The warmth and compassion and concern and joy you exude, comes back. I've seen cold interactions, and I know they're dull. And dullness is infectious, just as joy is," says Bedi.

I give myself an intellectual pinch. This is the headiest conversation I have ever had with a cop. Clearly, Bedi is a police officer who makes spiritualism pragmatic, but I take it a step farther and ask if she considers herself a spiritual leader.

"Spiritual *leader*? Oh my god. Not a leader. All I can talk to you about is what kind of human being I think I am. I am not as materialistic as I am spiritual. Because I'm pretty contented with myself. What I need is more inner food, rather than external belongings. If I were to choose between a diamond ring and a beautiful book, I would pick a beautiful book. For me, a diamond ring is a waste, but a book is full of knowledge and that's my food," she says. Her life certainly reflects these values. I lost the plot of police training details a half hour ago, and am focused on the broader implications of her holistic approach.

"It's not only duty. It's a mission," Bedi once told a reporter of her work ethic. "You are in it all the time. You have to invoke the creativity of five thousand years which is just lying dormant."

"There's a more visible humanitarian ethic here compared to anywhere else I've ever been," I begin, "and—"

"Well, India has reasons to be both happy and angry," says Bedi.

"What are they?"

"Happy—they're settled with themselves; they're contented people—"

"But why?" I press, as the notion of broad-based contentment seems far-fetched. Angst, rather than contentment, is the norm in my socio-strata. And India is famously stratified. And famously impoverished.

"Why? Genetically," she says, with too small a laugh for me to know if she is serious.

I laugh, uncomfortably.

"Really? It's not the three hundred thirty million deities?" I ask, half-joking, drawing on a figure I have come to consider specious.

"I think every Indian has a habit of looking for an anchor. Sometimes you look for an external anchor and sometimes you train to be internally anchored. And once you have an anchor, I think you're very well put, aren't you?"

"What is their anchor?" I ask.

"An anchor could be a deity, could be a god, could be a church, could be a temple, could be a parent, could be a teacher, could be a guru, could be an exercise, could be yoga. And once they are anchored and if they're convinced, they're settled, their search stops," she explains.

It strikes me that most Americans spend a good forty years looking for their anchor. Anchoring early could leave you more time to jump off the boat and go swimming.

"I think *anchor* basically means where you can go if you are in distress. And you can get an answer. You can get help," Bedi says.

"You started this by saying there's a lot to be happy about and a lot to be miserable about," I say, still trying to understand a fundamental dichotomy.

"Yes, a lot to be miserable about. I think Indians are looking for better governance at all levels, whether it's civic administration, village administration, state governance, or national governance. There is an anxiety in every Indian. How do we get better enforcement of laws? Better justice? Greater prosperity? More employment? We have overriding secular tension. Overriding caste problems. Imbalance in development—if one state is rich, another state in this country is very poor, so it brings down the overall national income," she says, listing just a few of India's myriad challenges.

"Yesterday," I say, "there was a rally—an anti-WTO demonstration—and thousands of people with placards were peacefully walking to Parliament in central Delhi. I would ask them, 'Is this a protest?' and the response was always, 'No, no, it's a rally.' It certainly looked like protest."

"By and large, India doesn't protest. But that doesn't mean—being contented and at ease—you don't want progress. Yet you will not find riots; you will find people still at ease, settled down because they have their anchors. And a lot of toleration. Toleration too is a very strong Indian spirit. It tolerates a hell of a lot of nonsense," she says soberly. "Even in the neighborhood, even within family. They think it's duty to tolerate. If you have a deviant son, you don't put him on the road. We don't send out aging parents," she says.

Gandhi promoted toleration. "Mutual toleration is a necessity for all time and for all races," he said. But he also knew when things could not be tolerated, leading a number of nonviolent demonstrations (I would call them protests) against British occupation and other injustices. So it seems knowing when or what to put up with is part of the art of wielding power—personal, political, institutional—responsibly.

"I've been hearing a lot about the notion that we all have divinity within since I've been in India. What do you think of that?" I ask, tentatively floating a nutgrab.

"I think each one of us defines divinity the way we're brought up, and if you're brought up in a value-based environment, then you see divinity in another person. I was trained to look at divinity in service. Divinity in humankind. In fact, when I was taking my unit public-service examination, there was a column in the form called religion. I could have written Hindu; I could have written anything," she says, her hand poised in the air as if she's still holding that pencil, "but I remember as a twenty-year-old woman when I was filling in the form I wrote *humankind*. That for me stood for divinity. Every one of us defines divinity," she said.

"What happens if there isn't enough, uh, humility in the mix?" I ask, reflecting my theory that hubris gums up the works in everything from interpersonal to international relations (and, well, by extension, any shot at divinity).

"If there isn't? I think we would all be animals. We would all be biting at each other," she replies, the very few lines around her eyes now showing themselves, "because there would be nothing but a clash of egos, and always warfare. There would be no gratitude."

The Bush administration comes to mind.

"After following you around today and talking to people, I'm convinced you have no fears. But you must. Do you have any?" I ask.

"After I lost my mother, I'm fearless. There's no more fear," she says simply, and warmly.

There is a hitch in the breath of the universe. Julie looks down; Cheryl's eye leaves the lens. We all have an immediate, visceral understanding of what she's said. I'm glad she continues talking because I have no follow-up.

"You're afraid of something you love most, of losing something you love most, and I lost her. And I think after this there's nothing more to lose. I loved her so much—I could still be a little girl when she was around," says this police chief with a sparkling, open-hearted grin.

"She's gone and it shows, you know, how everything is so transient. There's nothing permanent. But the point is I have no more fears. How long I live—what's going to happen to me. I think the key is what I do with what I have today. Because today is going to be yesterday and tomorrow is going to be another today. But what you *do* in that day *is* probably in your control," she says with conviction, her eyes never straying from mine.

"So the transience makes you more invested in the moment, rather than less?" I ask.

"Yes. The transience makes me focus more, because I know it's going to go away."

Kiran Bedi's leadership goes beyond the stuff of management books or celebrity charisma, and enables her to survive in an environment in which not everybody wants change. She has magnetism, as a guru might, but the power she exudes over others is mutually sustaining and endeavors to enlighten rather than control.

Bedi stands and firmly shakes our hands. Her old wisdom and new tools will continue to tackle contemporary challenges, and I silently wish her well in the inevitable battles. She hunches slightly to put on her cap and then walks away, alone, through two perfectly aligned rows of trees. Their solid lower trunks are painted red, to prevent disease, and higher up, the branches shake freely in the wind.

TO: HOLLY
FROM: JEANNIE
SUBJECT: EMPIRE UPDATE

Michael is making good progress on recutting Cuba into two half-hour shows but will need some rewriting, direction, and rerecording from you. Site is good: Kate did a wonderful Eritrean homepage (with Jill's profile of the war-poet), and Inga la Gringa ruffled feathers with her "How to get your sex toys past customs" column. Lotsa hits. Still working trademarks but we'll need $$$$$. Are you interviewing the bandit?—Jeannie

The subject line of Jeannie's e-mail and Bedi's insights on humility and enlightened leadership have made me think a little harder about our Diva rhetoric. We've been playfully using terms like *empire* and *divadom* to make a point about corporate media and entertain ourselves, but there is the possibility that by wielding the master's tools we would get cooties. Sometimes, the best way to fight fire is not with fire, but with water. Gandhi and other Indian leaders undermined the British army not through self-aggrandizement and armed struggle (the favored tactics of imperialists) but by changing the rules—by using self-restraint and nonviolence.

On our most idealistic, caffeinated days, we hoped we were, in our own small way, doing something in that spirit of originality. That is, by building an independent, uncompromising, pro-woman "empire," we could create an alternative model to corporate-run media. And by highlighting and linking divas around the world, we could imagine new models of power, leadership, and—as important—individual potential.

But until we could figure out a way to get by without additional investor capital, and until we could dream up a new, nonimperialist rhetoric, we would just have to keep improvising.

"Okay, then, you must all wear long-sleeve shirts and clean clothes," says Raghu, an investigative journalist who is moonlighting as our fixer. Raghu is lanky and mustached; he speaks judiciously and wears unwrinkled collared shirts. Often pastels. Foreign-paid fixer fees in India are much better than local salaries, so we have been able to persuade Raghu to spend his vacation from his journalism job with us.

Raghu, no doubt, is secretly glad to have a legitimate opportunity to upgrade this underdressed crew (except Julie, of course). "You cannot show disrespect in the temples," he says, glancing toward my threadbare 501s.

As we head toward the temple, Raghu uses his cell phone to call Phoolan Devi's residence for the fourth time today. He has been calling her handlers repeatedly, trying to arrange for us to meet Devi. He has never received a yes; but then again, he has not received a no, either, so Julie and I encourage him to keep trying. Phoolan Devi is from a low caste of fishermen and, as is usually the case among the low castes, is illiterate and does not speak English, so Raghu (rather than any of us) must make the initial contact. Illiteracy might disadvantage Devi, but she is said to compensate for it in spades through cunning, smarts, and charm—skills that probably helped in her outlaw days. I must admit to a romantic fascination with this Robin Hood–like figure, who actually did steal from the rich and give to the poor. A legend in her own time, Devi is regarded by many as a champion of the lower castes.

The narrow street that leads to the Kali temple is lined with vendors in wooden stalls and crowded with beggars begging, goats bleating, incense burning, children playing, and hundreds of the faithful preparing to enter the temple. Unpleasant brass bells gong every few seconds. Vendors peddle offerings to be presented at Kali's altar, as well as likenesses of the deity in 2-D, 3-D, plastic, wood, and porcelain; the street is filled with Kalis, large and small. I buy a garland of yellow marigolds for three rupees and continue on up the concourse of mayhem. Mounds of blood-red *kumkum* powder dot the way to the temple. I idly wonder if it is like a Grateful Dead concert where all the really interesting action happens in the parking lot or if this level of sensory orgy could be sustained inside the small, circular, white marble temple itself.

The moment I breach the entrance, I realize the latter is true. The interior of the temple pulses with Kali devotees boisterously doing *puja* (prayer). Throngs of people are tussling and pushing to get near a giant red poochy orb with a tree growing out of its top that anchors the center of the room. To my eye, the amorphous, globular manifestation of Kali (that looks nothing like the tchotchkes outside) is more curious than divine. People are rocking against and rubbing its marble base. Teenage boys bless worshippers by tapping their foreheads with a red cinder. Women bow, then dab cinders on their foreheads and down the parts in their long, pulled-back hair. Men sway, bellowing *puja* with their eyes closed. Bells clang mercilessly, erratically, as if to throw a wrench in the possibility of order, and sweet, sweet incense engulfs the entire overripe scene.

"Not exactly a Quaker meetinghouse," John, our cameraman, says about the atmosphere he'll be hard-pressed to capture on tape.

While the important blob might lack the features one might expect of a tough deity, the images of Kali that glare down from all 360 degrees *do not*. Yowza. This manifestation of the fearsome goddess has a red flailing tongue, dances with glee on the corpse of Lord Shiva, and shamelessly wears a garland of severed limbs and human heads that are dripping blood.

Goddess Kali, who is popular with the Bengali population, is believed to be a fierce, creative, and destructive manifestation of divine energy. Julie introduces me to a soft-spoken Bengali woman of about thirty-five who, with her family, tends the temple. She tells us that this ferocious deity that inspires so many signifies the divine and wicked forces within all of us. Kali's skirt of sev-

Kali

ered limbs suggests the transitory nature of human values and signifies the slaying of evil (thus the need to be mighty ferocious). In short, Kali is harsh, but truthful. Devotion to her is supposed to reduce tension and fear—fear being one of the primary things she bravely slays.

The Bengali woman leads me up to the altar, and I feel bad because I get cuts in front of a real devotee who is twice my age and missing an arm. A young boy blesses me with a smudge of red *kumkum* on the forehead and tosses a woven, sparkly red cloth over my head. Being blessed in the name of a goddess who dangles bloody heads and severed limbs like charms on a bracelet is surprisingly . . . uplifting. Kali, like Cuba's black Madonna, is much more exciting than Mary, whose lot in life always struck me as a bit dull. At least Kali gets to dance and slay things. Mary, in her time, was a maligned, celibate single mother. Need I say more?

At home I am comfortable with being fairly aspiritual; and while I'll never get caught burying a placenta in my backyard, India is tweaking in me the possibility that I might be overlooking something *big*. The need for ritual, the want of existential explanations, the affirmation of common truths; I get the need for a spiritual life, but it's the vehicle that always trips me up. Hinduism's acceptance of all beliefs and forms of worship is by definition agreeable, and the sassy deities are more appealing to me than Christian martyrs. But, as I wade against a current of worshippers to get out of the temple, I conclude that India feels like a spiritual petri dish: rich with life's delicious goop, but not something I'm entirely prepared to eat out of just yet.

I put my hand in my pocket to pay an eight-year-old boy for watching my flip-flops, which were bought at Target in Seattle but were made in India. Child labor, spiritual tourism, First World economic fascism, and simple gratitude all pass through my mind in the time it takes me to hand him the five rupees.

John and I climb to the roof of a building across the street to get a wide angle of the temple; I pull back a laundry line so he can get a clear shot. I smell blood and curry and feces and cooking animal flesh; I hear people wailing, and bells, and crying children and meditative chanting. Pure red and pure yellow and lots of gray, and so, so many people fill up this picture.

"Tape's out," says John, and we walk back down the stone staircase to the temple to find the rest of the crew. Raghu is sitting on a brick wall still holding his cell phone, looking more frustrated than ever. Apparently he has had another nonstarter conversation with Phoolan Devi's people. "Politicians. They are the same all over the world," he says about her elusiveness.

"We can't give up," I say.

"Are you sure?" he says. Raghu doesn't think we should be pursuing Devi. He is less forgiving than I am of the murders Phoolan Devi committed during her tenure as a bandit.

Personally, I can't resist the story of a low-caste woman who escapes a brutal child marriage to become a bandit, lays down her arms on her own terms, uses her populist power to negotiate the length of her prison term, and then goes on to become a member of Parliament.

Raghu can.

We have had this conversation before.

"But she was avenging her own *gang rape*," I say, referring to a group of higher-caste village men she ordered killed several months after they tied her up and brutally gang-raped her in a barn *for a month*.

Two cabs drop us at the Delhi train station to catch the afternoon train to Jaipur, capital of the state of Rajasthan. We lug our equipment on board and buy chai from a nine-year-old boy who carries a mobile metal tea set lashed to the front of his body by a white cloth sling. Julie downs her fifth hot, sweet, milky tea shot of the day.

Somewhere along the way—be it by siding with a murderess, general sacrilege, or that somosa I bought and snarfed on the street—I must have derailed my karma because I spend most of the train ride to Rajasthan rushing to the six-inch hole in the floor of a stinky train car (the bathroom) that is servicing my wicked bout of Delhi belly. When I am not squatting in misery, channeling my secret happy place, or necking the Imodium Julie has given me, I wedge myself fetal in my train seat to read Elisabeth Bumiller's *May You Be the Mother of a Hundred Sons: A Journey Among the Women of India*.

The book confirms that the ladies in India could indeed use a few more anchors. For every Kiran Bedi, who has had the tools, education, and class standing to realize her power, there are thousands of Indian women who fare less well. Seventy-five percent of Indian women (that's about 370 million) are illiterate and poor and live back-breaking rural lives.

Thousands of "bride burnings," in which women are killed because their husbands or in-laws are unhappy with the dowry, take place every year. Female infanticide. Sex-selective abortion among the middle class. Child marriage. The depressing list goes on. I am beginning to understand the widespread appeal of Kali, an avenging female icon.

Bumiller says that in the past two thousand years women's status plummeted. As wandering tribal clans began to settle, women became less involved in the means of production, and gender roles became more demarcated, with men (who brought home the bacon, or perhaps wild boar) taking a superior position. Bumiller also references historian Romila Thapar's theory that in India the oppression of women was part and parcel of preserving caste distinctions. (Apparently, some nasty fellow named Manu codified the caste system around A.D. 200 and also said this of us ladies: "Woman is as foul as falsehood itself." Whoa. What did his mother do to him?!) Caste meant controlling who married whom so that the gene pool did not get polluted (read: putting guys like Manu in danger of losing their power). Further, Bumiller quotes Thapar as explaining, "To avoid pollution, you must control birth . . . you lose control over birth if you lose control over women."

Et voilà, the institutionalization of oppression.

All this from a culture that worships millions of goddesses. This worshipping of women in religious practice and trashing them in real life is one of my favorite global-religious ironies, certainly not limited to the Hindu cultures.

Hypocrisy. Misogyny. Suffering. Organized religion. *Who needs it?* I think ungenerously, short-tempered with dehydration. I pop a Pepto-Bismol tablet, just to try something new. I wish I could ask Kiran Bedi about this. With her mastery of the spiritual, and direct vernacular, she could surely help me understand where orthodoxies fall apart, or at least where those in her own culture go astray.

Julie hails a horse-drawn flatbed wagon that will serve as a makeshift dolly, thus giving our low-rent documentary high-rent effects. Jaipur is the first place we've been that looks like the images of regal India of times past. We trundle past small palaces and Rajasthani men in bright red turbans and handlebar mustaches as we soak up the "Pink City" (a bit of a misnomer as the buildings are more of a hazy orange).

We arrive at our hotel, a former palace, to a frenzy of activity going on in the walled courtyard. Two dozen men are building platforms, draping yellow canopies, and stringing up twelve thousand bright orange carnations. Strands of lights and garlands of flowers are carefully arranged on an elaborate welcome gate. We have apparently stumbled on India's wedding season, an annual festival called Akha Teej.

If the twelve pages of matrimonials in today's *Times of India* are any indication, aside from caste, marriage seems to be life's personal and institutional tour de force. There are 3,012 "Brides Wanted" ads, broken down by the caste of the groom-to-be.

ALLIANCE INVITED BY A BRAHMIN
WELL SETTLED STATUS FAMILY for their son 34 ys, 5´6˝.
Professional handsome fair teetotaller well settled in business
(software engineer in Motorola Chicago USA) seeking extremely
beautiful, very fair, homely, slim, intelligent, convented girl from
reputed family background not more than 24 years.
SEND BIODATA INFO AND HOROSCOPE WITH RECENT
COLOR CLOSE-UP PHOTOGRAPH TO BOX NO BBV000R.

An example of one of the 2,712 "Grooms Wanted" ads:

A reputed Pune based WELL SETTLED CULTURED
MAHARASHTRIAN business family seeks alliance for their
CONVENT EDUCATED TALL ATTRACTIVE DAUGHTER
23/5´6˝ WT 60 MCM from a boy prof Maharashtrian
height 5´9˝ + well educated and smart.
SEND BIODATA PHOTO AND HOROSCOPE. WRITE: BOX NO Y000Y

"Homely" and "convent educated" aren't exactly plusses in the US of A, but the dating game is not *altogether* different than in the States, except that the priorities are a little different, the stakes are much higher, and the in-laws are notably more involved. For them, marriage comes first, and then love is generated as the bond grows. Indians think Americans are a wee bit unrealistic in our expectation that with marriage we get to have 1) the golden hue of falling in love, 2) a spouse with whom to conceive and raise children, 3) an intellectual match and companion, and 4) hot sex.

Yet, our (no doubt judgmental) queries about arranged marriage to the hotel concierge give even Julie and me pause. He asks us how many marriages in the United States are arranged, and how many are "for love." Julie and I respond, almost in unison (and a bit too quickly), "All of them are love."

"But," he asks sincerely, "what if you don't find love?"

Julie and I, both thirty-something and single (the Boyfriend in Seattle and I had gone our separate ways after I returned from Borneo), look at each other.

He nods slightly. "Yes." He pauses awkwardly and smiles. "Well, the wedding begins at seven, if you want to film."

Tonight's wedding in the hotel courtyard might be arranged (purportedly around 90 percent of them are) or for love, or some combination thereof, but a lot of the marriages taking place during this year's two-month-long marriage season are between children. Rajasthan, one of the most traditional states in India, has the highest incidence of child marriage—a practical hangover from times past that, though illegal, is still common in rural areas. A little girl might be married off at, say, age three—or ten, or twelve—although she won't go live with the groom's family until she is in her teens. Arranged marriage ensures that she will not become an economic liability to her family in later years. Dowry and child marriage, while concepts antithetical to modern Western sensibility, were born of pragmatism.

Rajasthan is also home to some of the country's most progressive social activism. In recent years, a broad coalition of groups fighting for women's and human rights have confronted the local political establishment on a range of social issues. These groups were initially spurred into action in 1987 when young Roop Kanwar, who lived in the village of Deorala, was burned alive on her husband's funeral pyre in an attempt to revive that tradition, called *suttee* or *sati*. Among the thousands of activists mobilized by this event, one of the most prominent is Alice Garg, the person we are on our way to meet at her home on the outskirts of Jaipur.

"We should shoot her seashell collection," says Julie, who met Alice last week while scouting. "Shells in this dry, barren desert; an odd obsession, don't you think?"

Alice is the founder of the Bal Rashmi Society (*bal rashmi* means "raise up" or "first rays of a new dawn"), which advocates on behalf of the most disenfranchised peoples of this region. Discouraging child marriage is just one item on her very long agenda.

Alice and the Bal Rashmi Society have been frequently under fire for their work to bring attention to—and end—atrocities against those in the lowest castes. Alice was involved in a campaign to bring to justice a group of gang-rapists, one of whom was the deputy superintendent of police. Alice quickly became a target. Before we arrived she e-mailed us about this experience: "I do not know if you are aware of the politically motivated attack we had to face. Nine cases—rape, murder, attempt to murder and rape, exploitation, fraud, misuse of funds, etc.—were registered against us." The Bal Rashmi office was raided; Alice and her associates were taken into police custody and tortured, and one died in custody. Since then, the ruling government lost assembly elections and was replaced by a new party. The case against Alice was reopened and dismissed. In the end, she and her colleagues were fully exonerated by a human rights commission.

"As a result of this, all our programmes have suffered greatly," Alice wrote. "However, there is plenty going on once again," she concluded her e-mail, encouraging us to come.

Alice Garg opens the front door and greets us with a subtle head cock and a warm smile. I notice that one eye wanders ever so slightly. She wears her salt-and-pepper hair in a tightly wound bun at the nape of her neck, and a chunky red *bindi* centers her forehead. She is wearing a white sari with red trim as, I later found out, she always does. Seventeen years ago Alice made a decision. "I am not against fashion or anything, but I feel that we women waste a lot of our time in selection of our dresses. Also, white matches everything."

She also intimates that she could spend the money she might have used on clothes on acquiring seashells, or on a trip to the seaside to pick them up herself. Her seashell collection is housed in a glass case, and she shows us this almost immediately after tea. "These are from all over," she says rhapsodically, taking small pinkish shell after small pinkish shell out of clear plastic bags and displaying them to us.

After an hour of filming the shells and watching Alice peddle on her exercise bike in her sari (and consuming a total of sixteen cups of tea and four primary-colored sugary treats each), we are all bumping along a dirt road through a scrubby desert landscape in a jeep, on our way to the village of Soan ka Baas, to follow Alice for a typical day of fieldwork. Once in a while a weak-looking tree asserts itself onto this seemingly inhospitable environment. As we drive, Alice tells us about her life.

At eighteen she married the wrong boy next door (as in wrong caste, wrong religion), which led to being disowned by her family. Her activism took shape shortly thereafter, and in 1972 she left her job as a high school teacher to start the Bal Rashmi Society with four thousand rupees (about ninety dollars). "I have seen poverty, extreme poverty, I've seen people suffering, you know, without any complaint. That motivated me," says Alice. In the early years, when Bal Rashmi was still fledgling, she took "untouchable" orphans into her home and cooked and cared for them. At least one out of six Indians are Dalits, or untouchables. *Dalit* means "crushed" or "stepped on," but Gandhi called them *Harijans,* or "Children of God."

These Children of God are often brutally persecuted and are victimized by violence including murder and assault, and they are often banned from worshipping at temples. Untouchables are thought of as too polluted to count as human beings, untouched by even the supreme Hindu deity. They are so low on the Brahmanical order that they are not really even on it; they are a caste predestined to deal with human waste and dead bodies.

Alice's latest project is the construction of an enormous water-retention site for the drought-ridden village of Soan ka Baas. "This is the third continuous year that we are facing drought," Alice explains. "We are trying to create a big facility in order to catch the runoff water from the rains. We do not want the water to go to waste."

We drive over a berm in this dry, butterscotch-colored wasteland and stop when we see at least fifty women, from teenagers to the elderly, dressed in stunning, bright saris that stand out like gems against the parched landscape and the hazy, pale blue sky. The women have carved out a vast depression in the dry earth and are busily picking and digging and hauling buckets of soil to the surface. A line of women emerges from the hole, each balancing a heavy, round, metal, saucerlike bucket—heaped with earth—on her head while holding a veil over her face and negotiating the steep grade. They pass by one another, often trading smiles, in the hundred-degree heat as they make their way from the bottom to the top, where each transfers her bucket to another woman. The curves and poise and sharp fuchsia and lime-green and bright aqua moving over a dead landscape make for a most graceful and extraordinary chain gang. I am loath to glamorize this back-breaking work in this sweltering environment, but there is something uncannily serene about the women's movement, and indeed, the entire scene. The run-off well that they are creating will radically change their lives.

"If the water is there, then there is some relief at least; it is the women who bring water for the whole family. They are always the one," Alice says, wheezing just a bit from the dust-filled air.

The men and boys, in white cotton pants and shirts with blue and green turbans, are looking *particularly* serene, as they are lounging on a ledge that forms the perimeter of the construction site where the women work. Alice yells at a group of idle men and explains that since they never have to carry the water, they don't care how close it is.

Alice surveys the sweltering, dusty work site, which covers a few acres. She scuttles quickly over tough terrain, unself-consciously hiking up her sari when necessary; we scramble to keep up. This is no tour for us; this is a typical work day in which Alice might cover two hundred kilometers and oversee several projects. Alice constantly barks directions, in a piercing, gravely voice, at those who are not working, and sometimes at those who are.

Her brashness is forgiven because it is a part of "Didi" (a moniker of trust and intimacy used by those who are digging the well), a woman who has won respect by years of working to empower the disempowered and to improve communities.

"What's the status of women in this region?" I ask, when we finally get Alice to stop moving for a minute.

"She is considered to be nothing. Nobody knows the women's names in the villages. They live anonymous lives. Day and night, unpaid servants," she says, gesturing to the chain gang, and her brusque managerial style softens.

"The caste system seems to create a double whammy—both caste and gender oppression," I say. Although caste discrimination is officially illegal, Alice confirms that it is still the most operative force in people's lives.

"Yes, [caste] plays a very major role. Oh, it exists very much, you can see it, you can feel it," Alice says, with that strange little wheezy cough that has been with her all day. She goes on to talk about how it takes a long time for cultural reality to match laws.

"We have a law, for example, against child marriage, but it continues. We have a law against female infanticide—you cannot just go kill the girl in the mother's womb. But it continues.

"Women in Asia are not even living in the Third World; we are living in the Fourth World. You don't have a right to be born. You don't have a right to live; you don't have a right to your future. The women are tortured and treated badly by the family and other people because they think that she will not open her mouth."

Alice goes on to explain the ways that oppression is institutionalized in contemporary India.

"I call the family an institution, because we in India, women especially, we're born in the family and we die in the family, we don't have any separate identity. So, the institution—like family, police, administration, religion—women are not safe anywhere in these institutions. Anywhere—including the family."

"Not safe from what?" I ask.

"Unsafe means their development is not considered; and unsafe in other ways, too. She can be killed for dowry in the family itself. We have seen rape cases in our police stations, by those who are supposed to protect women." Alice's voice cracks, and she pauses to compose herself. Working with everyday atrocities has clearly not hardened her.

"But now, women have started raising their voice against it," she continues.

Alice explains that laws will not change the adverse affects of deeply rooted mores and caste oppression. Change must come through people and through the social order.

"Why do you do what you do?" I ask, wanting to better understand her personal motivation. But she responds with the mission of her organization.

"We are working so that women can understand their situation and start making their own decisions. So she will be able to have her own identity as a woman, not as somebody's daughter or mother or sister, but through her own work, identity, through her education. We always tell them to raise voice against them. They should not feel ashamed. It is the women who need to change the social values now, in their favor.

"The mothers say, 'We have seen what our lives are like, and we don't want our daughters to face the same thing.' "

First water, then school. We leave the site of the well and drive to one of the twenty-nine rural villages where Bal Rashmi has set up schools. Alice and I walk through the tiny village, followed like Pied Pipers by a small parade of children. We settle in next to one of the caramel-colored mud huts to talk. Alice sits cross-legged on a bench and the villagers gather around to watch. Little girls, maybe six or seven years old, in pigtails with carefully tied, tattered ribbons, skip along the dirt road in front of us with buckets of water on their heads. They are in navy blue skirts and blouses, school uniforms—the only clothes they have. They are the first generation of girls from this community to go to school.

"Education is the best resource for a woman. If she can improve her economic situation, she can take care of so many things. She can also stand against the caste system and the so-called untouchability."

Alice wants to be sure I understand the gravity of the situation in these disenfranchised communities. Making us, the press, understand is critical, and thus she is willing to talk as long as we want. She seems unfazed by this long day under a brutal sun, but working against such a tide of ignorance and facing such a monumental challenge—not to mention political persecution—must take a personal toll on her.

"Do you have fears?" I ask, thinking of the sometimes dangerous circumstances of her work.

"Now I don't have any fear, I don't have any fear. This attack," she says, referring to the former local authorities who persecuted her and her colleagues and tried to destroy Bal Rashmi, "has made us stronger, because we have seen a lot—a lot we could never have imagined, you know? That is the difference between us and them. We will do this good work again, with full strength." As Kiran Bedi articulated regarding the death of her mother, when you confront your fears directly, you transcend them.

"Are you . . . happy?" I ask, as fearlessness and integrity, while admirable, don't necessarily add up to joyful living.

"Oh yes." A mellow expression replaces the serious intensity with which she has been speaking. "It gives me happiness when I work. It gives me happiness when I reclaim something which was going bad. I am not powerful. I am not in the politics. I am not a rich man's wife or daughter. I don't maintain any status. I am a social worker. But I will not stop. Now nobody can stop us."

This combination of personal humility and fierce determination seems to be part of a long-standing Indian tradition, with Mahatma Gandhi as its most famous recent exemplar. "The best way to find yourself is to lose yourself in the service of others," Gandhi said, and Alice, like Kiran Bedi, seems to have taken this maxim to heart.

Alice's commitment to her work is total. She has forfeited her own status (and possibly her health, from the sound of that cough) rather than exercising it at the expense of others. That ethos—and the small pink seashells that are her passion—are the wells from which she draws happiness.

It is long dark by the time we start our two-hour jeep ride back to Jaipur. We, the crew, are exhausted, heads bobbing with fatigue. "Alice," I ask after a long silence, "what's a diva?"

"Diva?"

"Yes, diva, does that word mean anything to you?"

"Diva is, like, lamp."

"Yeah?" I say. "Nothing else?"

"You said 'diva'?" says Alice.

"Diva. D-I-V-A," I say.

"Yeah, it is a lamp, which gives lots of light to others and goes on burning, you know?"

She looks out the window at what seems to be a small cluster of lanterns a quarter mile in the distance. "We must drop off this chalk for the school," she says, and the jeep begins to downshift.

Only later would I find out that *diya* means "lamp" in Hindi. Perhaps Alice misunderstood me, perhaps not.

Our cab whizzes along Mumbai's Chowpatty road. We pass a bawdy billboard that screams *HUM DIL DE CHUKE SANAM!*, which looks to be a recent hit movie. The billboard's lusty, big-eyed couple, in what you might call aggressive repose, welcome us to Bollywood: *Palm trees. Movie stars.* The city's thriving film industry, which turns out hundreds of feature films a year, is just one indication that Mumbai (formerly Bombay) is the country's economic powerhouse.

We decide to take the rest of the day off. John and soundman Doug take in Bollywood's latest at an air-conditioned theater and Julie, Cheryl, and I go our separate ways to explore Mumbai. I buy a plastic rendition of Kali that plugs in and makes the goddess's garland of severed limbs flash in bright red, and I get my fortune told: "You make a good friend and a bad wife." (And I paid for that?) Cheryl buys a poster of a leisure-suit-clad guru Si Baba, plucked from a bin of a hundred deities. Julie gets oil dripped on her forehead at an Ayurvedic health clinic.

Later, the three of us meet to swap stories over an early dinner. "I told the Ayurvedic guy I was seeking treatment because I was having trouble sleeping," Julie tells us, passing the chicken curry and some herbal chutneys clockwise. "He asks me why, and I tell him because I broke up with my boyfriend before coming to India. He looks at me puzzled, then says, 'Well, get a new one.' I'm telling you, there's a really different relationship to attachment here," she concludes drily.

On our walk back to the hotel we come to a bridge that crosses a river. I stop, and delicately ask Julie about what has become a slightly touchy subject.

"Julie, any luck on finding us somewhere to fish?" I say, looking down on a strangely deserted river's edge, in what is a very populated city.

"Holly, *give it up*," says Julie, who has been irritable with a bout of something lately (or maybe just a sad heart). "All the rivers in India are either *dead* or *sacred*."

Well, looky whose Ayurvedic treatment didn't work, I think.

The water *does* have an odd green hue, not dissimilar to the Chicago River on Saint Patrick's Day.

We return to the hotel and find John bellied up to the bar and looking sulky. Something is wrong.

"Half of Cheryl's film is blank," John says.

"What?" I say, praying I misheard him.

"Blank. Nothing on it, they say."

"Did they put it in the wrong soup?" Cheryl asks. "I marked the black-and-white explicitly," she adds, teeth grinding.

For two minutes we spiral into a finger-pointing frenzy in which we call into question the competence of Kodak, the Indian film industry, Cheryl's film cameras, the blasted hot sun, and my judgment about developing the film in situ rather than FedExing it home. It is a stunning display of the virulent strain of ass-covering that is endemic to the TV industry.

Weak from days of fever, I lack the horsepower to reach the high road, much less take it, so my response to the ruined film is to find Julie an hour later and have a *meltdown* about the waste of precious money, the heartbreaking loss of images, and the goddamn incessant heat.

"Holly, I will fix it," says Julie, with all confidence.

She gives me two Cipros and two Advil and slips in a sleeping pill and some unidentified orange tablet. I wash it all down with a Kingfisher.

It is Tuesday.

I float off to a fuzzy otherworld, thinking Julie is off to war with the local Kodak people to get our money back and somehow sprinkle magic dust to reconstitute the footage. But as an experienced producer, Julie knows that sometimes the best fix is to simply knock the director unconscious.

I wake up Thursday, without a fever and optimistic.

We have an appointment to meet with a composer and tabla musician named Anuradha Pal at her home near Mumbai's Chowpatty Beach. "She's a demi-diva," Julie says over a breakfast of puri, pakora, and black, steaming coffee, "so we can start late. Nine A.M."

Our India research was so chock-full of strong candidates that we have taken to calling some of our subjects demi-divas. What may sound like a catty divatocracy is really just practicality. Anuradha, since she is *merely* a world-renowned virtuosa and musical genius, is relegated to demi-diva. That is, in all likelihood she will only get about five minutes in the show. The bar is high in India, a country where immense social problems create immense divas who draw on a long tradition of fighting poverty and injustice.

Just before independence, a musical renaissance for women began. Only in the past sixty years has it been possible for a woman who did not belong to a family of hereditary musicians to take up music as her life's work. Despite the renaissance, Anuradha Pal is an anomaly, because the tabla, a two-piece drum and one of the most popular percussion instruments in India, is still very much a guy thing.

Pal lives in a swank high-rise with her parents and their small white stringy-haired dog, all of whom have welcomed us into their home with a kindness and savvy that indicates they are well versed in receiving the press.

Anuradha has a wide face, long brown hair with curly bangs, and a zeal for both her music and her family, to whom she attributes her opportunities and considerable confidence. While John sets up, and Julie and I knock back chai, Anuradha changes her outfit four times (old-school-diva behavior) and simultaneously educates us on the tabla.

"The right, treble side of the two-piece drum is usually referred to as the tabla," she says, "and the left, which makes a bassy sound, is called the baya. The tabla is played with every part of the ten fingers—the tips, the middle, and the base of the fingers where they connect with the palm." When Anuradha picks up the instrument and begins to play, my snooty reaction to her multiple wardrobe changes evaporates into the searing heat of her pure, unfathomable *talent.* Now I understand why *The Hindu* magazine touted her as having "the most pliable fingers in the world" and how she dazzles crowds with her virtuosity. Anuradha delivers ten minutes of genius in motion. We will end up threading her music throughout the program.

We sit down to talk about the historical and cultural implications of her music-making. In a global music landscape of remixes and sampling, Anuradha Pal creates new music within very old frameworks.

"What does it means to be creating within a culture that is five thousand years old?" I ask, thinking about how Kiran Bedi said she draws on time past for her creative solutions.

"I think it's a great legacy to live up to. Absolutely, you have to be very individualistic, and as a musician you're not performing set compositions. I'm talking about the pattern of improvisation. You're creating new, but it's coming from something of the past. You have to be very well rooted into what your tradition is, but be able to look ahead, have a broad vision and move from today into tomorrow.

"You're not doing things that just your guru has taught you. You have to go ahead. You have to give it your own individuality," she says, pushing back the red sash on an otherwise bright orange sari.

When one's body of knowledge about something is considerable (five thousand years considerable), the brain is then poised to ignite—to leap to a higher plane of creativity. (Knowledge + magic intuitive potion = inspired creation.) I can't relate musically, but I understand this phenomenon from fishing. Anglers can approach a river, full of generations of fish facts and strategy, as writer Howell Raines noted, but in the end it is a mysterious intuitive message that tells us exactly where the fish are. Anuradha's description of inspiration sounds like the same thing.

"Tell me about your gurus. The concept of guru is—I think, um, it means something different to me than it does here," I say.

"What does it mean to you?" she asks.

"Well, guru in my mind is someone to whom you have sort of a blind devotion," I say, treading lightly, thinking *Jim Jones! Jim Jones!* "And my sense of what it means here is, um, more of a teacher," I say, with tentative diplomacy.

"Well, actually, it *is* a blind devotion. It is a teacher—but more than a teacher. You know a teacher is somebody who can teach you anything, you can go learn science, physics, math, whatever from a teacher. In the case of the guru, what our Indian tradition tells us to do is a *surrender.* It's love, worship, and devotion towards a particular guru, his music, his style, his approach to music and you're following that with a degree of not only devotion, but a certain surrender. Which I think is alien to the Western rational mind," she says.

My Western rational mind does flinch when I hear the word *guru.* The moniker conjures up fat cats in white Mercedeses cruising along wide Texas roads. But what Anuradha seems to be describing is a very intense mentoring relationship. So intense that the guru's power, for his or her part, must be responsibly wielded.

"But how do you become an individual? How do you express your individual creativity within that context? Isn't there a conflict?" I ask, wondering, *Must we surrender to evolve?*

"Oh there's a huge [conflict], but that's a very good question, because that's exactly what I was saying—that you have to have this improvisatory attitude while sticking to the traditional setup. And that is where the challenge is. We are interpreting according to the moment, so that's why you would hear the same artist perform it differently depending on what that audience gives him," she says.

I think of the Penan's *mal cun uk,* "following our feelings," which allows them to navigate the Bornean jungle with only pure intuition to guide them.

"Basically the tabla is within me. I mean, I think rhythm has gotten inside," she says, touching her sternum, "and there is a need to express it. So if somebody were to take that away, oooh, I'll be dead. Playing tabla for me is a need; it's something that's necessary to my survival. It's a spiritual experience, because when I practice, when I sit onstage, that's when I'm feeling at peace with myself. It's what delights my soul, like nothing else," she says.

Crap. I thought we would have a simple five-minute virtuosa bio (shoot, write, edit, *easy*) but once again life, death, and the universe have been invoked and "the story" is anything but straight ahead. India seems to be a place where spiritual sustenance, through anchors, drumming, service, or other practices, is integral.

I look at Anurhada's *bindi* and suspect, not for the first time, that the ubiquitous red dot ties into India's spiritual story. By now Anuradha and I have a rapport going, so I charge ahead with the gusto of a rhino and the protective shield of a cultural ignoramus.

"What does—*that*—mean?" I say, pointing to the red dot on her forehead.

Turns out that the *bindi* is decoration for some, like lipstick, but at its purest, a *bindi* symbolizes the powers associated with the third eye. For the aware woman, the *bindi* is the gathering place for her whole person and a reminder of her spiritual dimension.

"Imagine wearing evidence of your spiritual agency—your spiritual self—smacked on your forehead," Julie says, as we leave down the stairs.

"I can't. Americans are too individualistic—or maybe narcissistic—to publicly admit that we're giving it up to something larger than ourselves," I say, thinking this is at least true for my urban life-after-God, post-everything, we'll-be-damned-if-we're-gonna-be-duped-by-some-higher-power-hoo-ha generation. Then again, people in rural Utah or Texas (not to mention Venice Beach yoga classes) might disagree.

Mumbai undergoes a transformation at seven P.M. The streets, which mellowed in blazing afternoon sun, now hatch with new movement and are awash in a golden light, a scene softened by the filter of polluted air. Stores that have been shuttered in slumber open. We steal glances into cracked doors for transitory peeks into life's backroom details.

Kurla train station is a hive of activity, a unique bedlam. There are dozens of tracks in the vaulted main room with trains pulling in, pulling out, bodies leaping on, leaping off. Legless beggars rolling like cylinders to the rhythm of the chai vendors' sales chants. Heads piled high with suitcases or bundles of food or blankets or jungle-gyms of lashed-together pots and pans. Chaos with a deliberate step.

If I keep looking long enough, I feel certain that a pattern will emerge.

We are taking a train to Kamathipura, Mumbai's infamous and historic red-light district. Kamathipura is one of the biggest and oldest red-light districts in Asia. The British established a brothel district here in the nineteenth century for soldiers in the service of the British Empire. British authorities issued licenses to brothel owners on the condition that they keep "their girls disease-free." Almost sixty years after the end of the British Raj, the area is still a haven for the sex trade, and it was the setting of the 1988 Mira Nair feature film *Salaam Bombay!*

Our taxi creeps down streets alive with man, beast, rickshaws, and cars through intermittent glittering lights and shadowy movement. Women linger in doorways, some sitting, some standing, their silhouettes cocked against the doorjamb in the international pose that says "Come hither." A girl of about thirteen lounges in a long mint dress next to her more matronly colleagues—an anonymous group of solid pinks and reds and blues. The image of girlish pink headbands collides with glittery jutted hips on the same person. Here, sex acts are performed for as little as fifty cents (U.S.). Kamathipura isn't merely a promenade, it's a slum where thousands of women in prostitution live with their children. On Raksha Bandan, a Hindu holiday on which sisters tie bracelets to their brothers' wrists in order to symbolize their brothers' duty to protect them, prostitutes give bracelets to their local politicians.

We are going to meet self-proclaimed muckraker Ruchira Gupta at her office in the heart of the red-light district, a million miles away from the tinsel of Bollywood. Ruchira's work on the award-winning film *The Selling of Innocents,* an exposé of the flesh trade, is what inspired us to track her down. A print journalist by training, Ruchira made the film after she visited Himalayan villages and noticed they were emptied of women between the ages of fifteen and forty-five. Many of these women, she found, had been sold by their families into the sex trade. More than a million girls and women are trafficked worldwide each year.

Julie, Cheryl, and I unload at what looks like an old abandoned building, once sturdily built with cubes of strong stone but now fallen beyond disrepair. We open a metal gate, collared by a chain with an unlatched padlock, and make our way up three floors toward the only lit room in the building. Little laughs trip down the stairwell to meet us. We arrive at the fluorescent-lit room and Ruchira ushers us in with a Western shaking of hands, and complete ease. A woman introduced as Surekha, rail-thin and in a long teal dress, sits with her six-year-old daughter, Shanti. *"Namaste,"* she says, welcoming us with a nod, hands touching in prayer in front of her heart. *"Namaste,"* we respond in kind, with a bow.

The thick tension of the night melts away as the six of us fill this room of two desks, two chairs, and a single bare bulb hanging off a ceiling fan that whines and clicks with every revolution. Ruchira pours tea and rolls up the sleeves on her yellow linen shirt in a futile attempt to appease the sticky Mumbai night. She tells me how she came to cross the line from journalist to activist.

"As a journalist, I've covered war, famine, riots, and I've always moved on to the next story. But when I began to work on this documentary on sex trafficking, I just couldn't move on. I had never seen this kind of exploitation—this level of human degradation. I was so outraged about what was happening inside the brothels. I felt that nobody deserved to go through this," she says with a sweeping arm that indicates her comments take into account not just this neighborhood, but an entire state of existence. We are at Apne Aap (which translates to "Self-Help" in Hindi), a resource center that Ruchira started after making the film.

"What happens when the women arrive at the brothels?" I ask.

"When they arrive they are locked up in small rooms. They are raped repeatedly until their spirits are completely broken. And then they are forced to service about twenty clients a day," says Ruchira.

Surekha speaks almost no English and has been quietly talking to her daughter in Hindi throughout our conversation. Ruchira tells us that Surekha grew up in a village in a Mumbai suburb and came to the city with an older boy who professed his love to her. When they arrived, he sold her into prostitution. She was fifteen.

"Mera ghar dekhna chahate hai?" ("Would you like to come see my house?") Surekha asks.

"Yes," I respond. Julie stays behind to make arrangements for tomorrow's shoot and, with Ruchira as our translator, Cheryl and I join Surekha and Shanti on their walk home to the brothel.

We step out onto the hot, unlit street, and a chilling number of eyes fix on our small entourage. Two other prostitutes fall in line with us; clearly they are protecting me and Cheryl. We are with Ruchira, and that is all they need to know. Surekha admonishes us on two points: Stick close, and do *not* film the clients.

We wend our way down a series of dark, rotty-smelling, dirty alleys, past several fires burning in barrels, and finally duck into a door. The two other prostitutes peel off and we climb a set of narrow wooden stairs. A fire sputters in a tin drum at the top of the stairway. A woman with gaunt Nepalese features is brushing her long, dark, straight hair. Children, and a few men, are moving from door to door. The place has an air of getting ready to open for business. A middle-aged woman (the madam, Ruchira tells me) barks at Surekha and I do not have to speak Hindi to know that she does not like our camera pointing at her women. Cheryl lowers her camera and, as is her style, begins to shoot from the hip.

The women in this brothel are the last link in an institutionalized food chain. A pipeline from villages to cities is supplied by traffickers, boyfriends who turn into pimps, and impoverished parents who sell off their daughters to support the rest of the family. Part of Ruchira's work is to try to change the mind-set that allows little girls to become the first resource in the face of desperate poverty. The most chilling scene for me in Ruchira's *Selling of Innocents* is the one in which a father is negotiating the sale of his young daughter, who is sitting right there by his side—an excited, clueless, nine-year-old girl.

"What happens is that normally in a village, a couple has a small child, and if she's a daughter, and the couple is in desperate need of money, they might mortgage the child to the local agent—everybody knows who the trafficker is in the village—and they might say, 'Give three thousand rupees now, and when she's seven or eight or nine, we'll give the girl to you.' The girl comes here, to the brothel district, and she's sold off to the madam by the trafficker. The madam may pay between five and six thousand rupees, which is like fifty to sixty dollars, for the girl, and she would try to keep the girl to herself for five years, during which period, the girl would get nothing. She'd be locked up in a small room, made to service a couple dozen clients a day."

"The little girls?" I ask, disgusted.

"The little girls, sometimes they are even premenstruating girls, and the madams force them to have sex with men, they say use ice and they say if you're bleeding, then the ice will stop the bleeding, and they just force them, and the girls have no way of trying to get out of the situation. At other times, the madams encourage the girls to become dependent on drugs and alcohol because then they cannot run way."

Surekha ushers us through a dark rabbit warren of tiny wood-framed rooms, almost like container boxes. She motions to one of them.

"My house," she says, in English, and with pride.

"Bedroom, kitchen," she says, pointing to two bunk beds and a hotplate, in one corner of a long corridor of many beds. "A-C," she adds, pointing to a hole torn in the ceiling which I suppose provides a modicum of ventilation. It takes me a few seconds to understand that she's saying "air-conditioning." The space is not more than twenty cubic feet. Her son is asleep on the top bunk. A young woman with a shy smile in a floral-patterned sari offers us Coca-Kolas (Coke knockoffs). She puts a straw in each of them, as if knowing we will be concerned about hygiene.

"Holy shit," whispers Cheryl from behind her camera, "this is unbelievable."

"I know. It's . . . it's . . ." I stammer. "Are these apartments, or . . . ?" I finally ask Ruchira.

"Beds, everyone sleeps at different times, in shifts, and if there is a customer, then no one gets to sleep at all," says Ruchira.

"So this is part of the brothel?" I confirm.

"Yes," says Ruchira.

I look at Surekha's hovel again, which she is clearly proud of, as many of the women here have no space of their own at all. As if reading my thoughts, Ruchira says, "It's like a hole in the wall, as you can see, there's no window, there's no ventilation, there is no light, and yet this is what they live in. This is all that they have for eight hours, then they have to give it up to the next person. They are servicing their clients in the bed and the children are playing on the floor at the same time. They cook, they clean, they eat, they service their clients, they look after their children all in that same space of four feet by four feet."

"The police try to extort money from them. These girls also have to offer free sex to the police. Sometimes the policemen say, 'We don't want sex with you, we want you to get us a young girl.' So they have to give one of their daughters," says Ruchira.

The conditions in this brothel are inhuman, but the atmosphere is vibrant, which must be what prevents me from sliding into an inert depression. I try to feel beyond the choking parameters of the abysmal setting and the exploitative, usually fatal, flesh trade; I note the rapport among the women, the laughing, the way they care for one another's children.

I feel the respect the women of the brothel have for Ruchira—someone who has created, in concert with them, a resource and hope beyond these walls, and who does so without judgment or condescension.

"So the center is an outgrowth of your film?" I ask when we meet again at Apne Aap the following morning.

"It is. Because some of the women that I worked with while making the film pushed me into starting it. They said, 'You will come, make the film, and go away. How will our lives change?' I told them, 'Your lives will only change if you want to, I can't do anything.' So they said, 'But we can't do it right, we don't know anybody.' So I said, 'Well, I can be a facilitator, but you have to organize.' And through that process, we set up this organization in 1998 informally, and in 2002 as a formal legal entity. People come here, make promises, and go away, so there's a lot of faith that I have to live up to," says Ruchira.

For the first couple years Ruchira funded the organization out of her salary, then friends and family began to make donations. Eventually, the Mumbai government contributed the building space, and Ruchira got some small grants from the Global Fund for Women. Ruchira is about to launch five additional community centers in red-light areas of Kolkata, Bihar, Delhi, and Mumbai.

Ruchira tours me around the building. "This is our office and the girls come in here and we register them as members of Apne Aap. This membership gives them a sense of belonging, and restores a sense of identity. With this ID card," Ruchira shows me a white card with a passport-type photo on it, "they belong to an organization. They have a sense of who they are," says Ruchira. "These girls didn't have a sense of being citizens of any country. And so they have no sense of what the country owes them—what citizenship rights they have."

Ruchira tells me that with these Apne Aap identity cards, the women are less likely to be turned away from hospitals and other institutions that often reject them.

"You know, you can keep talking about rights in a vacuum, but until you have a sense of what rights mean, how you can exercise them, it doesn't mean anything. So we are trying to tell all the women about what their rights are, how to fight the police, how to tackle the disease of AIDS. Sometimes it's just a matter of information; the second part, of course, is organization, because you have to mobilize."

"How many members?" I ask.

"Two hundred and six. We have a waiting list."

We walk to the next door and poke our heads into a room with a single mattress on the floor. A woman and her small baby are fast asleep on it.

"Most of our women don't have a home. What they do is rent a bed for eight hours every day and then they're thrown out. So then they try to sleep on the sidewalk. If it's too hot or crowded, or somebody pushes them off, they just wander around the streets sleepless," Ruchira tells me.

"It is so nice to walk in and see the women sleeping peacefully," she says, closing the door quietly. "They're not scared, nobody is harassing them. They can take a shower when they wake up, have a cup of tea, and that goes a long way toward just restoring dignity in their lives," she says.

I've noticed a number of women and young girls scampering around the halls, preparing for something. "Two of our members died this week, of AIDS, and the group is having a memorial celebration in honor of them," Ruchira says, explaining the energy.

"Most of the women in our organization are HIV-positive. One of the problems of course is, what are we going to do to help them? But the bigger issue is, what's going to happen to their children? These children could literally be growing up on the streets when the mothers die. The boys will become part of gangs, and the girls will end up becoming prostitutes," Ruchira says, answering her own question. "We want to get the girls placed in boarding schools and the boys given some vocational training classes."

Ruchira tells me that they are also trying to educate men in the community.

"The customers or the partners?" I ask.

"Some are boyfriends, some are pimps, some are sons, and some are customers. We try to reach sailors, the police, taxi men's unions. We explain to them what sex with a minor means, what it means to that little child. Her childhood is lost, her body gets destroyed, she has no chance of building a life for herself ever again. Many of these men think sex and violence are the same thing, they haven't really understood what it means to have an equal relationship with women. We try to redefine masculinity because sometimes men come to the brothels thinking that they have this sexual urge, and the macho thing is to go and look for a really young girl and find an outlet for this sexual urge, but they don't realize that it is so exploitative. They think that masturbation is wrong, it will make them blind. They think that sex with a virgin will cure them of AIDS." These myths are not uncommon in communities around the world.

Outside, the memorial has begun. Fifty people, mostly women and girls, are gathered to honor the lives of the two women who died. Ruchira stands up and gives a talk, and a few others also speak to the group. Then six girls who look to be about thirteen or fourteen begin a Kashmiri dance, to Bollywood pop music that comes over a tinny loudspeaker.

"We try to build self-esteem through music and dance—and that goes a long way—but we come to a dead end at one point when the girls turn thirteen or fourteen, just at puberty. We know that the brothel madams are going to put them into prostitution," Ruchira tells me as we watch the dance.

"See that little girl in the green dress?" She points to a girl of about thirteen, with thick black bracelets and a green *dupatta* scarf. "Her name is Lari and she hasn't been in the business yet. She was somehow protected because the brothel madam liked her a lot and she thought she could get more out of her when she grew older, she was kind of skinny, and I was . . ."

Ruchira continues on, but my heart stalls.

She was kind of skinny.

Somehow this small phrase, which Ruchira includes almost parenthetically, horrifies me most of all. A little meat on her bones would change her price, and her destiny.

". . . I was telling the madam," Ruchira continues, "that Lari wants to be a doctor—let her stay in school and study for another year or two. I was literally trying to buy time, so I had to sit and negotiate and negotiate and negotiate and finally the madam has agreed to give us one more year."

With the time she buys, Ruchira tries to find sponsors to support the children and get them in boarding schools out of harm's way. Sometimes the brothel madams agree to this, and sometimes not.

In the last seven years, Ruchira's work has taken her through the global network of sex trafficking, from Bangladesh, Myanmar, Thailand, Cambodia, and Laos to Kosovo, Czech Republic, and Slovakia, as well as to several countries in Africa and most major American cities. While awareness of trafficking is growing, so is the industry's institutional strength via the Internet, telecommunications, and the well-oiled machine of organized crime.

"What we want to do is actually eradicate sex trafficking and prostitution as a work choice for women. Prostitution is inherently exploitative and women have the right to other nonexploitative options," says Ruchira.

"What's the good news?" I ask, not really expecting any.

"The good news is the women are willing to fight. Six years ago they were so timid and they were so scared, they were not willing to even talk to each other," she says without even having to think about it. "They did not let outsiders in, and today, you can see the laughter and the joy that they have. They were willing to talk to you, they were asking you straight-out questions. They're no longer timid, disempowered women. If you work with people and tell them about their rights, they're willing to stand up and fight, and I think that is a challenge to the human spirit, and its response is the biggest and the best news," Ruchira says.

"Has *your* spirit changed since you moved from journalist to activist?" I ask, loving her clarity, her warm but no-nonsense style, her respect for the people with whom she works and serves.

"Yes, because as a journalist you go so far and then you back off, you know, you just want to tell the story—you don't want the responsibility of changing the world. But as an activist you go, you push, and you push and you push and you push until you feel that you actually get a paradigm shift. I feel I'm doing something beyond muckraking. Journalists make a very valuable contribution. They expose the problem, and activists add on by trying to change the way people look at the problem and changing the situation altogether," she says.

Her embodiment of both activism and journalism resonates with the Adventure Divas approach to storytelling. And her on-the-road life, dictated by the international nature of the trafficking issue, inspires me. I figure her kind of commitment must have a particular source.

"A lot of the women I've met may be artists, singers, professionals, whatever—but they're also committed to a grassroots activism," I say.

"I think that comes from the freedom struggle," Ruchira responds, referring to India's struggle for independence, "and it continues in all kinds of ways—social work and commitment to changing things. Life is not just about living for yourself; we have to contribute something back to society. It's almost as if the thread of the freedom struggle is going through us. The women's movement in India actually was born during the freedom struggle in a way. Politics are very much a part of women's aspirations on one level in India; on the other hand, you'll find a seven-year-old girl sold into sexual slavery and she can do nothing about it. So the contrast is great in India, and some people have the luxury to be activists, and other people don't. So the people who have the luxury to be activists, it's almost like an additional responsibility that you do it."

"Is there anything you fear?" I ask Ruchira, thinking back to Kiran Bedi and Alice Garg—and to Kali, the protectress.

"Fear is not, um . . . well, there are moments of fear, but nothing long-term. For example, when I was making a film and was inside a brothel, I had refused to take help from anybody to make the film—no power structures, no cops, no NGOs—and a man pulled out a knife at me and said, 'How dare you make this film here?' There was that momentary sense of fear that, oh my god, I am going to lose my life here. On the other hand, the women with whom I had been making the film for eighteen months came forward and surrounded me and said, 'We have let her in and she is making the film to get our voices out, so you can't stop her.' So their strength gave me strength and it was inspiring, you know. It's almost like a commitment that this is the bond we've created. They trust me, but my strength also comes from their trust; and so there is no fear because of that."

Ruchira goes to speak with a woman in a purple sari about an upcoming workshop designed to educate men about condom use. Cheryl and I sit silently and watch the final dance. These girls' lives give new meaning to the term *at-risk youth:* fourteen, living in a brothel, and their mothers are all dead or dying of AIDS. The village girls sold into sex slavery are appallingly abused victims, but with support and voice, they aren't powerless. I think about the prostitutes who gave bracelets to local politicians for protection. Apne Aap has created a new system of protection, a system through which women support and protect one another. Ruchira would never call herself a warrior, but she is one. I look at this building, which is a refuge amid a war zone. Strange how the brightest light comes from the darkest places.

Lari, the skinny girl who's been granted a brief reprieve from the sex trade, is twirling, slightly awkwardly, the tassles of her long green scarf following her. She passes her hand across her face as the music stops.

My torso hangs out the open side of the train and my dry, wide-open eyes watch India scroll by, vivid and blurry at the same time; an old life passing by in fast-forward. We are riding the rails again, back to Delhi for a day before making a final journey up into the Himalayas. I fixate on the waterways we chug over and alongside. All the rivers tweak my devotion to fly-fishing, a response that feels strange and indulgent after the brothel experience. A few hours outside Mumbai a particularly special emerald snake chases our tracks, like a playful child. I imagine a stolen afternoon of laying lines, and wily reflections. Fish do represent spirituality the world over, so my obsession is not completely without context here in India. The truth is, life never feels more holy to me than when I am thigh-deep, midstream, battling a lunker or simply watching arcing lines play out over water. Fishing is a meditation—my tabla—that keeps me on point, alive.

I walk back to our seats, and can't resist raising the issue, once again.

"Julie," I say tentatively, "what do you think?" I point at the green river that promises me sleek flashes from another world. She pulls her head out of Arundhati Roy's *Power Politics* and looks.

"Dead," she says, nodding in the direction of a bloated sheep carcass floating mid-river.

"There might be some fingerlings," I mumble hopefully.

"Dead," she reiterates, and goes back to *Power Politics*. Roy, a Booker Prize–winning novelist and activist, was on our diva list. While we could not arrange to meet her, her insights reverberate among the crew members as we pass around her book, a challenge to the globalization of the world economy, the privatization of India's power supply (usually by U.S. or multinational companies), and the dams that are displacing hundreds of thousands of citizens. Roy says, "Is globalization about 'eradication of world poverty,' or is it a mutant variety of colonialism, remote controlled and digitally operated? . . . The answers vary depending on whether they come from the villages and the fields of rural India, from the slums and shantytowns of urban India, from the living rooms of the burgeoning middle class, or from the boardrooms of the big business houses." By the time Julie finishes the book, she will most certainly add "dammed" to her reasons why we will not find a suitable river to fish in.

The train makes a stop and the crew stumbles out to attend to myriad bodily functions. We have been going down, one by one, with parasites. "This is the last one in the course," Julie says, tossing a Cipro to John as he shuffles off to find a bathroom. Julie is like Scarlett O'Hara, tenaciously tending to moaning Civil War soldiers; she refuses to let a mess get in the way of the production at hand. Julie gets busy counting cash and pills and I run across the street to call Jeannie.

"I'm so glad you called. Where have you guys been?" she asks over a crackling international phone line.

"Ruchira Gupta—the sex trafficking story—just completely consumed us for a few days. It was amazing—scary and horrible, but amazing. The divas here are *huge*. Oh, and we lost some great footage to bad processing, which was heartbreaking."

"That's really a shame. But listen, listen, I've got excellent news. REI is in! They want to be an exclusive underwriter and will pay more for it."

"Oh my ghaad. *Fantastic.* Exclusive?"

"Also, *USA Today* says that we are 'Firing up souls!' So I hope whatever you're getting over there can deliver on that," she adds with a laugh.

"I don't know how we're going to capture this country in fifty-two minutes. Jeannie, there are a *billion* people here."

"Who's next?"

"Well, the Bandit Queen, if—" The line cuts out as a diesel-belching Tata Steel truck rumbles by the yellow phone booth. I see Julie waving to me frantically, and I run back through a cloud of exhaust for the train, in time with the whistle toots, just like in the movies.

I am anxious to breathe the pure air of the Himalayas, but haven't given up on Phoolan Devi, the elusive Bandit Queen. Devi, along with a New Zealand writer named Keri Hulme, has been on our list from the inception of Adventure Divas. But our window of time for meeting Devi is closing. We must leave for the Himalayas in twenty-four hours.

"Let's just go to her house tonight," I say, exasperated, when we arrive in Delhi and still are unable to reach her. "We're out of time. What's the worst that could happen? We get thrown out."

At eight o'clock that night we are dropped off in front of the open tall wrought-iron gates that surround Devi's residence on a main drag in Delhi, less than a mile from Parliament, where she works. A man stands in front of the residence, his orange cigarette cinders one of the few bits of light. Raghu stops to speak to him near the front gate. While they're talking in Hindi, Julie and I slip by and head up the driveway and toward a back door, maybe a kitchen door, that seems to be ajar. "Could it be this easy?" Julie whispers.

"I've never shot in D.C. but I can't quite imagine dropping in on Tom DeLay or Denny—"

"Tom DeLay? Why in the world—"

"Ao" ("Enter"), we suddenly hear from inside.

Julie and I push open the wooden door and step into a small, windowless rectangular room with white walls full of twelve very serious-looking middle-aged men in pale pastel shirts, who sit in chairs that line three of the room's four walls. The men stare at us: two American women clasping our hands in *namaste,* bowing slightly, more times than necessary, because we do not know what else to do and are buying time, hoping like hell Raghu shows up. At the front of the room, taking the fourth wall, holding court behind a large wooden desk, is a cute (no other word suffices), poised woman with a wide face and flat cheeks: Phoolan Devi.

The Bandit Queen, in the flesh!

She flashes us a charming, almost shy, inquiring smile.

Raghu steps in behind us—*thank god*—to explain our presence; Julie and I continue to smile and nod. Raghu expresses our apologies for barging in, explains who we are and our mission. Would she do an interview for us? he asks.

There is ardent discussion among Phoolan's cronies. She nods and listens quietly as they, one by one, appear to give her advice. It's like *West Wing* in Hindi, with a diva in charge. "Raghu, what's happening?" I say, still smiling at Phoolan Devi.

"Batao pach hazar dollar" ("Ask for five thousand dollars"), one of the men says. And then Phoolan Devi speaks, for the first time.

"She wants ten thousand dollars," Raghu translates.

"What?" I say. "Have you explained that we are making a documentary? We can't *pay* for interviews. Did you explain *Adventure Divas?*"

Raghu continues in Hindi. The cronies keep saying *"Americana."* I hear one of them say something about CNN. *No, no,* I panic, *she doesn't understand.*

"Raghu," I whisper, tugging on his shirt, "explain PBS—*public* television. You know, donations, groveling, cheap graphics."

Raghu continues to explain. Given the wry laughs that bubble up among the cronies, our ethics argument, and pleading poverty, are, I'm afraid, ideas lost in translation. On several levels, we are speaking different languages.

"Oh my, I think we're being extorted by a diva," I whisper to Julie.

The room suddenly falls silent. Phoolan nods at me, and smiles. *"Das muit ke liye, dosh hazar dena. Kal mera ghar ko telephone Karo,"* she says.

"Ten thousand dollars for ten minutes," Raghu translates. "She says we should call her residence tomorrow if we want to set something up. We must go now so they can continue their meeting."

We leave, silent and demoralized.

The seven-hour drive up into the Himalayas has given me ample time to stew on our interaction with Phoolan Devi. That we only had $462 left, rather than 10k, was moot. We could not feature Devi because highway robbery—literal or figurative—is not a trait we want to condone. From a production aspect, we were, for the first time, faced with the question of what to do When a Good

Diva Goes Bad. Failure to land Devi exempted me from a quandary I would have eventually faced in the edit room: Would I fan the flames of her legend, mythmaking in the name of good TV?

The money issue may have ended my pursuit of Phoolan, but the entire experience has led me to reexamine my motives for wanting her in the first place. I was caught up in her legend. I wanted to believe in a strong, female archetype, a leader who championed the lower castes and avenged atrocities against millions of women in India (and, by example, across the world).

I was drawn to the sexiness of Phoolan Devi's *story,* but overlooked the truth of her life—which lacked the character, the deep and examined moral inventory, that is a hallmark of divadom. *Robbery, murder, bribery, deception—* these are the words that now resonate as I read more about her during our long journey into the Himalayas. A master at reinventing herself, and with many who've known her now dead or in jail, Devi has a history that is hard to decipher. The more I read, the more it seems Rahgu might be right. Phoolan Devi is more bandit than queen.

Then again, I wonder if it is fair for me to judge a low-caste woman who used whatever it took to revolutionize her life. If one is of low caste, *must* one be a bandit to become a queen? If every institution condemns you, is bloody vindication justifiable?

Gandhi and Martin Luther King, Jr., and Sojourner Truth didn't think so. And I have a feeling Alice Garg and Kiran Bedi and Ruchira Gupta—the everyday archetypes I was looking for in Phoolan Devi—wouldn't think so, either.

Kali may be ferocious, and slay the evil in her path, but she is not an earthbound deity, she is an ethereal myth that brings comfort to millions of people who drew life's short sticks of poverty and caste oppression. And this is the way in which Phoolan Devi, too, is important and valid. What she represents is what matters, and she represents a challenge to the country's most egregious atrocities. "She is tailor-made for the Indian imagination," columnist Sunit Sethi says in an *Atlantic* article about Devi. "Since ancient times we have had an inordinate capacity to make myth out of any story, and to demythicize the most epic into the mundane. Phoolan is a do-it-yourself goddess who can rapidly demonize."

"It'll be interesting to see if she has as much impact as a career politician as she did as a bandit," I say to Rahgu.

"You never know," he responds. "We'll see."

But we won't.

Three months after we met Phoolan Devi, she was shot dead by masked men in front of her Delhi home. Some say the assassination was politically motivated; others say it was revenge by the families of the men she murdered. Her death, like much of her life, is surrounded by mystery. Hundreds of thousands of people took to the streets at the funeral, to honor the now-martyred Bandit Queen.

We continue to drive up a pilgrim route into the Himalayas, a range called the "abode of the gods," to meet our final interviewee, a mountain climber. People come from all over the world to walk into the foothills to visit and worship at a series of Hindu temples. In a couple of months there will be thousands walking this route, but as it is now we are passing a pilgrim, usually dressed in white or orange and carrying a tin pail, every quarter mile or so. Traveling is traveling, but a pilgrimage is a spiritual act, an exercise in devotion. With each shoot—what with our deepening investment in the project and the people we've met along the way—creating this television series is beginning to feel closer to the latter. With each day, my respect for the women we are meeting grows (excepting Devi, of course), and, production challenges aside, my desire to bring their stories to a wide audience increases.

We gas up our minivan and continue our loopy switchbacks into the foothills, shadowing the Ganges, and ours does feel like a progression filled with meaning, though of what kind I am not entirely sure. I blurt out one of the Buddha's rallying cries: "You cannot travel the path until you become the path," hoping it will inform our journey on this sacred route. It thuds like the non sequitur that it is.

"You cannot catch a fish until you become a fish?" offers Cheryl, in one of her game attempts to understand my passion since we fished together in Cuba. We stop for a chai and sit by the river, not too far from its source, the Gangotri Glacier, a massive chunk of ice measuring five by fifteen miles. The glacier rests above us in these foothills, at about fourteen thousand feet above sea level, and melts into the river Bhagirathi, which flows into the Alaknanda River to become the Ganges.

"Julie, what do you think?" I ask, nodding at the clean, wide, robust stretch of river.

"Holly. It's the *Ganges*," she responds with a laugh. *"Sacred."*

And indeed, the towns that dot this stretch of the Ganges seem to attract spirit seekers from all over. Flyers for gurus, yoga, crystal readings, and chakra adjustments abound. ENRICH YOUR LIFE USING CRYSTALS AND GEMS! a cement wall entices. WELCOME ALL QUALIFIED SEEKERS OF THE TRUTH, says a billboard. HEALING THE SEVEN CHAKRAS and THE DIVINE LIFE SOCIETY blare out in primary colors on a sign that a *sadhu* is leaning against. My personal favorite is PIMPLES, WRINKLES AND BLEMISHES—with absolutely no follow-up sales pitch. Perhaps the sign painter was not unionized and walked off the job.

Two young Western women with shoulder-length brown hair and gauzy skirts stop to chat. "This is where the Beatles met their guru," they tell us.

Another young Westerner named Daniel—shirtless, with long blond dreadlocks and a well-defined six-pack—pulls up on a beat-up motorcycle. Daniel is from Germany and spends two months in India every year. I try to imagine what molecular leap takes place when German chromosome meets Eastern chakra. When I did a shoot for Pilot Productions at a Native American sundance in Oklahoma, the only people sweating it out besides Native Americans were Germans. Are the Germans simply committed travelers, like the Aussies, or is there some stickiness to this Germano-spiritual trend?

"Has your time in India changed you?" I ask Daniel.

"Yes, of course it changes you, of course. You get much more open-minded like this, take things easier, not like running on a normal system like Germany."

Normal.

"I am staying at a local ashram. Do you want to come to this afternoon's yoga class?"

My idea of an ashram is a swarm of middle-class white kids who padlock their trust funds and come here in their eagerness to find themselves.

"Sure," I say, and he hands me a flyer. I'll be damned if I'll be out-evolved by a German.

ASHRAM RULES AND REGULATIONS:

- No meat, fish, eggs, alcohol, tobacco and narcotics.
- No personal checks.

- No refunds.
- Playing rock music is not allowed, only chanting.
- No tight pants, shorts, or sleeveless dress allowed.
- It is difficult to maintain the pure vibration, so we request that you abide by the above rules. If anyone disrespects them, serious action will be taken.

My first-ever yoga class takes place at magic hour on a real live ashram on a gorgeous, red-slate terrace overlooking the Ganges. Hot damn. We grab our pads and fall in line with twelve other gringos warming up. A yoga veteran, Cheryl quickly engages in a contorted backbend warm-up thingy.

"Check that out," I whisper to her, and nod toward Daniel, who is somehow balancing with his arms on a railing, suspended in midair with his legs crossed. His six-pack is a veritable half-rack. The pose and the abs both defy physics.

That's what happens when Germanic order meets tantric ambition.

"Oh yeah . . . he's serious," says Cheryl, unwinding a leg from around her ear.

A bell tinkles and the guru sashays in, wearing a flowing gold robe. "The breath comes in . . ." he says to begin class. My lower back crinkles with every Upward Dog, and something called a *vakrasana* sends me to the floor in a sprawl. I peel my cheek off the tile, embarrassed, and decide it is ruder and more disruptive for me to stay, so I slink out the back of the class.

I trundle down to a deserted edge of a Ganges tributary, sort of bothered by the trappings of the sacred served up for gringos. An orange robe, a bunch of *om*s, and an excess of crystals shouldn't annoy me so much. I sit by the water and worry about the loss of footage. I worry that persistent irreverence can be as constricting as blind reverence. I wonder if there's a middle ground between the "dead" and the "sacred." I focus on the river flowing by.

We drive deeper into the Himalayas, passing an increasingly thick stream of pilgrims. We are heading for Uttarkashi, a village in the Garhwal region that is home to the mountain climber Bachendri Pal.

Pal was raised on the backbreaking work known to all rural people of her low caste, yet time and again she resisted pressure from her family to leave school and go to work. Most village girls never get educated, much less manage to stay unmarried, but as a rebellious dreamer, she resisted arranged marriage and fought all the way to college, earning two bachelor's degrees and a master's degree. Along the way she kindled her love of mountains, and escaped to them regularly. At college she was trained to be a teacher and studied Sanskrit, knowing that its literature was rich with images of the Himalayan mountains that had bewitched her since she was a child. After graduating, she again defied expectation, tradition, and her family's wishes. Rather than teach, she enrolled in mountaineering courses and was soon identified as an "Everest prospect." Pal doubled her firewood and water loads. She trained relentlessly on the steep grades of her home village, leaving her fellow villagers perplexed and amused (though they worried when she started carrying rucksacks full of stones up nearby foothills). Pal excelled in a mountaineering world considered far beyond the grasp of rural village women, and eventually she was selected for an elite Everest team.

Bachendri Pal would become the first Indian woman to summit Everest, which made her an instant celebrity and a folk hero for rural women and girls who live in the villages we are driving past. Pal has often said that her life's hardest battle was not the grueling toe-kicks that got her up Everest, but what it took to transcend the limitations prescribed by her rural, low-caste place of birth.

I am charmed by the small villages that nestle against endless circular terraced hillsides until I realize—"God, are these the villages drained of women between fifteen and forty-five—the ones Ruchira was talking about?" I say to Julie, who, like me, has been consumed by the sex-trafficking issue since our time in the brothel.

"I bet so," she says. "I bet they are."

Bachendri is wearing a black windbreaker, khakis, and light, generic sneakers when we arrive at a set of tents at the base of a river, next to a mountain. "Welcome to base camp," says Bachendri softly, almost demurely. She is shy about her marginal English.

Part of Bachendri's work these days is to provide an Outward Bound–type experience for executives of the Tata Steel company. Bachendri takes away their PDAs and tosses these young manicured execs from major industrial centers into the natural world in order to build confidence in themselves, and one another.

Bachendri and I set off for a hike along the Ganges to talk about the Everest summit that transformed her life. We are hopping over chunky gray boulders, making our way upriver to a trail that will take us to the top of a baby Himalaya. Bachendri moves steadily and delicately. She does not seem particularly tough or strong or well-versed in speaking in sound bites—all things I associate with elite veterans. I am fixating on her unlikely generic sneakers when a silver streak pans by in the water just to my right.

"Bachendri," I ask, excited, "are there fish in this part of the river?"

"Yes," she says quietly, then adds, "It is written in our sacred texts about the purity of the water. People worship the Ganges."

Figures. There are fish. But the river—definitely sacred.

I ask Bachendri about her draw to Everest. She'd had a love affair with the Himalayas throughout her youth, but the big mountain must have been special. "When I first saw Sagarmatha [Everest], I bowed my head in reverence," Bachendri says as we turn up a trail and start our ascent.

"Did you think you would summit?" I ask, trailing her, my eyes on her sneakers.

"No. I was not sure. But I was confident about my physical condition, and mentally I was very strong," she says matter-of-factly.

On Everest, she faced that moment every climber fears: avalanche.

"It was midnight and I was sound asleep. I was hit on the back of the head suddenly, by something very hard. And I heard a very loud explosion, so then I realized there was a very big avalanche, and I was really waiting for the death, and I thought, 'I am going to die. I am going to die.' "

Bachendri's limited English has conveyed the shorthand version of a harrowing experience. At twenty-four thousand feet, she and nine others in her climbing party were sleeping in their tents when they heard a thundering sound from the glacier above them. Enormous tumbling blocks of ice and snow developed into a massive avalanche that rumbled down the mountain and buried Bachendri alive in her tent. Fortunately, she was dug out by one of her fellow climbers.

"I was carrying a small image of goddess Durga-Narishakti. *Nari* means woman, *Shakti* means power. Woman power," Bachendri tells me.

"But aren't you supposed to carry a very light load?" I ask, knowing climbers are religious about every ounce they pack. "And you carried a goddess up there?"

"Yes," she says, laughing quietly, for the first time sweeping away a bug.

My arms have been moving constantly to keep black biting gnats at bay.

In the book *Leading Out: Stories of Adventurous Women,* Bachendri describes what the deity meant to her on the climb: "Well before dawn we began to dig out our equipment. I was terribly worried about the image of Goddess Durga which I had in my rucksack."

Durga, as I learned back in Delhi, is worshipped as an embodiment of female energy. She takes different female forms and goes by many names; one of them is Kali.

"Every morning and evening I took it out and drew inspiration and strength from it. So my first act on finding my rucksack was to thrust my hand into the side pocket. To my relief my fingers encountered the ice-cold metallic image. I held the holy image tightly and, placing it on my forehead, felt that I had everything I wanted. I had Shakti in my arms—the Shakti which had saved my life a few hours earlier and the Shakti which, I was sure, would lead me onwards and upwards. The experience of the night had drained all fear out of me."

Miraculously, nobody was killed in that avalanche, but Bachendri explains that the team, injured and in shock, was in disarray. When the rescue crew arrived the next day, most of her team returned to base camp, abandoning their bid for the top. Bachendri took another route.

" 'So what do you want to do?' I say to myself. I am alive after this life-and-death situation. So I said, 'I must try.' And that decision was the turning point," she tells me. Shaken yet determined, she kept climbing.

"I was literally on top of the world," she says of her summit on May 23, 1984, with climbing partner Ang Dorjee. After digging their ice axes in for security, Bachendri reported of her summit moment, "I sank to my knees, and putting my forehead on the snow kissed Sagarmatha's crown."

Writer Alain de Botton explains how places such as the top of the world compel you to hit your knees: "Sublime places repeat in grand terms a lesson that ordinary life typically introduces viciously: that the universe is mightier than we are, that we are frail and temporary and have no alternative but to accept limitations on our will; that we must bow to necessities greater than ourselves. This is the lesson written into the stones of the desert and the ice fields of the poles. So grandly is it written there that we may come away from such places not crushed but inspired by what lies beyond us, privileged to be subject to such majestic necessities. The sense of awe may even shade into a desire to worship."

Bachendri's reverence in the face of success is refreshing compared to the bawdy swaggerers we get so much of in the media of today's "extreme" sports. Competition and goal orientation too often muffle the subtler glories.

"Did you enjoy the climb?" I ask. Except for the summit, it sounded like a miserable experience.

"After coming back," she admits, with a laugh.

Bachendri Pal's 1984 Everest summit was a beginning. "After that I wanted to promote adventure sport among youth and women. Why not rural women? Rural women work very hard. Adventure should be a part of everyone's life. It is the whole difference between being fully alive and just existing," she says. With the public support of India's then leader Indira Gandhi, Bachendri began to put her philosophy into action.

"The biggest hazard in life is not to take risk," she continues, offering me some water before taking a small sip from her canteen. "If you want to achieve something you have to take risk. One of my big dreams was to lead an all-woman expedition up Everest." Bachendri accomplished this in 1993 with several young rural women from her own home village. I notice she tells this story with considerably more pride than that of her own, first Everest summit.

We are both panting now, and say less. The modest summit of this baby Himalaya is about a hundred yards in the distance. We scramble upward, and I am recharged by the burn in my thighs. For the first time in weeks the quease in my stomach is gone; I do not feel unmoored. We are scrambling, without ropes or protection, but I feel anchored.

"Do the mountains feel . . . holy to you?" I ask.

"Oh yes, yes," she says switching to Hindi, as if this is a question that can only be answered in one's native tongue. "I really worship the mountains. I consider the mountains an ideal. Mountains offer self-discovery; a chance to understand our limitations and to understand our strengths."

The natural world as a place to look inside and worship makes sense for the secularly minded like me; and the out-of-doors is a reasonable, inspiring temple. There is no overarching institution susceptible to human foible involved to muck things up, and no pearly-gate fantasies are required. It is a sure bet that in the final chapter we will all be communing with mother earth. Ashes to ashes and all that. Worshipping what we *know* to be our final destination makes some real sense to this rational Western mind.

We reach our small summit and in the distance we can barely make out giant, sharp, lumbering mountains, the kind that make you hold your breath, feel tiny and unburdened and excited all at once. Up here, in the temple of my familiar, the sacred doesn't feel scary, and surrendering to it doesn't feel like weakness.

"What do the mountains teach you?"

"My potentials. They teach me to believe in myself—to look up, and look straight in your life. With guts of great, and confidence," she says with stumbling, yet no less profound, English. "That is very important whoever you are—an officer, an administrator, an engineer. To have that confidence, that gives you tremendous self-respect. I think nature is a great teacher and a great purifier. And that is why I look at every peak with respect. I revere them as my inspiration."

For Bachendri the mountains are an "anchor." And brawn, and rampant ego—a charge leveled at climbers the world over—seem absent from her approach. By insisting, with a quiet voice and a triple load of firewood, on chasing her own "potentials," she got up Everest. She is a regular person who worked hard and summitted a mountain, and then parlayed that success into living her ideals.

I wonder how these unusual qualities, in this soft-spoken world-class climber, will translate to TV, a medium not known for subtlety. Bachendri ties the shoelace of her right sneaker, and lightly brushes dirt from the cuff of her pants. We take the descent in silence.

I jot down some thoughts as we drive from Uttarkashi to Hardwar. We cruise down the switchbacks at double speed, gravity now on our side. I worry out loud about the challenge of capturing the complexities of India on the screen. "The good news is a picture tells a thousand words," says Julie, ever tuned in to the upside of fate, and nodding toward our box full of shot film and tape.

Except for the few rolls mysteriously destroyed in Mumbai, we're not missing anything.

The Ganges flows out of the Himalayas near the city of Hardwar, where we stand watching thousands of pilgrims dip in the holy waters. A constant chant bellows out over the dozens of tinny loudspeakers that line the river: *hey-beda, hey-be-da, hey-beda.* Even when the order of the day is reverence, the atmosphere is buzzing with energy.

In Cuba, you hear something before you see it; in Borneo, you feel it before you see it; in India, you smell it before you see it. Diesel exhaust. Crushed marigolds. Smoldering cow dung. Old hot cooking oil. Milky chai. And always, incense. The smells of India swirl around us. "We'll need to make a scratch-'n'-sniff film to do this country justice," notes Julie, handing me a chai.

Colorful porcelain statues of Shiva, Ganesh, Kali—practically the whole gang—perch in the water, the river parting around their brightly colored torsos. I snap a picture of Sky Dancer at the water's edge. The plastic base from which she launches delicately divides the water just like the rest of the pantheon. In every direction there are people, pilgrims—orange, white, red, young, old, men, women, beggars, lepers, *sadhus*—all of them sweeping holy water onto their faces and over their heads, making *puja.* Bowls made of woven leaves and filled with marigolds, each centered with a white, softly flickering candle, float down the river as offerings.

This is a parade of worship as far as the eye can see. *Guts of great.* I think of Bachendri's words as hundreds of people unself-consciously prostrate themselves to the unknown. To faith. Maybe finding the divine in the everyday simply lies in the service, devotion, and ritual we see in the divas, and before us now.

I bend down to launch my own boat-of-flowers offering into the Ganges, and feel something new climb on board. The boat floats off, and I stand and just watch the carnival of the sacred splayed out before me.

4.

SHORT-ROPED TO HEIDI'S GRANDFATHER

—

Climb if you will, but remember that courage and
strength are naught without prudence, and that a
momentary negligence may destroy the happiness of a
lifetime. Do nothing in haste; look well to each step;
and from the beginning think what may be the end.

—EDWARD WHYMPER,
CIRCA 1900

"Yeahhh, well, Bradley Cooper just pulled out of the Matterhorn shoot. Are you available?" says Ian Cross, over the phone from Pilot Productions in London.

Keeping up with Bachendri Pal on a day hike was one thing, but tackling the Matterhorn is another issue altogether. Bradley, a strapping lad of about twenty-five—the perfect television profile to conquer a classic mountain—is my male counterpart in the trekking series. He needed to be in Hollywood for auditions, and I had to decide if I could fill his shoes.

"The day rate is especially good since it's a short shoot," Ian says enticingly, noticing my hesitation. The QuickBooks data comes up with a single click of the mouse. I look at our Adventure Divas bank balance. Alarmingly few digits appear before the decimal point.

"I'd love to do it, Ian."

"Bloody good then."

Ian tells me about the rest of the production team, all guys, two Brits, two Americans, then we hang up.

This will be my first time, ever, working in an environment that is so X-weighted, chromasomally. The job will bring in a much-needed infusion of cash, but the experience of immersing myself in high-altitude mountaineering, a legendary bastion of maleness, could be the real sociological pay dirt. I start doing push-ups and prepare for a new kind of cultural exploration.

Twelve days later, as my ice ax is being confiscated at Sea-Tac airport, I make last-minute cell-phone calls before boarding a Boeing 777 to Heathrow, and then Zurich. Ever since a flash-flood scare while shooting a canyoneering show in Arizona, I have taken to calling loved ones prior to departure. Road life is tough on relationships. Cell phones help.

"Dad," I say, walking down the gangway, "just wanted to say good-bye. I'm kind of worried." He's the right person to talk to. My lust for action comes from him, and he's been a strong supporter of Adventure Divas and my business risks (if a bit bewildered by their estro-focus). Competition. Male-dom. These are the NFL's human resources (and his) and what I might be tangling with on the mountain.

"Well, lots of people have climbed it," he says by way of support, but I only hear the challenge. "I saw it up close once on a tram," he adds.

"One thing's for sure, you'll never look back as an old woman and regret not experiencing the world," he says, almost whimsically. "Call me when you get back, baby. Good luck."

In order to acclimatize, and add another element besides the Matterhorn climb to the program, we are scheduled to spend three days "warming up," climbing around the Brenta, the Dolomites' stunning mantelpiece of limestone spires and towers. The shoot begins on a sunny August day in the Dolomites' jagged Via Ferrata ("Iron Route"), which rests in a stretch of mountains in the northeast of Italy. The team spends two days in a hotel at the base of the Brenta before the climbing begins. The team consists of Keith, who just lost twenty pounds filming on K2; Digger, a seasoned climber with guiding credentials galore and a new baby (not with him); a Tall Blond Quiet Man named Paul, who is a seven summits veteran and perhaps the most *deeply* mountain among us;

and dark-haired, medium-build director Ben, who I have not figured out yet. Quiet Thirsty Girl may be their impression of me, as I drink glass after glass of water in the hopes of staving off a bladder infection.

We sit together in the dining room surrounded by very coifed Italians whose lipstick and nail polish match. We have had several meals together, yet an awkward silence lurks at our table like a giant, boring, clay-blob centerpiece. We have dissected every technical aspect of our forthcoming climbs, three times, and now grope for things to talk about. I keep thinking this stilted atmosphere between us will crack, and a "joie de road" will hatch. After all, three of the five of us—Digger, K2, and TBQM, that is, the *real* climbers—already know and like one another well. A paid work trip like this can only be gravy for them. They should be having fun. This is the first all-male team I have worked with. I look around at the guys and wonder about communication, or lack thereof. My years in feminist publishing lent themselves to overprocessed meetings, perhaps, but hardly ever silence.

Maybe this is normal?

"What kind of cheese is this?" TBQM asks, revealing a new twinkle in his eyes. I file away "cheese" as a topic we could pursue at our next meal together.

We hem and haw, and snap long, thin Italian breadsticks over the white linen tablecloth until finally, after much awkwardness, we stumble on a topic we can all engage in: a sunken submarine. CNN is reporting that a Russian nuclear sub has plummeted to the deepest part of the Barents Sea with a crew of more than one hundred on board. "Can you *imagine* what's going on in their heads?" says Ben. "God, and the pressure."

We have found something besides the climbs at hand, or climbing in general, to chew on. The submarine situation speaks to basic human fears and tragedy. We share a dark intrigue about the *Lord of the Flies* scene that might be taking place fathoms below. I wonder whether the sailors, when they took off from shore, had thought of it as a job or as an adventure.

Most likely the former. The sailors down below are poorly paid family men from a country with a dashed economy. We are affluent folks who endure risk, even chase it, for what must be entirely different (and often elusive) reasons.

"Everyone have extra beeners?" asks Digger before we set off the next morning. Everybody nods. Each person on our team—director, talent, camera—gets a "guide" to cover him or her mountainside. Digger covers Ben; Paul, a.k.a. TBQM, covers K2, and my guide is a local expert named Pierre

Giorgio. Pierre Giorgio is a lean, dark Italian who, like many of his colleagues, comes from a long line of mountaineers.

With stumbling, earnest English, a genuine love of the mountains, a fuchsia cell phone that matches the piping on his outfit, and the balance of a tarantella dancer, Pierre Giorgio leads us through the Dolomites with the style of, well, an *Italian*.

The jutting rocky peaks of the Dolomites are a majestic playground for any mildly competent mountaineer. The towers of rocks were once a coral reef that was exposed by a receding ice age. Among the climbing routes ten thousand feet above sea level you can find fossils of prehistoric sea creatures. The Via Ferrata is fully "protected," meaning a climber can always be tied or clipped in; no free soloing necessary. The routes were originally developed by troops in World War I who used their considerable alpine skills to advantage during battles. Later, the routes were improved by mountaineers who wanted to shorten the time it took to get to popular climbs in the Brenta Dolomites. The result: magnificent climbs protected with cables, ladders, and fixed pitons, making otherwise dangerous terrains accessible.

Carabiners, or "beeners," are our best friends as we traverse the Via Ferrata. At any given time one or two active carabiners are clipped from the harnesses around our waists into the fixed protection. The climbing is not technically difficult, but it demands stamina and a steely stomach in the face of sheer, brutal drops and great heights. I never could relate to Jimmy Stewart as he teetered miserably at the top of a bell tower in *Vertigo*. However, the frequent waves of queasiness that roll through my abdomen tell me that scampering at these heights is an unnatural act for the human animal. After all, we have soft feet and big brains—rather than, say, hard cloven hooves deft at negotiating jagged stone and mountain-goat-size brains that don't dwell on cosmic hazards such as mortality and self-actualization.

"Vun clip eez okay here," Pierre Giorgio says when there is only a thousand-foot drop. Later the fog rolls in and I cannot see the five-thousand-foot drop that lies below the four-inch ledge we are negotiating.

"Two clips here at all times," Pierre Giorgio urges. He suddenly looks less relaxed. A new tendon defines his neck. A gap in the icy fog opens, but it does not reveal a crisp, heavenly view. Instead, I get a glimpse of the hellish abyss below. *"O mio dio,"* I say to Pierre Giorgio, repeating a phrase I picked up from him.

"*Due* cleeps," he reiterates with a smile.

"Don't look down, don't look down, don't look down," I create a mantra, and think about Sky Dancer. She is currently wedged at the bottom of my backpack. If I spun her off this ledge, she would sail, arms up, blue tutu billowing around her chest, twirling for minutes . . . down, down, down in graceful circles until she plummeted into the rock thousands of feet below, shattering to bits. We'd have to erect a plaque in her honor. "Sky Dancer: She died hiking up much more than her skirt."

I sing "Edelweiss" to distract myself until the tune inadvertently morphs into Tom Petty's "Free Fallin'." I stop singing.

A group of three young and brightly Gore-Texed guys climb up quickly behind me to pass. *Shame spiral!* Oh, to be passed on a route! I check that the carabiners are soundly clipped to my harness and to the steel rope, then plaster myself, bladder first, flat against the fifteen-million-year-old sedimentary rock. In the ruckus my nine-dollar gas-station sunglasses go sailing down down down and meet the fate imagined for Sky Dancer. The men scuttle around me—*grazie bella*—and zoom ahead *unclipped*. Well! I shoot a glance to Pierre Giorgio. "Spaniards," he says, as if that is an explanation.

A perhaps obvious, but noteworthy, word about ropes and clips and other forms of "protection." One might think from afar (as did I before I began to climb in college, and later for television) that they offer some sort of *help*. They do not. "Ah, well, at least we won't be free climbing," I used to naïvely think as I trailed a zealous college pal up a 5.7 route, or was asked to do a standup from a precipice with massive exposure. True, if your body is about to hurl off a cliff, protection will stop your fall, eventually. But does it make it any easier to climb? No. Does it change the psychological component? No. Hedge fear? No. As when using other forms of protection in life, the rigor, the glory, the emotional drama is always present. Protection, in climbing as in the bedroom, curbs the consequences of a misstep, to be sure, but our hearts pay little heed to it in the heat of the moment.

We huff and puff and struggle up Scala degli Amici—the Ladder of Friends—a rusty iron sixty-seven-rung ladder that is bolted to a sheer cliff. To distract myself from what is the region's most dramatic drop, I tick off the names of all the Von Trapp kids: Gretl, Fredrich, Brigitta, Marta, Louisa, Kurt . . . damn, there's one more. Louisa, Brigitta, Friedrich, Marta, Gretl, Kurt. Hmmm. A rung suddenly snaps under my left leg, which slips and flails unanchored into the universe. Both carabiners lock in under the pressure of my weight—*clllaaang!*

"Caaareful," says Digger, and I scramble up to the next rung, my heart pounding. I'm embarrassed that the camera is catching my every struggle (though admiring of K2, who also has to get up these heights ten steps ahead of me—all the while filming—in order to do his job). At the eleventh hour of this, our second day, my legs quivering, I try to remember that each hard step now will better my chances of getting up the Matterhorn next week; that each blister that is born, pops, and calcifies in my stiff new blue suede mountaineering boots will toughen me up for the *real* challenge . . . and that each ibuprofen taken now is one less I will have later. These thoughts, along with endless spectacular vistas and a deep need to outrun my own fermented stench from consecutive sweaty days *sino* shower, keep me at a steady pace despite the pain.

"One more hour, yes," Pierre Giorgio says, also noting that moment when day gracefully downshifts toward evening.

A hut system that offers spare, communal accommodations to dozens of climbers is smattered across the Dolomites and links one day to the next. Before dinner I have bent myself into one of the stacked, narrow bunks and am cleaning out raw blisters when I overhear my colleagues outside the hut's glassless window making bets about whether or not I will make it up the Matterhorn. Odds are even, apparently. *"Yeah." "No." "Well, it's going to come down to her state of mind."*

Why the mediocre expectations? My inexperience? Would they be laying bets if I were a guy?

I slip into a quiet, lonely funk.

I hide my irritation as we carb up on piles of pasta puttanesca at long, narrow wooden tables. No freeze-dried stroganoff in these Italian Alps. I jab and twirl the noodles, and say little throughout the meal. At other tables tiny but indelicate glasses of grappa slosh with revelry before going down. My colleagues are experts at sussing out their clients, and it is now clear that this climb in the Dolomites is as much to observe my skills and whip me into shape as it is to add a story to the show. There are four possible outcomes of a Matterhorn climb: injury/death, client quits, the guides "call" the climb due to dangerous conditions or a failing client, and a summit success. I am too tired for anger, but a renewed determination to get up that mountain gestates inside, like an alien.

After dinner we liberate our sleeping bags from our rucksacks and bed down in the bunks. A cacophony of snoring in several different languages blankets the night, inspiring in me as much awe as the heavy rack of bright stars that ignite the sky, which I stare at through the window frame. One sleeping Norwegian displays an odd, nighttime Tourette's attack in which potty expletives are seamlessly lodged into the flow of his snore: "Fuck-en—eeeeqqqqq—sheeet—eeeqqqq—fuck! fuck—eeeeeqqqq—shit shit shit!eeeeeeeeqqqq."

The next morning after Tourette's-a-go-go, I invest in earplugs, one of very few items (another being grappa) that can be readily bought in the huts.

We head out to the trail and I catch myself counting the plaques that dot the landscape, marking spots where climbers have fallen to their deaths. "That's twenty-four," I say to Ben. An hour later we stop and film a stone shelter adorned by simple crosses that houses pictures of smiling, once-vital, now-dead men in their twenties and thirties. Daniele. Valerio. Franco.

There seems to be a calm acceptance that life in the Alps exacts its sacrifices. Pierre Giorgio is a consummate professional; safety-minded yet relaxed, hardworking but not neurotic, and completely blasé about the cameras. He hits his stride at altitude but is clearly grounded; I notice the faraway look endemic to mountaineers in his eyes. At the risk of imposing a chin-jutting Marlboro-man stereotype onto our Italian host, I venture that Pierre Giorgio is full of respect for these mountains, and for the community that stoically weathers a certain number of humans lost every year. That said, climbing's accident rate is low compared to the sport's public perception. But as with airline disasters, accidents that do happen resonate deeply in subconscious chambers.

At the top of Cengia Alta, Pierre Giorgio introduces us to the old man of the mountains, ninety-three-year-old Bruno Detassis, who has beaten the odds time and again and lived a long life as a famously aggressive, first-ascent climber. Detassis dreamed up the Via Ferrata decades ago. Pierre Giorgio's father helped make that dream a reality by camping on ledges, summer after summer, installing permanent protection in the form of iron cables to make these routes safe and accessible for "wannabes" like us. Droopy-eyed, but with ass-pinching spirit intact, Detassis is a revered mountaineer. He chats with us about glory days and then makes a memorable departure in a wire trolley basket (usually reserved for food) wearing a traditional Alpen climbing hat and trailing pipe smoke down the mountain. "That's the best image in the show so far," says K2-Keith with a grin.

One might expect three-thousand-foot drops and fourteen-hour climbing days to be the main source of clenched jaws, but instead our strange and still stilted group dynamic seems to be the real source of a palpable tension, and the biggest obstacle to the task at hand: making a decent show and having plea-surable—nonfatal—experiences.

Jeez, Ben and Digger really need to pull it together, I think. The two of them have been engaged in a power struggle since day one. Director Ben is in charge of the filming, Digger is in charge of the safety and climbing. Who trumps whom when the demands of their respective departments dictate different ac-tion? Strap on a bit of competitive spirit and ego, and a sunny walk amid the Alps can turn dark indeed. *Boys can be so catty,* I think.

The lesson that communal quarters can be devoid of privacy, yet full of loneliness, crystallizes the next night when I overhear a conversation between K2 and Ben on my way back from brushing my teeth.

"No, no, Keith, the shooting is not the problem, our *presenter* is," says Ben. A hunk of crow goes down, ripping the soft pink flesh of my throat along the way. Me? I'm the problem? I don't want to hear any more. I turn and go out-side. I sit, knees to chest, huddling in my down parka, against the hut's wooden planks, feeling like a failure. I watch my breath until a star pings off to the right in my peripheral vision.

I get fetal in my bunk and stew, using my headlamp to scribble in my jour-nal: *"Am I just lonely, sore and in over my head—or do these guys just thrash out, rather than pull together, under pressure?"* I shove in my ear plugs and resolve to talk to Director Ben in the morning; to be a professional—detached, unemo-tional, anything but personal, despite the fact that we as a climbing team hold one another's lives in our hands on a daily basis and are intimately familiar with one another's bodily functions.

"Ben, can we talk? Things aren't going well," I say the next day, standing up straight, emboldened by the potential inherent to mornings. Ben and I walk off about a hundred yards, out of earshot of the others.

"Working with you is like beating a dead horse" is his pull-no-punches opener. "Clearly you'd rather not be here." (And clearly, Ben has been stewing too.) Ben feels, it seems, that my on-camera performance is lacking vitality.

Oh where oh where are my nurturing feminist publishing colleagues of yore? Never again will I complain about potluck professional events, having to "check in" at the beginning of meetings, or even Judy Chicago posters. Give me estrogen over testosterone any day.

I *may* be a bit low-energy, but it is hard to toss off witty one-liners to camera when every last electrolyte is going to the climbing task at hand. And, well, as an American, with a slight insecurity about the superiority of the British intellect, I *may* be overcompensating with excessive irony . . . crossing dangerously over the line into cheap sarcasm. I concede all this in my head, but of course, don't give an inch. Instead, I lash back, "Well you, you, you just roll your eyes when you don't like pieces to camera." Ben has not overcoddled me as directors are wont to do, but his disdain for my work has been fairly obvious, which has sent more than one painful pulse to my vulnerable bladder. "How about a little constructive criticism?" I ask.

While we are scrapping I steal a glance over at the crew. Pierre Giorgio is picking up his messages on his fuchsia cell phone; K2 is tinkering with his camera; TBQM is looking wistfully into the distance, thinking of far-off summits . . . or gouda. I turn back to Ben and lob more euphemisms about his insecurity under pressure; he kicks up scree about my lackluster performance. And after about ten minutes we are done. *Basta. Finito.* We both moved a bit, with me conceding that the physical challenge has dampened my host-perkiness quotient, and him alluding to fears about getting all of us working in concert, and up that mountain. We agree that our union is crucial to the team's success. As the "creatives" on this project, the two of us have to work together to pull off this show.

We continue to scramble up and along rocks, and the magnificent landscape begins to buff the edge off the human tension. On our last night, having completed the Dolomites, we have a few grappas, loosen up, and discuss the sub that still gurgles in the depths of the Barents Sea. Will they survive? Can they cope with the dark and cold? We can relate to the sailors and to the Cold War atmosphere that is affecting decisions. What's more important, saving the sailors or protecting whatever mission they were on? "I can't believe the Russians haven't asked for submersible aid from other countries," says Ben. We all agree, shake our heads, and bond in our disapproval.

The bright red Glacier Express train carries us from Italy and away we slip, like an oyster down the gullet, into Switzerland—a bastion of neutrality that can surely offer the level playing field our group will need in order to pull together and tackle the Matterhorn.

My youth was alive with the girl characters of these Alps. Sassy, how-do-you-solve-a-problem-like Maria . . . Maria . . . ? What was her name before Von Trapp? Anyway, Julie Andrews was so much fun until she married the captain. After the nuptials, gone were the days of puppeteering and play-clothes-made-from-curtains! And Heidi, she kicked some alpine ass and had a very progressive thing going with Hans Peter before she got shipped off to the city. I can't remember what happened to her after that.

We start to unpack Swiss stereotypes by interviewing a champ yodeler in front of the gargantuan Aletsch Glacier and learn that the art is not simply background music for "hoist another stein" moments in the Alps. It is an ancient tradition, first recorded in the fourth century and born from the cowherd's incantatory call across valleys to his charges, to his cowherd colleagues, and to the gods. Some even say the origin of the yodel is the cowherd's reaction to stunning scenery and a reflection of the human soul. "A real yodel is a wordless communication," the champ explains before she belts out an amazing string of sounds.

"You try it, Holly," Ben says.

"No," I clip.

"I'm sensitive to you not wanting to make a fool of yourself on telly, but give 'er a belt," urges Ben.

"Absolutely not," I say firmly, skirting the edge of our delicate truce.

Fondue is everywhere, and this is one cheesy cliché we can all agree on and participate in. Long, tough Swiss winters used to mean there was only old, unpalatable cheese to eat. Out of necessity fondue was born: Toss in a little wine, heat it up, and presto, cheesy fondue that made even stale bread tasty. Eating from one pot was symbolic of communal dining, and the Swiss to this day still show manners and kinship by keeping to their corner of the pot.

The five of us sit in the bar of our hotel in swish Zermatt, chasing kinship through the gurgling mass of Gruyère before us. Our pokers clank against one another unceremoniously, creating a significant attrition rate. But after we discuss the flavor, the best way to twirl, and the consequences of losing one's chunk of bread in the pot, the inevitable lull ensues.

We once again take up . . . *the Tragedy*. The sailors in the submarine are all dead. They had survived for a while, as a note in a dead seaman's pocket reveals: "All of the crew from the sixth, seventh, and eighth compartments went over to the ninth. We made the decision as a result of the accident. None of us can get to the surface." Did they combust? Freeze? Suffocate? Most importantly, who made the fatal mistake? We are talking about death in the depths, but secretly our minds are on altitude. *Adventure tragedies are due purely to human failure* is the comforting lie that silently passes among us and goes down with the next glob of fondue. I look around at our quiet, chomping group. Like the sailors sealed together a hundred meters below, film crews and climbers also share a forced intimacy and interdependence. I am by turns excited and scared about climbing the Matterhorn; feeling both strong and weak; clinging to the thought that guts and Kodak courage can overcome a serious lack of skill and experience. I climbed Rainier last year, but that's a cakewalk compared to this. I try not to think about the sailors whose adventure turned to tragedy—how they awaited their deaths, the world pitying them.

The Matterhorn hangs in a funny balance between icon and cliché, a situation exacerbated by the town nestled near its base: the touristy, car-less town of Zermatt, which is like a postcard of itself. Zermatt is a spendy stop on the global tourist route and makes big bucks off those who will pay to experience risk. The town crawls with cell phones, top-flight mountain gear, an endless hawking of all things Matterhorn, and Internet cafés that serve triple chocolate cake.

TO: JEANNIE
FROM: HOLLY
SUBJECT: BASE CAMP

Jeannie—Dolomites were tough but am stronger now. Was pressured to yodel (I know, I know: tone-deaf). We're in Zermatt awaiting the Assault. (That's what the books call it—an Assault.) Did those football players you used to interview ever talk? These climbers don't. What's happening at hq?

TO: HOLLY
FROM: JEANNIE
SUBJECT: CASH POOR

Hol—No venture capitalists have come on board, unfortunately. The economy is really beginning to slump and the dot-com bust still has everyone feeling burned. You didn't yodel, did you? As for the talking, well, that generation of jocks mostly expressed intimacy through butt slapping. I'm sure your guys are all just worried. A lot of pressure to get up a mountain and make TV.—Jeannie

We take a clean, modern tram up to a viewing area in order to get some long shots of the mountain. The tram-train is filled with tourists and a few climbers. Who falls into which category is easy to distinguish by what comes tumbling out of their mouths upon seeing the Matterhorn for the first time up close: *Is my exposure set right, honey?* or *Shit, have you ever seen such massive exposure, honey?*

A middle-aged American tourist in blue fleece hears that we are to climb. "I wouldn't do that for a million dollars. No *danke.* Six people died last week up there. But honey, I feel you'll be all right," she says, patting me on the thigh, "and I'm a bit of a psychic."

"*Six* fatalities in one week?" I say to the psychic. She nods solemnly, as if to reiterate her no-*danke* stance. Digger does not look up from his magazine.

"Lots of people have climbed it"—my dad's parting words collide with the psychic's—and lots of people have died on it. The indifferent stone citadel that fills the train window has claimed more lives than any mountain in the Alps, which may be why it remains a siren to climbers worldwide.

I tire of my own melodrama and spend the rest of the tram ride playing travel Scrabble with an Australian teen. "A-N-C-H-O-R. Anchor," she says, eleven points.

The next day, we walk through Zermatt's climber's cemetery before setting off for Hörnli Hut, our starting point. Ice axes drape tombstones that bear the dates of birth and death of those who have died on the Matterhorn.

DAVID ROBINSON OF WAKEFIELD AND BANGOR NORTH WALES WHOSE UN-TIMELY DEATH AT THE AGE OF 24 YEARS OCCURRED WHILE DESCENDING THE HÖRNLI RIDE HAVING CLIMBED THE NORTH FACE OF THE MATTERHORN, says one. Another reads simply: TAUGWALDER FRONZISCUS "I CHOSE TO CLIMB."

Edward Whymper was the first to summit the Matterhorn in 1865, along with six others in his team—four of whom died on the descent and are buried here. Whymper and his contemporaries were an understated lot who took to the mountains in the name of the Queen and good air; this was long before the commodification of "adventure." No Gore-Tex, no helmets, no crampons; they roped to one another and learned through experience, some of it tough. Their hazards will be ours—falling rock, avalanche, the fatal misstep—but because they could not rely on modern equipment and cell phones, they must have been far superior mountaineers to those of us who try it today. They also had *time*—to watch the mountain, to make many attempts, to talk to one another. They did not have to dash back to the office on Monday morning. Whymper, who was a lithographic artist and illustrator by profession, had been hired by a London publisher to make sketches of Alpine peaks, a job that gave him time to conjure and do reconnaissance missions that would inform his eighth, and successful, attempt on this mountain long considered unsummitable. "Toil he must who goes mountaineering, but out of toil comes strength (not merely muscular energy—more than that), an awakening of all the faculties; and from the strength arises pleasure," wrote Whymper in his golden years. There was a good deal of competition regarding who would first summit the Matterhorn. Those early attempts seem, through the lens of history, so pure compared to ours. A relatively few men blazing unknown trails. In a funny way, we compete against ourselves, but they . . . well . . . they looked right down the barrel of the unknown. They thought: *Can it be done?* We think: *Can I do it?*

Why climb if you can die doing it? What is it that makes us intentionally tango with the Maker? The draw seems more than just getting to a beautiful place to commune with the secular power of nature. The yearn to climb has to do with mortality and vitality being inextricably wed. The delicate glacier, the narrow ledge, the capriciousness of the elements all require us to Pay Attention—to our moves and our lives. Thus, fear gets transformed, through action, into vitality. To live in that complete present is the goal, the moment of the take. To feel, for an extended period of time, that any moment may be your last (which I did every time my leg slipped off a ledge or ladder in the Via Feratta) makes you realize that you like—and want to keep—your life, and switches *vita* from black-and-white to color. Bachendri Pal calls it "the difference between being fully alive and just living" (N-U-T-G-R-A-B, sixty points).

So is it merely competitive machismo that drives mountaineers to high places with little oxygen and plenty of hazards? Or is the act—for the viscerally inclined—one of leaving entropy behind and chasing a perfect bit of prose poem, a rhapsodic bolero, the last answer in the Sunday *New York Times* crossword?

Whatever the answer, I'm sure it didn't apply to the guys in the sub.

We hike several hours up to the Hörnli Hut, launching point for the Assault. A few relieved and giddy climbers who have already summitted sit at nearby tables, basking in their success and the sun. To the right and straight up looms the Matterhorn, in all its 14,690-feet-above-sea-level glory.

When my aunt Donna heard about my going on this trek, she banged the mountain up on the Internet and wailed from the other room, *"Haaahleee, good God, don't do it—have you seen how pointy it is?"* Her words come to me now as I crane my neck and take in the sheer, pointy, unfathomably vertical rock before us.

Already-high tension peaks to a sour pitch. The mountain seems different to me after hearing that it claimed those six lives. We all make ourselves feel better by saying it must have been those "crazy Czechs" who never rope up, since they were so recently unleashed politically (a superficial analysis that bounces among climbers, and that we readily accept). Digger says the plan is to conquer the mountain in one day. Light packs. Stealth filming.

"Vee vill have good veather," says sixty-four-year-old Ricky Andematten, who has met us at the Hörnli. Ricky has a bushy salt-and-pepper mustache and a matching thick bunch of hair on his head. He will be my personal guide as well as the team's lead guide. Like Pierre Giorgio, Ricky has climbing in his blood. He is a fourth-generation Swiss Matterhorn guide.

We do not all bunk in the same room in the Hörnli Hut, which is a blessing as I have lost my earplugs. Ben and I, the tension between us now at a very low simmer, are roommates for a couple of days. Aside from our potentially lethal-smelling socks, our room is a sanctuary from the stories of mountain fatalities zinging around the hut. There is no escape, however, from the periodic buzz of helicopters on rescue missions ("Those damn Czechs!"). We look out our small window and see orange sarcophagi chained below the choppers as they zoom by. One time the limbs that hang out of the sling have the limpness of death. Two times they do not.

We eat sauerkraut. We prepare ourselves mentally for the mountain. We grieve the lack of cheese. Preclimb rituals take the form of obsessively fiddling with equipment and an endless recitation of stories about climbs gone awry. I hear about losing hands to frostbite on Denali, bodies tossed down crevasses on Everest, glorious barroom brawls, and women's fat asses. We talk about the weather. A lot.

I can relate to exactly none of the conversations. One part of me can swagger with the best of peak baggers, a frequently useful trait. Another part of me thinks it is strange to have so many conversations devoid of emotion when emotion is actually the addictive opiate of the climbing experience. I opt out and funnel my trepidation into watching the handsome young guides who take clients up the mountain. An entrepreneurial idea comes to me: a Men of the Matterhorn calendar. There are a few other women in the hut also waiting to climb, and I briefly consider asking for their nominations.

The nature of my nerves reflects my own internal dichotomy. I fear not getting up the mountain and screwing up the show as much as or more than I fear becoming a statistic. How twisted is it that I fear professional failure more than heart failure? Traditionally, professional drive has meant working to publish a book, launch a business, or film a diva, not climbing fourteen thousand vertical feet in six hours.

"Tomorrow you will suffer," my guide, Ricky, says as he goes through my backpack, purging nonessentials on the eve of our attempt, "but later you will see the world differently. You will be a proud girl."

"This," he says, pulling Sky Dancer out of the inner pocket I hid her in, "stays behind. No extra weight."

———

Four A.M. and the dark, crisp, clear skies come as a relief—if only because they put an end to a fitful night of anxiety dreams. Though he has a climbing past, Ben shares my trepidation and charmingly confesses to scratching out a will. "Everything goes to my girlfriend and my kid, with the exception of my record collection and cameras . . . my brothers get those," he says soberly, showing me where the will is stashed. Being devoid of assets and any significant equity, it occurs to me that this could—cosmically speaking—be an okay time for me to "go." Nevertheless, I sneak Sky Dancer back into my pack for good luck. After all, Narishakti worked for Bachendri on her climb up Everest.

"Ben," I ask, as we make the final cinches on our small packs and swing them from our cots onto our backs, "what do you think happened down there in the last moments? In the sub. Do you think they turned to, or against, one another?" I ask.

Ben looks down and shakes his head slowly. There is a long silence. "I don't know," he replies quietly. "But you gotta hope they reached some sort of peace in the end. All they had was each other."

It's 4:15 A.M. and the temperature reads fourteen degrees Celsius. We scramble around in the dark clicking on our headlamps and putting on our gear. With dozens of other silent hopefuls, we toss back some tea, and set off. All of the young guides—March, September, January—are tying on to their clients and rushing out the door so they do not get stuck in an alpine traffic jam.

Ricky and I, too, are short-roped together. Since the Everest tragedy in 1996, I've considered short-roping a dirty word because, on Everest anyway, it can lead to a shameful situation in which one climber virtually hauls another, weaker climber up a mountain. On the Matterhorn, however, short-roping is the most common and safest method, as the density of climbers makes belaying a partner (fixing into the mountain with protection and belaying with large stretches of rope between you) far too hazardous. With short-roping, the idea is that if one partner slips, the other can dig in and prevent them both from falling. Ricky and I only have each other; there's no protection. Worst-case scenario: If I go, he goes—and vice versa.

In the pitch black we walk in single file across a snowfield. I look up and see a trail of lights, a weaving troupe of fireflies, inching its way up the base of the mountain ahead of us. "Gently, gently," goes Ricky's mantra as we set out with only our headlamps, his expertise, and our combined enthusiasm to guide us. The stars wink above as if conspiring in a bit of a laugh. Zermatt slumbers below, making its leisurely living off the sweat of us naïve thrill-seekers above. Part therapist, part drill sergeant, and part Heidi's grandfather, Ricky will be my savior.

"Left hand here, right hand there," he says. "Good girl, zat's my champ," he encourages, with his kindly accent. "Steady, steady, gently, gently, watch my feet. Step where I step."

LOVE Ricky!—despite the "good-girl" stuff and that he has me on a leash.

I feel lucky. Our pace is fast, but my body and mind harmonize and remind me that this is the kind of place and circumstance that make me most happy. My eyes sting and adrenaline rushes down legs that only knew needles of pain a few days ago. Ricky encourages me to play with the mountain and the moves, to breathe, and to synchronize my legs and arms; he teaches me a certain mountain dance, a choreography. I am not alone. He and I are a team that will succeed or fail together. Ricky does not approach this as an assault. Ricky, a guru of the Alps, is wise enough to be humble.

Dusty orange quietly emerges in the east until, from the crux between two peaks, a blazing star of light bursts forth, turning into a new day.

"Good Holly, you do vell," says Ricky.

The first two hours of the climb are very rigorous but—almost—enjoyable. "Liesl!" I blurt out, suddenly remembering the name of the other Von Trapp kid. Ricky looks back and nods, as if this is normal behavior. I realize that the suffering on the Dolomites paid off. That struggle made me strong. Starting the climb in the dark helped, of course, as I can develop a rhythm without the added pressure of seeing the consequences of a misstep.

Hour four. Misery gains a toehold, though the spirit remains intact. "Gently, gently" starts to grate on my nerves; my thighs burn from overuse as I grind up the Upper Mosley Slabs. An eight-inch hunk of rock zings by my ear, having been kicked loose by a climber above. I try not to look up or else I'll take in the massive totality of this endeavor and become overwhelmed.

I stop on sheer slope and struggle with my crampons. I spent an hour taking them on and off last night, but the fruits of my practice desert me in this critical moment. I chuck aside my ego, and let a guide who comes up behind us untangle my straps.

One step at a time, usually a slightly jaded phrase in my lexicon, now becomes a totally earnest hold-steady loop in my mind. I care less about the view; I stop talking. I wish I could fast-forward this adventure. Whymper wrote: "We who go mountain scrambling have constantly set before us the superiority of fixed purpose or perseverance to brute force. We know that each height, each step, must be gained by patient, laborious toil, and that wishing cannot take the place of working."

Whatever, Whymper.

Hours five and six. Mild delirium sets in. *No WAY,* my mind and body holler as I confront the next vertical challenge on this narrow, narrow ridge. I forget the camera. I forget the crew. I look to the right, down the four-thousand-foot drop of the Matterhorn's north face, where four of Edward Whymper's seven-man party fell to their deaths on their descent from the summit in 1865.

Pain sends me crawling into my secret happy place. *You're all alone . . .* but I am decidedly *not.* An endless stream of climbers is directly behind me. I look up at the vertical cliff in front of me that leads, tauntingly, to the summit. A mental ticker tape of tongue-lashings begins. *Fuck this show. Fuck this mountain. Fuck Ricky and his goddamned lulling voice and incessant confidence in me. Fuck all these* guys. I remember, in Borneo, the headman's reluctance to sacrifice a cock for our good luck. My vision blurs with tears as my upper body screams for salvation. I look over at one of the guys. I'd do it, right now, sacrifice a cock, if it would relieve me of this mountain purgatory.

I want to quit. Ricky looks back and sees. He recognizes that his client has crossed the line. He twirls and delivers the emotional equivalent of a smack across the face. "Be a tough girl! You are a tough girl! Action! Action!" He morphs from supportive Swiss grandfather into snarling guide, determined to bring his client back from the edge. I gulp a hunk of too-thin air and begin to scramble up the cliff, crampons flailing, spitting out a considerable range of four-letter words.

Another forty-five-minute snow climb up a seventy-degree grade. "Quit stepping on your crampons: *beeeg* steps, *beeeg* steps!" says Ricky sternly when I stumble dangerously near the edge of the narrow ridge. My last reservoirs of anger and determination plow me onward.

I toe-kick with a vengeance, grunting with every hard-earned step, focusing only on the next one to come. I imagine my thighs as separate units that propel, without failing. I don't know how much time goes by, but I suddenly become aware of Ricky, who is touching me lightly on the shoulder, stirring me from my kinetic revelry. I lift my eyes and take in the totality of where we are.

Holy shit. "We made it?" I whisper to Ricky through the panting, my head slightly bowed with exhaustion. The narrow, hundred-yard summit, part Italy and part Switzerland, adorned by two crosses.

"Here vee are at the top of the Matterhorn," Ricky says. "I am proud of you. You vill alvaays remember this, my champ," he says, smiling, his mustache crusted with ice.

He is, once again, right. Alps and countries and rugged humbling peaks pour across the distance, and for the first time on this trip I see through another portal: gratitude. I am determined not to cry, or keel over with a heart attack, or plunge my ice ax into the sky in victory. Despite the cheese and yodeling, this is no time for clichés. All I can think of is apologizing to Ricky for turning into such a bitch ("It is normal, my champ," he assures me) and getting a picture of Sky Dancer on the summit. She made it!

I slog over to Ben. "Please take her picture," I say, and wedge Sky Dancer into the crisp snow in front of a hard-earned backdrop, and he clicks; her blue hair perfectly matches the piercing sky behind her. Ben lowers the camera and the weary but blissed look in his eyes tells me that we have all waged our individual battles getting up here.

Digger and Ben shake hands. Paul fastidiously covers Keith, who is shinnying toward the edge to get a better shot. It dawns on me that all of the tension these past two weeks was about the high stakes attached to our common investment—reaching this summit. So many things could have gone terribly, horribly wrong, and they did not. Caught up in my own nerves, and my own unchecked ego, I had failed to truly understand that each of us was packing a few extra pounds of pressure—but now I hear it hissing off into the nearly fifteen-thousand-foot ether.

Our time on top is brief, filled with a wordless communication. We relish our success in the cracks between doing our jobs—filming, directing, protecting one another. Our kind of yodel, I guess. There is no high-fiving, but there is a pure and happy visceral moment together.

We begin the descent, the most dangerous part of any climb. Adrenaline surged us up the mountain, but a new rhythm accompanies our troupe back down. Funnily enough, I don't see Zermatt, only layers and folds and jutting peaks of snow-covered majesty.

STROPPY SHEILAS AND MANA WAHINES

—

Stroppy sheilas are uniquely Kiwi gals with grit.
"Stroppy" . . . derives from the adjective "obstreperous,"
meaning boisterous and untameable. Stroppy
women . . . are feisty and hard to handle, and they are
viewed with a mixture of annoyance, wariness and re-
spect. "Sheila" is a curious antipodean colloquial term
for women—it's the other half of "bloke." Sheilas lived
down on the farm, wore print frocks and were good
sorts. . . . It's a term that's dying out—sadly, because it
has far more going for it than its decorative, defined-by-
their-tits-and-bums successors, such as the "chicks" of the
seventies or the "babes" of the nineties.

—SANDRA CONEY, AUTHOR
AND EXPERT ON
NEW ZEALAND'S
WOMEN'S HISTORY

"Okay, so keep the cameras low, focusing on the boots and hooves. Don't pull up until the last line. Is Ram Cam holding?" I ask.

We bought an old hi-8 video camera at an Auckland pawnshop and have spent the last hour rigging it with bungee cords and duct tape to the neck of a very smelly, very oily, very fidgety hundred-and-twelve-pound ram. Two local Kiwi farmers, wearing black singlets and gumboots, yip and shuffle to keep the herd of seventy-five sheep within some semblance of control. The occasional rogue sheep is chased down by a border collie, or by one of us. We have exactly one chance at this opening standup, as these sheep are going to be too traumatized, and scattered, for a second take.

"Okay!" I yell. The farmers start whooping and running, driving a heaving mass of off-white curly hair toward me as I start the standup.

"Waaay down under there are a quiet couple of islands"

Holy crap.

"where bucolic scenes can be deceptive, and rogue politics are the order of the day."

Oh shiiiii—

"It's a place where pastoral conservatism meets twisted brilliance"

A thundering cloud of terror-stricken sheep, who are unused to being Hollywood extras, begins to overtake me. Nanoseconds before impact, the cloud bisects and snakes around me with the g-force of spring runoff in a slot canyon. One. More. Line.

"where biculturalism is a verb—and it's all run by stroppy sheilas!"

I hit the dirt and protect my torso as the maelstrom passes in a final *baaaaah*ing melee.

"Uh, I think we got it," says Michael Gross, with a big, warm laugh. He gives me a hand up and we swap a the-things-we-do-for-TV look. Of medium build and height with dark hair, glasses, and a friendly, full-body slouch, Michael has been a creative conspirator on all things diva ever since he edited the Cuba show. For two unrelated grown-ups, he and I have developed an oddly fraternal relationship. Our shared sense of quirk led to this stunt, which will give sheep—which outnumber humans seventeen to one in New Zealand—top billing in the show.

Ram Cam lies trampled in the mud, detached from its four-legged tripod (quad-pod?). The camera is destroyed, but we spool the tape back into the cracked casing. "It can be salvaged," Michael says with uncharacteristic optimism.

"Right," I say, wiping a chunk of sheep doogie off my forearm. "Guess we'd better get going to the first interview if we're going to make it on time."

"Good morning Auckland. Today the burn rate is eight minutes, so be sure

to lather on the number thirty," advises Channel Z, Auckland's modern rock station.

"*Aoteoroa* is what the indigenous Maori people call New Zealand," says Simon Griffith, this episode's producer, who lives in Seattle but was raised in New Zealand. "It means 'land of the long white cloud.' But the cloud doesn't protect you from the hole in the ozone layer," he adds, scratching his brown beard with a burly forearm. Simon is unusually *lumberjack* for a producer. Must be his brawny Kiwi blood. He is driving us from the pastures farther into the farming communities outside of Auckland. In addition to Simon and Michael, our crew is rounded out by Liza Bambenek, a young, strong, Santa Fe–based camerawoman with a mop of short dark hair; and Jan McKinley, a local soundwoman, who will keep us from getting lost time and time again.

"Weird. You hear the burn rate statistics here like you might hear the price of pork bellies in Iowa, or weekend box office sales in L.A.," I say.

"Why New Zealand?" many people asked in the weeks running up to this shoot. "Kind of 'soft,' isn't it?" A seemingly domesticated set of islands was an unlikely location for one of our shoots. Yet, New Zealand's importance lies in its unique political reality: The country, quite literally, is run by ladies. On September 19, 1893, New Zealand became the first country in the world in which women got the vote—a full twenty-seven years before the United States. And as of this writing, women hold nearly all the key positions in the country: prime minister, Maori queen, Supreme Court chief justice, governor general, and attorney general.

Women run the country. *Interesting.* Outside of utopian sci-fi novels, my images of societies in which women head and control the power structure are limited to Amazonian legend.

What kind of sociopolitical tectonic shift occurred to create this reality? Is New Zealand a particularly fertile place for divas? If so, why? And there were other things that intrigued me about the country beyond its feminized politicians. New Zealand's progressive political reputation extends to race relations. Today's Maori, the country's first-nation people, and Pakeha, New Zealanders of European descent, are said to have created a relatively peaceful bicultural modern-day society, despite the shadow of British colonial rule.

Oh yeah, and there was a certain fish-loving writer on the wild and wooly South Island I wanted to meet.

In any case, we decided there was more than enough here to justify a *Divas* shoot. We hopped on a plane, mapped out a three-week road trip through the North and South Islands, and, striving to serve both fashion and function, rented a bright orange 1972 Valiant.

The Valiant is a sedan manufactured from 1966 to 1976 by the now-defunct Plymouth division of Chrysler. The quintessential muscle car, the Charger, might be considered its groovy uncle. Valiants were huge sellers in Australia and New Zealand and were popular as souped-up race cars. Attached to this particular Valiant's tail end, like a poorly buried lead, is a boxy, off-white caravan with an orange racing stripe, replete with faux teak-wood paneling on the inside: home.

"Hard to believe, but the Valiant was originally manufactured as a compact car. Got the same body type as the Duster," says Simon, who, along with fellow Kiwi Jan, will do most of the driving on this trip because the rest of us tend to veer to the right side of the road into oncoming traffic.

"I bet the metric system stuck here, too," says Liza, who joins me in having experienced the United States' debacle in metrics during grade school.

"I like the color—and the fact that it was made the same year Shirley Chisholm ran for president."

Liza looks at me, puzzled. She's not that old.

"Yeah, she's a fine old sheila," muses Simon (about the car, not Chisholm), tapping her dashboard with affection, apparently inured to the fact that the car is without brake and tail lights. His patience with the Valiant will serve us well, it will turn out, as Old Sheila will break down repeatedly over the next three weeks.

We drive Old Sheila through the bright green, lazy rolling hills and farm-land that surround Auckland until we reach Marilyn Waring's farm. Waring is a former member of Parliament (the youngest ever—she was only twenty-two when she first entered the hallowed halls in 1975) and author of the book *Counting for Nothing*, which is widely regarded as a seminal work of progressive economics. Trundling down the loopy driveway, we spot a person in a gray T-shirt, lumbering gumboots, and black khaki pants emerge over a grassy knoll. She has a stout, efficient build and short brownish-gray hair, and her thick hands are clapping together.

"Come on darlings! Come on!" she chortles to the hundred or so goats that trail behind her. This is our first—and unforgettable—image of the intellectual powerhouse who imploded some of the most sacred orthodoxies of economics, and made her country famously No Nuke.

We have one day with Waring. A busy academic, lecturer, and prolific writer, she made it clear we would have to join her routine in progress and interview her along the way as time allowed. So after perfunctory introductions we get down to business: farm chores.

CHORE #1: FEEDING THE PIG

"Here, shake this, Holly," says Marilyn, shoving a bucket of slop into my hands. "Tam! Tammi! You awake? Where are you, pig? There she is. She didn't feel well yesterday. Come on. Come on. Yes!"

"Uh, have you had her a long time?" I ask.

"Yeah, probably about six or seven years. We picked her up late one night wrapped in a towel at the local hotel, and she's named after the barmaid—come on, Tammi!—because, well, the barmaid was a redhead," she says as a 104-pound, wiry, auburn-haired creature lumbers its way over to us snout first and starts, well, *pigging out* on slop. Marilyn explains that Tammi is the resident garbage disposal, thereby keeping away possums and other scavengers.

"How long have you lived the farm life?" I ask.

"About fifteen years. When I was in Parliament I represented a rural constituency. Actually, Helen Clark's [the prime minister's] family home and her parents were in my constituency. I was so envious of the lifestyle."

"The lifestyle of your constituents?"

"Yeah. I knew I just couldn't live in town forever; I never really was a city person. I was forced to be in the city part of the time I was in Parliament but it's just not me, so it had to be a farm. You know, you have to be quite resilient," she says.

"Do you have to be more resilient to live on a farm or to be in Parliament?" I ask, knowing she was elected to Parliament three times, and trying to lead this discussion toward something less agricultural.

"It's completely different," she begins. "I found Parliament personally really brutal. Of course, in the 1970s there were only ever four women in the Parliament and for one whole session I was the only woman in the government.

"But the resilience that's required on the farm means really hard calls: Sometimes when animals are sick and cows are having calving trouble you have to make up your mind about life or death. Here," she says, nodding at the expanse of the farm, "you're working all the time with elements that are more powerful than any humans can ever be, and the only way to survive is to work *with* them. Whereas in politics humans assume they have power *over,* most of the time. So this is much better," she says, letting Tammi lick the last bit of grub from the pail.

CHORE #2: GETTING THE CRITTERS IN THE SHED

"Come on, come on, girls!" Marilyn says, somehow successfully guiding an organic mass of goats in the right direction simply by gentle command. I doubt her fellow Parliamentarians were as easily herded.

"You were twenty-two, right, when you entered Parliament? I mean that's—"

"That's a baby. But when you are twenty-two you don't think about it, and besides, you know, people in their twenties have a right to be there. Women have a right to be there. Indigenous peoples have rights to be there. It's supposed to be a house of *representatives,* so it shouldn't have been so quaint," she says frankly, referring to the largely white and male legislature she became a part of.

"Did you do something about that?" I ask.

"Well, in lots of ways I don't think I achieved anything. I can't show you a memorial or a private bill or anything that I managed to pass. Sometimes I think some of the most important [achievements] were stopping some of the worst things happening. In the seventies and early eighties it was a really important time in New Zealand for the women's movement and for me to act as a kind of a bridge and sometimes as an interpreter—just to be there, you know, screaming, 'Excuse me but . . .' "

No memorial, maybe, but in fact Marilyn is responsible for her country's antinuclear stance—a formidable contribution. Marilyn felt strongly that there should be no nuclear weapons inside New Zealand's sovereign territory and committed a now legendary act of political courage. In June 1984, she announced that she would vote against her party in favor of an opposition bill to ban nuclear weapons.

Marilyn's political party, the National Party, controlled the government, headed by Prime Minister Robert ("Piggy") Muldoon. In response to Waring's revolt, Muldoon dissolved Parliament and called a snap election four and a half months earlier than the election would have been held (some say Muldoon was visibly drunk at the time). The Labour Party, then in opposition, won the election in a landslide, bringing the Muldoon government to its knees and ushering in a proud antinuclear era in New Zealand's history.

All this was the result of a gutsy stand by Marilyn, who has just said to me, "I don't think I achieved anything."

New Zealand's antinuclear policy led the country to ban the United States from parking its nuclear submarines in its waters, a stance that strains political relations between the two countries to this day.

Marilyn picks a chunk of hardened mud from the nape of one of the goats. She might have been one of few women in government in the seventies, but things are considerably different now.

"With all the women currently in power in New Zealand, do you think there has been real institutional change?"

"Kind of. You know, with a woman prime minister and leader of the opposition and governor general designate and chief justice and mayor of Auckland. Having that range of women in important or figurehead positions still doesn't mean that you have a kind of substantive equality, but it *is* very different. One of the former women governors general used to tell this wonderful story about primary schools and one little boy putting his hand up and saying, 'Can a *man* ever be governor general?' " she says with a laugh, illustrating how quickly norms can change.

"It doesn't by any means change things like the distribution of wealth or racial inequity or the whole range of other things. . . . A lot of the women are in power in some of the very last bastions of patriarchal structures, to use the old language, so I guess they start to change language in small ways. They start to change the priorities that are on the agenda and some significant legal changes, of course. So, it's an evolution just as long as you're not too impatient," she concludes, somewhat hopefully.

"I've always thought of New Zealand as being conservative in a blokey-bloke kind of way, but in terms of women in power, in terms of women's right to vote, New Zealand has really led the way globally, right?"

"Yeah, there's some good stuff. It's because New Zealand is so small and so a lot of the politics are pretty transparent. It's very difficult to be highly corrupt here because everybody knows everybody and there aren't many of us."

Pub intelligence. When you are so small that the politicians and constituents share pastures and pints, it's tough to pull the wool over.

CHORE #3: MUCKING OUT THE SHED

While we are chatting, Marilyn mentions the goat shed, our next stop, more than once. The problem is, her accent, with its inflected vowels, makes it sound as if she is saying goat *shit* (*goat shiiiid,* in Kiwi). Every time she says *goat shed* I wince, knowing PBS censors won't like a potty mouth. And bleeping a diva goes against my libertarian principles.

"I'm going in there to sort this lot out," she says, entering the crowded wooden shed. "Excuse me, babies." She nudges a pair of confused goats in her way. "Just pull that gate," she tells me, "so they don't slip out. Push them. Push them! No, no push them up there," she yells as one dashes through my legs, snagging the wire from my radio mic and dragging it through a pile of fresh goat *shed*.

"What inspires you more these days, farm life or, ah, politics?" I ask, as I latch the wooden gate to curb further goat attrition. I delicately sniff my mic before clipping it back on my collar.

"Farm life!" she declares instantly. "Good intensive labor that keeps you fit but doesn't require a vast amount of cerebral activity. You're free to think creatively. I certainly wrote some of the most significant parts of *Counting for Nothing* in the goat shiiiid."

Wince.

"I probably have some of my best ideas in the goat shiiiid."

Wince.

Her best ideas resulted in *Counting for Nothing,* a book that posits the simple yet radical idea that women's unpaid work, and the environment, should be valued and figured into the global economy. Across the world, 65 percent of women's work time is unpaid, whereas men's unpaid work is about 30 percent of their total work time. Unpaid work includes housework, informal enterprises, and family businesses. In many of the so-called superpower First World nations, women account for 50 percent or more of the unpaid workers in family businesses.*

Why is it, Marilyn asked in her work, that market economies are all that count? Often economic policies pretend to be objective, but are in fact elitist and mask political agendas. Her ideas challenge many of the economic policies that drive modern-day globalization. Just as Jimmy Carter demonstrated that human rights can be a part of foreign policy, Marilyn Waring's is an unapologetically value-based economic paradigm. She says economic models should include humane ways of measuring quality of life, and that community well-being is data worth measuring. If only more of the world's thinkers spent their time in goat sheds instead of ivory towers.

"What's easier to handle, goats or members of Parliament?" I ask, stumbling after a kid that has wandered off.

"Well, goats are invariably all intelligent," she responds. "They can be very stubborn."

"Goats or Parliament?" I say.

"Oh, goats, but of course people in Parliament are stubborn. I mean, if I thought Parliament was easy I would still be there," says Marilyn. "Aren't you a little beauty!" she declares to a small angora. It's clear she doesn't want to talk about Parliament anymore.

"So do you think there is a direct correlation between being out here"—I gesture to the rolling hills and the shed—"and your economic philosophies?"

"Absolutely. Because there is a whole different sense of value operating out here," she says.

If policy makers the world over were the ones carrying buckets of water three miles every morning, like the women in India, policies might look different, and unpaid work might be a part of economic models. You value what you sweat for.

Marilyn wrestles one of the goats and brings the analogy even closer to home. She shows me the goat's ear, which is heavy with a brown, crusty

* All statistics are from Joni Seager, *The Penguin Atlas of Women in the World,* third edition, New York: Penguin, 2003.

square-inch chunk of . . . something. "It's cancer," she says when she realizes it's not obvious to me what I am looking at. "See, this goat's ear is developing a big skin cancer because of the ozone layer depletion. It's not something I suppose people in the northern hemisphere think about very much, but in terms of the hole over Antarctica, we here live with the effects of the discharge up north," she says. "The best we can do is try and wait for it to dry off a little bit and then actually just cut if off," she says, scruffing the animal's good ear, "to make it more pleasant for her. She's healthy, you know, at the moment, but I mean the ear is very close to the brain and she's an older girl. This is the kind of thing we're having to watch for all the time now."

"Does this kind of thing change the atmosphere around environmental politics?" I ask, petting the ailing goat.

"Yeah, I think it's hard to live in this country and not have a certain attitude about environmental politics. A huge percentage of New Zealand land is locked up in national parks and forests or reserves. There's a tremendous consciousness especially among those that have the privilege to travel," she says.

In fact, one third of New Zealand is protected as national parks and forests and wildlife areas. They are considered *taonga* (treasures) of irreplaceable value.

CHORE #4: COMBATING TOE JAM

"C'mon, it's time for a footbath!" Marilyn hollers to the troops. "In you go. C'mon, little beauty." She encourages a few rogue goats through a treated puddle. The solution of water and zinc combats skold, a nasty inflammation between halves of the cloven hoof that can cause foot rot.

"That's it?" I say after we hustle several more into the treated puddle.

"No, they are going to stand there for about ten minutes," she says. "In you go, in you go," she says, shoving a few more into the bath. She hauls the gate into place, leaving the goats to their pedicure soak.

"What sort of mistakes do people make, in terms of activism—environmental, political, feminist, what have you?" I ask, noting that this is the first time I've competed with goats for an interviewee's attention.

"Well, I think too many of us are taught to think that you have to embrace a political ideology, or it could be a religious ideology—any ideology. That somehow there's a central committee, you know, determining the right way to do something. Sometimes I think there is too much internecine warfare, even in terms of advocacy for the environment, for the feminist movement, or for the indigenous people's movement. There's not one way, you know."

Marilyn Waring doesn't seem fond of orthodoxy or fundamentalism in her political views. Reminds me of former Black Panther Assata Shakur in Cuba, who mentioned her evolving relationship to revolution, which I interpreted to mean a relaxing of orthodoxy, a recognition of the hazards of fundamentalism. Marilyn appreciates a diversity of methods in progressive politics. I wonder how strategic her political path has been.

"Have you ever felt or do you feel now that you have a mission or has life just unfolded?" I ask.

"Ahh. Life's just unfolded. I don't have a kind of zeal, you know. I've just happened to find myself in some unusual places at some unusual times," she says, with what I now understand to be characteristic understatement.

"But there are certainly times when I wish my brain would stop," she says, panting because she's just heaved aside a fence post, but I also sense another kind of fatigue in her voice, too. The fatigue of thirty years of activism.

"It's also one of the great things about farming . . . the fact that I can have a little bit of time off from, you know, worrying about the war crimes tribunal, or the conflict in Bougainville.* But of course, I can't stop worrying about foot-and-mouth disease." She laughs and wipes her hands on her pants. "Yeahhh."

"There's a real strain of independence, a real matter-of-factness among the people around here," I observe out loud.

"Oh, well for me, it's just that I don't want to make things complicated, and I want things to work, I don't want to waste time and I want to be able to do it myself. I'm trying to do really simple things like having tools the right size for a woman's hand. Getting things where I can maintain them. It's like, I don't need a beast of a machine that makes me depend upon somebody else."

Simplicity in farm or economic theories, I've read, is a Marilyn trademark.

"You're known for being able to interpret complex things like economic theory into lay language. I think you said during your time in Parliament you became 'the master of the simple question,' or something like that," I say.

"The art of the dumb question," she clarifies.

* An island province of Papua New Guinea in which a nine-year secessionist revolt ended in 1997.

"The art of the dumb question, yes, and, um, do you think that the fact that you were so *young*—"

"One of the things you learn is that nearly anywhere you are and you ask a dumb question, like three quarters of the people in the room are really pleased you did 'cause they didn't know either, and they were just gonna sit there and suck it up and just be ignorant, you now, and, um, it helps to cut through the bullshit, you know? Yeahhhh."

Or goatshiiiit or sheepshit or piggy(Muldoon)shit. We load up and Marilyn continues to work in the muck, chucking sheep into their proper pens, demonstrating, it seems, an important correlation between being up to your ankles in crap and the stroppy skill of cutting the crap.

"*People love her for* bringing down Piggy Muldoon," says Simon, as we drive back from Marilyn's for our last night in Auckland. "And what a great interview. Who would have guessed she would be so funny."

"Yeah, she really was," I say, grateful. Feminist Economist isn't exactly a title that ushers forth images of (prime-time-worthy) knee-slapping good times in the populist psyche. "And for a politico, she doesn't seem to get mired in politics—not the conservatism of the right or the knee-jerk reactions of the left."

"What's with this traffic? In Auckland of all places," he says, forced to hit the brakes three blocks from our hotel. Down the street we see the red flashes of a dozen fire trucks and cop cars. How annoying.

"Do a U-ey, Simon. Can we get to the back alley where we unloaded our equipment?" We begin to creep down the alley, avoiding the roadblocks.

"Whoa, looks like there's a fire in our hotel," I say. There is smoke billowing out of windows above.

TO: JEANNIE
FROM: HOLLY
SUBJECT: A LITTLE PROBLEM

Mom—the good news is that the crew and I are alive and nobody was hurt. Bad news is, well, we had a hotel fire last night. Two floors kinda burned.

Here's the deal: We went to do the Waring interview and when we got back to the hotel there were fire trucks surrounding the block, preventing our movement. But then we got closer and realized it was Our Hotel; and closer, and realized it was My Floor and . . . well . . . um . . . it started in My Room. Oops.

Not my fault! One of those crazy do-it-yourself, built-in Kiwi kitchenette stoves blew up. Or maybe it was an electrical fire (yesterday the outlet sparked when I plugged in my computer). Anyway, litigiously paranoid that I am, have we paid our insurance premium lately? I was surrounded by hotel security fellows and got the full-on good-cop/bad-cop let's-make-the-girl-cry routine. It almost worked. (I think they were in bed with the hotel's insurance company.)

In case the insurance people want to know, nearly everything was destroyed, including my black polyester Wranglers.
Also lost:

1. Mac G3 laptop with all my interview notes
2. Handspring electronic organizer (never figured out how to use it anyway)
3. All clothes and books
4. Canon Elph camera—cute but ineffective—got enough cameras on this shoot anyway
5. Walkman with favorite Trini Lopez tape inside (irreplaceable)
6. Maori language tapes

I'll borrow a shirt from camerawoman Liza as we're loaded up with divas for the next few days. No time for shopping. We figure the hotel-burning is a bad omen, so after we leave Auckland we'll sleep in our caravan, Old Sheila, which we rented yesterday. (We've pinned my orange half-burned Sleater-Kinney shirt on its wall.) Will be good for bonding and the budget anyway. Ever the optimist, and ever onward . . .

love, Hol

p.s. Sky Dancer survived! She was in the apparently fireproof bathroom. Her tutu got kinda sooty but she lives to fly again.

"Time to get on the road," Michael says sweetly when he finds me hunting and pecking around the charred, sprinkler-drenched ashes of my room the next morning for anything salvageable. I have been up all night, and he knows it.

"Yeah, I think we've worn out our welcome." Hitting the road sounds just right. Despite occasional four-alarm production hiccups, such as hotel fires, in recent months road life has made me feel alive and reminded me that I am my best self in motion. When I haven't been suffering, I have been very happy.

We spend the day driving through a part of the North Island where the oceanic Pacific plate slides under the continental plate. The volcanic plateau that fills Old Sheila's windows is rife with dramatic geological depressions and thermal pools. We are headed to a hotspot called Rotorua, a town where tourism and the natural world intersect.

The moment we breach the town limits we are swimming in a mix of twee colonial remnants, Maori culture, and sulfuric acid. We pull up at the Whakarewarewa tourist area to film its bubbling-hot mud pools, namely the spouting Pohutu geyser, which erupts twenty times a day, and a faux Maori "village" that features Maori arts and crafts. B-roll.

A package of German tourists are disembarking from a very large air-conditioned bus and being greeted by a young Maori who is doing *hongi,* the traditional Maori greeting in which foreheads and noses are pressed together. "Let's get a shot of this," Michael says to Liza. The greeter goes in for the reverent nose touch to a skinny white fellow in bermudas with binoculars around his neck. The white man gets flustered—*Why is this handsome young native entering my personal space?*—and in a dazzling display of poor, panicked judgment in the face of a confusing culture clash, he cocks his head and kisses the greeter *on the lips.*

Michael, Liza, and I double over in laughter.

The kiss, and its awkward after-moment, are a reminder that while New Zealand is at first glance a quiet, controlled place, cultural tensions simmer underneath its surface. Kiwi/Pakeha writer Helen Lehndorf wrote on adventuredivas.com that while "New Zealand has a good reputation for race relations . . . the reality is that Maori make up most of our unemployed, succeed less in the education system, and have lower life expectancy. The current government is attempting to address this discrepancy with 'closing-the-gaps' policies. Perhaps in time we can achieve true equality and real biculturalism."

Modern-day Maoris are the descendants of a Polynesian tribe that navigated by stars and wind and arrived in New Zealand (Aotearoa) a thousand years ago. In the 1700s, the British and the French showed up and were soon followed by an influx of whalers, traders, and missionaries. Concerned that the French would colonize first, the British rushed to offer the Treaty of Waitangi. Signed by tribal and British leaders on February 6, 1840, the controversial treaty gave the Crown rights to govern and settle, while giving the Maori citizenship and protection of their interests. But today, the treaty is being disputed and land rights debated, amid a growing Maori cultural and political revival. The movement has made major progress in land and cultural rights in the past twenty-five years.

"How much consciousness about the Maori renaissance was there when you were a kid?" I ask our Pakeha-in-residence, Simon.

"I grew up believing New Zealand was truly bicultural—but like most Pakehas, hardly knowing anything about the Maori culture or language. The seventies were a big time for the revival. Lots of sit-ins and protests. Most of it led by women, really," he says, pulling into a caravan park near Rotorua within whiffing distance of the sulfur from the thermal areas. Kiwi soundwoman Jan slathers Vegemite on white bread for our appetizer. "Mmm. Marvelous," she says, mooning over the fetid, brown, sticky yeast. Blech.

Hot greasy smells (now that's an aroma I can get behind) overwhelm the eau de sulfur and soon the back of the caravan teems with vice: unlit cigarettes dangle out of the sides of our mouths; poker chips and playing cards with late-1800s soft porn on the flipside glint in our lantern's light; and grease-splotched wads of newspaper, which held our fish-and-chips dinner, litter the floor. Between us we drink a half rack of Speight's and, quite possibly, ingest a half gallon of Bad Fat. "Four of a kind beats a straight flush," says Michael, incorrectly.

"No, *no* it doesn't," I contend.

By the time we arrive at Hawke's Bay the next day to meet pop music icon Hinewehi Mohi, we have mostly digested the fish and chips, but we are two hours behind schedule because we ran out of gas, thanks to Old Sheila's unreliable gauge.

"*Kia ora*," says a woman with long, dark, pulled-back hair who walks out of the house bearing the address Simon has typed on our schedule. I check the address. She is almost unrecognizable from her most recent music video, in which a sexy, almost feral Hinewehi strides in a long green dress through a dense rain forest (here referred to as "the bush"), furtively dodging vines. In person, she is all girl-next-door: orange crewneck sweater, brunette ponytail, no makeup, and a sunny, genuine smile.

"Hi, Hinewehi," I say, leaping out of the Valiant and introducing the crew. "We're very sorry to be so late."

I wanted to meet Hinewehi because this rock star next door has become a spokesperson for Maori culture and her commitment to *tino rangatiratanga*— self-determination for the Maori people—is well known throughout the nation. She's said to have lots of mana, a Polynesian term for a concentrated spiritual force. In 1999 Mohi shocked and galvanized the country by singing New Zealand's national anthem in Maori during halftime at a World Cup rugby game. Her radical patriotism (which was more meaningful and alarming than any Super Bowl "wardrobe malfunction") aggravated a stress fracture in New Zealanders' highly regarded commitment to biculturalism.

Today is a family affair. Hinewehi's husband, George; daughter, Hinerau-katauri; and grandmother, Nanny, all pile into Old Sheila, as we were due at their local *marae* an hour and a half ago.

"What's the deeper meaning of the *marae*s, Hinewehi? I mean, I know they act as community centers—but they're more than that, aren't they?" I ask.

"First, call me Hine," she says, the initial gesture in a long day that would become increasingly informal. "About the *marae,* well, we come together at the *marae* to celebrate life, as a mark of respect for the end of life, but also to bring us all together and acknowledge who we are and where we've come from, and the ancestors that have brought us here," Hinewehi explains as we unload our gear in a parking lot adjacent to the *marae,* a compound of sturdy reddish wood buildings and grassy lawns.

We cannot enter the grounds until we have been ceremonially invited. All of a sudden a woman's voice bellows out in Maori from the distance. "The women are always the first to call the visitors on," Hine says quietly, then lets float the most beautiful notes from her mouth. And so begins an ethereal call and response. We guests go through a small "receiving line," in which we *hongi* (touch noses) as a way of cleansing all the spirits, or anything bad that has gone before us. We settle into a line of folding chairs to be welcomed in Maori by the men of the *marae,* as tradition dictates. We are expected to stand and express our sentiments about being welcomed to the *marae.* Only men can perform this honor, and as a Kiwi somewhat familiar with the process, Simon stands and speaks on our behalf. "We are honored to be your guests . . ." Simon begins.

That women are forbidden by longstanding tradition to speak in certain contexts on the *marae* is a divisive issue. There is a shared pride in and commitment to rejuvenating the Maori traditions and cultures, but as was true in the civil rights movement in the United States, many women are not pleased about fighting the Man only to have to get her own man the coffee. As women and progressive men increase their *mana*-power in contemporary Maori culture, this is likely to change.

Hine tours me around the *marae.* She takes me into the main meeting-house, where every structural line and post of the building, or *wharenui,* is ornately carved with representations of ancestors, tribal history, and symbols of ancient legends. It is believed that the Guardian of Peace, Rongomatane, reigns inside the meetinghouse. Framed, crinkly black-and-white photographs of tattooed elders adorn the walls.

We feast for two hours on fried bread and *kaimoana* (seafood, in this case mussels) before driving back to Nanny's house to eat more. "I've made pavlova. You *must* have some," declares Nanny, more forcefully than one might expect from a seventy-eight-year-old in blue stretch pants and a floral top talking about a white fluffy dessert.

Nanny shows us through her own house, pausing at one of many picture walls sagging with photos, pointing with a yardstick.

"So this is the family?" I ask.

"Yes, this is the family, *whakapapa.*"

"*Whakapapa?* That's . . . ?"

"That's your ancestry. It is very important to the Maori people. It's very important to know where you come from and who you are. Very important indeed. But I see Granny is crooked there. I'll have to straighten her up," Nanny says, whacking the side of a picture of her own grandmother with her yardstick.

"Granny's got the *moko,*" I say, noting the dramatic, spiraling facial tattoo in the picture.

"Granny's got the *moko.* All the old ladies in the old days had their own *moko,* and it was just like a coat of arms to that particular family."

The black facial tattoos were traditionally carved into the skin with a bone rake and the ink, made from the body of a special caterpillar, was tapped into the grooves. Maori women usually only had chin or lip *mokos;* they were also sometimes tattooed in the pubic area. Maoris ended the tradition in the early 1900s to protect themselves from white colonists who liked to take tattooed warriors' heads back to Europe as souvenirs. But lately, the *moko* is coming back into fashion as Maoris reclaim the power of their ancestral traditions. I am fascinated by how its mesmerizing spirals eclipse any natural lines on these old, creased faces. In India, I admired women committed to the (temporary) *bindi* as a visible symbol of their spiritual agency. But to feel so secure in your identity that you're willing to permanently chisel it onto your face, that's real commitment.

Chin moko

"All my pictures," Nanny says, swooping her yardstick from the wall and around the living room. "There's nothing by Rembrandt or somebody fancy like that. It's all my in-laws, out-laws, my children, my grandchildren, my great-grandchildren, and my great-great-grandchild," she says with pride, and with a curious, mischievous smile. "Did you want to know that I started very early in life? I won't tell any more secrets."

"They're all on the wall," I say.

Hine and I sit down at the kitchen table for tea while Nanny is fiddling with the pavlova.

"What's your interpretation of mana?" I ask, setting down my mug decisively, trying to get to the essence of this Polynesian notion of concentrated soul power. It reminds me of the force said to be contained in those heads I saw in Borneo.

"*Mana* is a word that really . . . basically gives you a lot of prestige and a lot of strength of character," Hine answers.

"From inside? Or is it something you get from . . ." I gesture broadly to no cosmos in particular.

"There's lots of different ways of describing mana in Maori, like different elements of your innermost strength as well as your physical strength," she says.

"It's a special word that's pretty hard to say in English exactly what it means," adds Nanny.

"But is it tied to the spiritual?" I ask.

"Yes, spiritual strength and it comes out in what you do, what you say, or how you hold yourself or how you—"

"An aura," says Nanny.

"An aura, yes," says Hine, "an 'innermost ethos' is what they call it. For many it's a wonderful way of saying, 'I get my strength from way back, from my ancestors and from those that have gone before me who have set me up, and who continue to guide and look over me.' "

Mana, she tells me, implies prestige, power, and influence. Elders have more mana than the young. Supposedly you can see mana in great souls, people whom you respect for their inner strength and fearless inner calm.

Hearing this, it occurs to be that mana might just be the active ingredient in divadom worldwide. What is it, after all, that the Kiwi women I'm meeting share with those we spoke to in India, Cuba, and elsewhere? "Inner strength and fearless inner calm," is a good way to put it. Maybe diva = woman with mana.

In any case, some fearless inner calm must have been at work for Hine to use New Zealand's national passion—rugby—as a forum for declaring the rightful place of Maori cultural heritage in her country.

"What was the fallout from singing the anthem in Maori?" I ask Hine.

"Well, at first it was quite horrific, because the whole country was brought into the debate. We knew that it would create some problems because the rugby fraternity is a very staunch one, and not particularly embracing of things Maori," she explains.

"Well, they'd sung it in English for a hundred and sixty years. Why couldn't it be sung in Maori?!" interjects Nanny feistily. "This is our attitude," Nanny affirms, nodding vigorously. "*This* is our attitude." She punctuates her conviction with an index finger to the Formica, and thereby confirms my suspicion that there is more than one diva in the kitchen.

"A comparison would be if someone were to sing 'The Star-Spangled Banner' in Navajo or something, with no English. And probably similar to the response when Jimi Hendrix did a pretty wild guitar version of your national anthem," Hine says. "But it's turned around so dramatically since then that last year I was paid by the Ministry of Education to record and perform the national anthem in Maori for schools."

In fact, shortly after Hinewehi's brave 1999 performance, the law was changed to make Maori an official language of the anthem, thanks in part to the support of Prime Minister Helen Clark, with whom we have a date in exactly four days. The PM supported Hine's action amid a sea of other high-profile detractors.

"In the scheme of things, that change was quick," I note, thinking of Malcolm Gladwell's description of singular events that tip a balance—events that are like a match to an already existing pool of ideological gas. "Tipping points are a reaffirmation of the potential for change and the power of intelligent action," he wrote.

"Yes, and now I think everyone expects there to be a Maori and English version," Hine concludes, matter-of-factly, about a cultural shift ushered in by her creative action.

Sitting around eating pavlova on a blue-speckled Formica table in rural New Zealand, it's easy to forget that Hine is a mega-star. Her hugely popular band, Oceania, fuses traditional Maori instruments with hip-hop and reggae. Their gold album, with its Maori percussion and Western-style ambient tracks, is credited with reawakening native culture and fostering a new culturally based music renaissance among youth.

Hine's husband, George, wheels their six-year-old daughter, Hineraukatauri, who has cerebral palsy, into the kitchen. George and Hine beam at Hineraukatauri, whose pleasure at seeing all these people in her grandmother's kitchen eclipses her inability to control her limbs. Hine credits Hineraukatauri as her muse, though she is not saccharine about her daughter's disability.

"This sort of challenge is a real blessing to us," Hine says of Hine-raukatauri (named for the guardian of all Maori musical instruments). "She teaches us so much every day. Her needs are very basic—breathing, thinking; all the very basic things in life that we take for granted are a struggle for her. She has such a cool attitude," she says, brushing her curled finger across her daughter's cheek, "that you can't help but be inspired by that strength for life."

She explains that although each of her songs is different, they all celebrate her daughter's, and the Maori people's, survival.

"Do you think your creativity comes from way back?" I ask, wondering how much cultural legacy fuels her art.

"Yes. Definitely. Because I've been brought up with a real love and respect for who I am as a Maori. My father didn't speak Maori as a child because in Nanny's generation coming up," she says, looking at her grandmother, "kids were taught that you needed to get on with life in the world of Pakeha."

Nanny chimes in, "It was very difficult because the Maoris were second-class citizens. And it wasn't until after the Second World War that gradually the Maoris were recognized. The Maori girls went to boarding schools and were taught to be good housemaids, that's what they were. That was their station in life. But that was in the old days. We weren't allowed to speak Maori in the playground, we always got the strap. We had to speak English."

"Are creativity and power tied together for you, Hine?" I ask.

"Yes, because of my creativity—my work—I have a high profile and a responsibility to take my language and culture to the world. People look to me to be doing things right for the Maori people. So it's a powerful position, and of course power can be used in a good way or a bad way," she says, reiterating the idea that a great responsibility comes with possessing mana.

"Reflecting our culture to the world makes young Maori feel good about themselves. We are trying to regenerate a whole sense of quality and expression of who we are, and what we have to offer," she says, then adds with a grin, "It's cool to be Maori.

"Oh bugger, we have to go," she says, glancing at her watch. Hine has arranged for us to go over to the girls' school where she was educated. She wants to show us her roots, but, more importantly, what the new Maori generation is up to. "Can we take the Valiant?

"I'm driving, vroom! vroom!" Hine yells as she walks out the screen door;

Nanny grabs her floral purse and trots after her. George and Hineraukatauri will drive over in another car and meet us.

Liza and I unhook the caravan from the Valiant and climb in the car's backseat. Nanny rides shotgun (the left side).

"Rock and roll! I feel like a petrolhead!" Hine yells as she guns it around a roundabout.

"Twin carb!" yells Nanny. Liza is laughing so hard at this septuagenarian's automotive expletives that she can't hold the camera steady.

"Nanny, teach me some Maori," I say, holding onto the headrest for stability as Hine takes a curve.

"Ahhh. Pakehas always want to learn Maori words. Well, of course we teach them the swear words first. Like *tonanane*."

"What's a *tonanane*?" I ask, warily.

"A *tonanane* . . . is a *teke*," Nanny says, giggling like a schoolgirl. Hine chuckles under her breath as she guns it down Hastings's quiet main road.

Suddenly, Nanny turns around to Liza and me and the rolling camera and bellows, "IT'S A VAGINA!"

Good god. First the goat shit and now the vaginas; brilliant, divalicious moments to take home to the PBS censors.

Liza grips the small video camera and gets a close-up of Hine banging the thirty-year-old gear shift into reverse. *"Mana wahine"* ("powerful woman"), she says to nobody in particular, and I wonder if she's referring to Nanny, or to Sheila's uncanny ability to hug any curve.

Believing in the birds-of-a-feather theory, I ask Nanny and Hine for some leads for other divas to interview. "Hey, who do you think we should go see on the South Island?"

"Oh. Keri Hulme," says Nanny. "Keri Hulme would be just the one. She's a famous author; she's very down to earth, sort of in your face, a 'do what I bloody well like' sort of person."

Yes. I know of Keri Hulme. "Is she there now?" I ask, excitedly.

"No idea. But she doesn't stand any nonsense or any crap from anybody," says Nanny.

"Oh, that's the bugger," yells Hine.

"That's the bugger. Should have turned left," agrees Nanny.

Chugging into the parking lot of the girls' school, Hine cuts the Valiant's engine and hops out of the car. Liza and I follow, trying to adjust her mic as we walk. Hine lets out a holler at the sight of one of her old teachers.

"Hine, you're a role model now," I say emphatically, nodding to the girls who are piling into an auditorium to welcome her with a performance. All the girls are buzzing at the sight of such a big star.

The auditorium looks like a church, with rows and rows of benches and an elevated platform at the front of the room. Hine now stands on the platform, with Hineraukatauri in her arms, brimming with dignity, facing a hundred Maori girls in their school uniforms: white collared shirts, blue skirts, stockings, and pointy black dress shoes. With a resounding *thump* of their daintily clad feet, the girls begin to sing, a few guitars mere backup to their powerful voices. Their lithe, brown, young arms move in unison; then they perform the traditional *kapahaka* dance, a high-impact warrior art of strength and empowerment. Many credit the *kapahaka* as a first introduction to their own Maori roots.

"*Hey ya kay. Hey ya kah. Hey ya ka, hoomph! Hoomph!*" they sing as one. *Stomp. Stomp. Stomp.*

The collective power of these little girls claims all the space in the room, and more.

One girl leads.

> *Ka mate! Ka mate! Ka ora! Ka ora!*
> (It is death! It is death! It is life! It is life!)
> *Ka mate! Ka mate! Ka ora! Ka ora!*
> (It is death! It is death! It is life! It is life!)
> *Tenei te tangata puhuru huru* (This is the hairy man)
> *Nana nei i tiki mai* (Who fetched the sun)
> *whakawhiti te ra* (and caused it to shine again)

> *A upa . . . ne! Ka upa . . . ne!*
> (One upward step! Another upward step!)
> *A upane kaupane whiti te ra!*
> (An upward step, another . . . the sun shines!)
> *Hi!!!*

White collared shirts and black patent-leather shoes melt into a blur of mana and now what stands before us is a phalanx of young warriors. The schoolgirls are gone—they are an *iwi*, a people. The room's instant transformation is eerie and humbling. Hine is crying. I am crying.

Hine holds Hineraukatauri, a child who has struggled for her own existence, and rocks her almost imperceptibly in front of this roomful of hope; in front of *whakapapa*—ancestry—which makes hope seem almost plausible. I guess I am so moved because these girls are not fifty, or forty, or thirty; they are thirteen, fourteen, fifteen, and they already know where they come from.

They pound and thud and holler together, playing guitar, their muscle reverberating, spiraling into the world. One hundred fierce girls belting out their past, and claiming their future.

A upane kaupane whiti te ra!

It is time to confess: The single most compelling reason I wanted to do a show in New Zealand was to meet the author Keri Hulme, the writer Nanny mentioned in the car. Since the inception of Adventure Divas it was Keri Hulme—novelist, angler, and enigmatic literary icon—who was firmly planted in my brain as *the* diva template: a creative, independent, "do what I bloody well like" person (as Nanny put it). I have been obsessed with Hulme for fifteen years, ever since my first reading of her Booker Prize–winning novel, *The Bone People.* The book's fusion of Pakeha and Maori worlds with dark, poetic storytelling is strangely seductive. And the book's protagonist, Kerewin (like Keri herself), fishes for whitebait, a bizarre translucent migrating fish about five millimeters long that, for a few special months of every year, becomes a Kiwi obsession.

Hulme's quirky talent and creative independence inspire in me a shameless admiration not in keeping with my normal anti-pedestal stance. (Sure, I tried to shove Phoolan Devi up there, but that was an uninformed, must-make-it-so producer's yearning for a sexy bandit story.) I know about Keri Hulme, and I have been a bloodhound on her scent for years. In the past decade I have, as a fan, editor, fellow angler, and aspiring filmmaker, come up with various excuses for contacting her: "Can I publish your work in a women's fishing anthology?" *Yes.* "Can I option *The Bone People* film rights?" *Absolutely not.* And now, "Will you appear in this documentary?"

A few years ago I received a benign "if you're ever in New Zealand" invitation at the end of the fax that denied me film rights. I've had it on my bulletin board ever since. I took her invite at face value and attempted via fax to confirm a meeting with Hulme prior to our departure from Seattle. No luck. Now, halfway through the shoot, and four more unresponded-to faxes later, only Michael is aware of the degree to which meeting Hulme is consuming me. I feign emotional stability to the rest of the crew, yet privately I rant to Michael.

"For twelve years I've been wanting to meet her," I say. We gave up on camping and I am now kicking ice cubes around like soccer balls in a hotel room one day's drive north of Wellington. "This is killing me."

"If we can't get her, how about we make the story about the quest?" says Michael. "Your obsession is enough to drive the story," he adds glibly.

"You mean like *Sherman's March* or *Roger and Me*?"

"Yeah."

"Oh, I don't know. I don't know. I want *her.*"

"Why is she so important to you?" he asks.

I tell him the story of how *The Bone People* got published. How after twelve years of writing, Hulme was turned down by every major publisher in the country; how three women created the Spiral Collective in order to publish it; and how the book then began a viral path to popularity and success that eventually led to the Booker Prize, and to her status as an unlikely literary heroine.

"What's the book about?"

"Well it's about a mute kid, a bicultural loner artist, and a loving, brutal guy. But in fact it's really about independence and passion in a crapshoot, culture-clash world."

"Uh-huh," says Michael.

"I guess it's not just her, it's all she represents. She and her book are inextricably wed in my mind. She's quirky and independent, kind of an allegory for New Zealand itself, and I'm hoping an interview with her can help cinch up our story of this country."

This last comment seems to resonate, and Michael nods. And I don't say this to Michael, but even though Hulme's driving me *nuts,* I kind of respect her freaky reclusiveness.

Except for late-night tête-à-têtes between me and Michael, my obsession with Hulme stays under wraps while we advance the stated premise of the program, to investigate estro-leadership in New Zealand. We are scheduled to be in the country's capital of Wellington, which is nestled in the southern tip of the North Island. I have to shelve my Keri fixation long enough to meet with Prime Minister Helen Clark.

Jeannie, bless her well-connected soul, reached back to her Chicago roots and contacted former Illinois senator Carol Moseley Braun (who was then the outgoing U.S. ambassador to New Zealand) and enlisted her to help us set up the meeting with the PM. We made a dozen calls to Clark's press secretary and promised to fax the questions ahead of time, all for five minutes with a prime minister who, I am told, *doesn't suffer fools.*

Clark grew up in the countryside and became politicized during her time at university in the 1970s. She joined the Labour Party in 1971, and she has been ascending the ranks ever since, focusing on issues ranging from housing to environmental conservation to health. She became prime minister in 1999, when the Labour Party was elected to govern. *Time International* magazine notes her candor with journalists and says Clark represents "a paradox in the national psyche: tolerance with an authoritarian streak." Under her leadership, New Zealand has pursued some controversial measures, including legalizing prostitution and enforcing the ban on nuclear warships from the country's ports. She is currently involved in a battle to defend Maori affirmative action, which has become a central issue in New Zealand politics. Clark, it's worth noting again, stood in strong defense of Hinewehi Mohi when she sang the national anthem in Maori.

The Valiant, once again tugging our caravan, pulls up to Helen Clark's office, next to Parliament, which is a gray stone building with lots of columns. Simon and I dash out of the car, late and underdressed as usual. Since the hotel fire, my wardrobe has been exceedingly limited. I am wearing a (clean) white T-shirt, jeans, and a mint-green leather coat streaked with smoke damage. Entry could be questionable, ambassadorial endorsement or not. Simon, at least, is in a collared shirt.

"What do I call her?" I ask Simon, puffing, as we take the stairs to save time. "Madame Prime Minister? Her Honor?"

"She's known as the Queen Bee around here," he says, "and *here*"—he ominously gestures out the window toward the beehive-shaped Parliament building next door, "is known as 'Helengrad.' "

Doesn't suffer fools.

We make small talk with the PM's young, sandy-haired, navy-blue-blazer-clad press secretary in the lobby as we wait. "Do you know Keri Hulme?" I ask. "Know of her, certainly," he says. "Sounds like she's doing more fishing than writing these days," he says glibly, referring to her long-awaited follow-up book to *The Bone People. Hiss!* I want to lash out and defend Hulme against this dapper, wet-behind-the-ears flunky who has probably never written more than a dehydrated position paper.

We are ushered into the prime minister's office, which is as you would expect. Clean. Dignified. Well lit. I get the impression that none of the real work gets done in this room. The prime minister walks in with a small entourage. She is just as I'd read in articles: formal, direct, tall—and, I might add, somewhat *manly*. None of the press ever mentions that. As someone who's been called "manly" from time to time, I take some comfort in our shared characteristic, and relax a bit. We sit down and talk, man to man.

"Thanks for taking the time to see us. I, um, well, what we're trying to do with this program is understand the character of your country . . . through its people . . . so, um, can you offer a bit about the character of a New Zealander?" I ask, sensing that launching softly is the tack to take with this formal leader. I feel awkward, but she saves me.

"New Zealanders are very practical people," she says. "They are do-it-yourselfers. They're the weekend mechanic. You've got the strong farming industry background where people did it themselves, fixed it themselves, made it themselves . . . so all that's deeply ingrained in the culture," she responds, incredibly matter-of-factly.

I've always admired Kiwi literature and film's curious strain of independence, twisted black humor, and deft politics, so I ask, "What's your philosophy toward funding the arts? New Zealand produces brilliant filmmakers and writers." I'm thinking of filmmaker Jane Campion's *Sweetie,* Lee Tamahori's *Once Were Warriors,* Gaylene Preston's *War Stories Our Mothers Never Told Us,* writer Janet Frame's *Faces in the Water,* and, of course, Keri Hulme's *The Bone People.*

"I've given a lot of priority to the arts because I think that through the arts and culture you express the soul and heart of your nation," she responds.

I stop myself from asking her about Hulme, because this interview is all about the show's nutgrab. If the Queen Bee can't explain the country's estro-power, who can?

"Could you talk a little bit about women's contributions to social and historical developments in New Zealand? I understand that Maori women were at the head of the renaissance in Maori culture, and I know women got the right to vote quite early—twenty-five years earlier than in the United States. What happened here as opposed to other places?" I ask.

"Well, I think it's partly due to New Zealand's being a pioneer society in the nineteenth century, when women worked pretty hard. Not having your right as a citizen to get your vote recognized is tough in those circumstances. Obviously women got out and led the campaign for the right to vote; I don't recall too many men. The women were on the front line demanding it, and they had a little government at the time which was prepared to go along with it.

"But unfortunately it took many decades for women to actually come into power. They were really represented in very small numbers until the late 1980s and 1990s," explains the prime minister.

Okay, we're getting there. You're out there digging fence holes right along with the blokes, so you should have the right to vote. But run the country?

"Right now there are lots of women in top power positions, and I'm wondering if you feel this power is really institutionalized. And what's brought it about?" I ask, pressing the thesis.

"It's partly a function of the new voting system we adopted. Prior to the system, we'd reached a level of twenty percent women in Parliament, which by U.S. standards is quite high, but it's really not high by northern European standards. We're now up to over thirty percent. And it still needs to go somewhere yet. Is it institutionalized? Yes it is, because for political parties now to do well electorally, they have to appeal to women; you can't just shut off half of the population. And there are parties who do very well by, for, and with women, and there are parties who don't," she says.

"Why do you think the States is not doing as well?" I ask.

"It's partly a function of the electoral system. In New Zealand, when you had the single-member constituency, it was often easier for parties to portray the males as the character who would be the local representative. That's the way it always was. But when you move to a proportional system, parties have to attract proportions of votes for a party, then they have to pay a lot more attention to being representative, and that's when women do get a lock-in," says the prime minister.

Huh? How totally unsexy. I wanted mana, and virile rogue strains of Amazonian DNA, or secret cults or, or, or, annual summits of powerful women in the country's equivalent of Sun Valley; but she's telling me—I think—that it boils down to a revised electoral system. I could barely follow what she was saying, it was so mundane. But essentially, it seems to go like this: After Marilyn Waring dissented over the nuke question, and the Labour Party won the election of 1984, Labour appointed a nonpartisan commission to investigate the long-held claim that New Zealand's electoral system did not properly represent the politics of the people. As a result of the commission's findings, a mixed member proportional (or MMP) electoral system was developed in the mid-1990s in which voters cast two ballots, one for a local member of Parliament and one for a party. While conventional (white male) candidates tend to fill the slots for MP, the parties often try to balance their tickets by running women and minorities on the second ballot. Across the board, countries that use proportional systems like this have more women and minorities in public office than countries that use a "majoritarian," winner-take-all system, like the United States.

In New Zealand, the new system meant more women and minorities got elected into office, and thus, their power became institutionalized.

Meeting Helen Clark and digesting the banal details of electoral system theory made me recognize Adventure Divas' movement, throughout my travels, toward dwelling on the spiritual and personal characteristics of divadom. I set out for Cuba sensitive to the individual lives and work in the context of the communist political system; by the time I left India, I was ready to trade the blockades and voter registration for a good sit with the Dalai Lama. Helen Clark has brought me back to center and reminded me that sometimes the hard work of improving the lives of women is rote, and that divadom is as much about political construct as it is about personal potential.

The demands of production sometimes make me a user. A hateful admission, but true. This is what I am thinking as I slug back some Earl Grey on a windy front porch in Wellington with filmmaker Gaylene Preston.

Prime Minister Clark's commitment to the arts helps make filmmakers like Preston, who is widely regarded as *the* maven of Kiwi film, thrive. But I'm also here because Preston is the only filmmaker ever to get Keri Hulme to talk to her at length in front of a camera. Preston used Hulme's devotion to whitebaiting as a structure for a documentary called *Kai Purakau*. My tri-weekly faxes to Hulme ("We'll be in your area in late April, might you be willing to meet?") have finally been receiving some response, albeit spotty and noncommittal. I want Gaylene to help me understand Kiwi film *and* land the elusive Keri Hulme. I'm desperate. And I'm a user.

I know Gaylene knows how to get an unlikely film made. Her best-known documentary is the internationally acclaimed *War Stories Our Mothers Never Told Us*, which is about the generation of women who stayed home and ran New Zealand when all the men were off fighting World War II. The documentary's success was a complete surprise, most especially to Preston herself.

"*War Stories* was an idea that I immediately tried to make go away for a good two years because I thought, you know, I felt it was a really bad career move. If I had a career, and I wasn't sure I did," she says, brushing the brown bangs off her forehead.

"After your eighth film?" I ask, figuring if that's not a career, what is?

"Making a film about seven old ladies talking about the world isn't exactly a good career move, you know. It was a local film that was going to have a local audience that was just for us. It wasn't intended to travel internationally," she said.

"I had seen these women who had told wonderful stories in our archive and I was scared someone was going to die, so I started filming without any money. The women weren't in any way encouraged to be stroppy sheilas, but the stories they tell and the way they tell them, that's them coming out of the closet. So I think I only make films about stroppy sheilas," she says. "Stroppy sheilas," Gaylene and I had determined, was the Kiwi equivalent of *diva*.

Gaylene's penchant for unorthodox heroines extends into her feature films, too. Long ago I noticed that tough, un-Cinderella-like heroines people the Kiwi media-scape. Perhaps it is no coincidence that Xena, the Warrior Princess, is from New Zealand.

"You know the famous film of the heroine who somehow kind of gains autonomy. Gets independent, becomes in charge, and everything's tickety boo.

That's the happy ending. Well, I'm challenging that," she says, leaning forward for emphasis. "I'm likely to make a film about somebody who doesn't know what she's doing. I find it much more interesting, you know, than the driven, sort of focused, hero. We're not leaving them—Thelma and Louise—we're not doing that suspended . . . suspended," she dramatically dismisses the idea with a sweep of her hand and a roll of the eyes, "over the Grand Canyon in a freeze frame—"

"Well, *that*'s the point," I interject emphatically, as Gaylene touches on one of my least favorite moments in an otherwise acceptably adventurous (if a bit paternalistic) film. "For them to be liberated, they have to *die.*"

"No, nooo, not in our film," says Gaylene, meaning the Kiwi genre. "I'm taking Thelma and Louise and they're going to Mexico, *dammit,* and when they get there everybody better watch out. Because Thelma and Louise are not the women they were when they set out, and one of them is fairly *mad.* So we're saying this liberation thing isn't just . . . it's . . . actually quite dangerous." Gaylene nods to a common theme of subversion and madness in Kiwi art.

"But you can live through it," I add.

"You can live . . . you can live and cause trouble!" she says, waving an index finger in the air with cheerful emphasis. "So this is what we're up to and we're trying to get a large audience worldwide to go along with this idea," she concludes, and takes a sip of tea.

"You take on a new spirit and challenge with each of your projects," I say, thinking of her diverse films, which range in topic from haunted cars to storytelling old ladies to the pro-democracy movement in East Timor.

"This is no way to run a career, if you're thinking about it," she responds, putting down her teacup.

"Okay," I say, considering my precarious global gig tracking down people who sometimes don't even want to see me. Publishing certainly offered a consistent paycheck and less smoke damage.

"Don't do it," Gaylene warns again, seriously.

"Okay. But, um. What was it like making a documentary with Keri Hulme?" I ask, twitching from the Earl Grey, no longer able to keep my full agenda under wraps.

"I got in touch with Keri, which wasn't easy. She was under siege. *The Bone People* had just been published in Germany and she was getting a lot of unwanted attention. Anyway, I knew from anecdotal things that Keri was elusive, that we could go all the way down there [to the South Island] and find that she wasn't there for all sorts of good reasons. That she's shy. And she's an artist protecting her work, actually," Gaylene says, obviously respectful of Hulme's curious choices.

"I've got this strange fax relationship going with her but I can't figure out if she'll actually see me . . . but—"

"Has she been drawing on her faxes?" Gaylene asks.

"A little bit," I say, remembering an odd snail-like figure that appeared on one.

"Yeah, well, you know, that's a good sign," says Gaylene. "There's something to be said for just showing up," she adds, opening up the possibility of trespassing.

I leave Gaylene's with a copy of her Keri Hulme documentary and emboldened by her tenacious commitment to bringing unorthodox heroines to the screen. To me, Hulme is the real live version of the unorthodox, subversive heroine Gaylene refers to. I imagine that Hulme, who is part Maori, lives (like Hinewehi Mohi) *rangatiratanga*—self-determination—every day, especially as it relates to her creative life.

Meeting Hulme has taken on sacred meaning. Buoyed by Gaylene's suggestion that we just show up in Okarito, armed with some top-shelf whiskey, we pack Old Sheila onto a ferry and leave the North Island for Picton, on the South Island.

Hulme, I've heard, doesn't use the telephone. Since the press has come down on her as a dilatory genius she has become even more elusive. (So she is going on eighteen years since publishing her last novel. Please, people, think Thomas Pynchon! J. D. Salinger! Henry Roth! and other such laggards.) My image of Hulme is wed to *The Bone People*'s protagonist, Kerewin, who is a bit of an outcast and seeks unlikely relationships to quiet her roiling soul.

That night I receive a disturbing message from Keri: "Chances of us hooking up are slim. But can fax."

My spirits crash.

"Well, we got the prime minister, that was a coup," says Michael to combat my fax-induced glumness.

"But we need Keri to anchor the show. If she's not in, we're fucked; no Keri, no show," I sulk.

to: Jeannie
from: Holly
subject: Prozac?

Jeannie—Epic effort to get Hulme but still no confirm. Situation bad. May need to extend shoot to dig up new diva. Send Prozac.

to: Holly
from: Jeannie
subject: Lawsuit

Hang in there, honey. We had a 6.2 earthquake here in Seattle. No major damage to HQ but we've been declared a disaster area (I could have told them that!) so we get an extension on our corporate taxes, thank goodness. Oh, the insurance guy wants to know if you put your clothes in the stove?—Mom

My fax relationship with Hulme has become a curious exercise in approach-avoidance behavior: I try to get Hulme to commit to see me, and she, sprinkling her writing with Maori and fishing references, avoids the issue. One evening Gaylene calls our cell phone.

"Keri called me," says Gaylene. My heart sinks. "She used a *phone*?" I ask, knowing this must be a bad sign.

"She says her nephew is sick and she doesn't know if she can meet you."

"Shit. What does that mean?"

"I think she's getting cold feet," says Gaylene. "She needs to look you in the eye, is my guess. You can use any footage you like from my film," Gaylene generously offers as consolation, which depresses me. I am discouraged and confused. Will she be there, or not? Will she see us, or not? The fan in me understands her elusiveness; the editor in me respects that she protects her artistic space; the producer in me is annoyed.

Teha ra ko, e Holly, Ya it's a pity you won't be here 5 a.m. first of
September and 9 p.m. 14th of November which is the season for
whitebaiting on the coast. Anyway, I'll be heading over the hill shortly.
I'll be in touch when I get back.

—Keri

(Whitebaiting. Argh. I want to net *you,* not fish.)

We spend the day moping around the outskirts of Christchurch, shooting
b-roll of seals and burning up too much 16mm film trying to get a shot of Sky
Dancer landing in a gumboot.

"Time to throw yourself at her mercy," says Michael, handing me yet another greasy packet of fish and chips. I stand in a hotel lobby early on a
Tuesday, faxing off what could be the final groveling request. I pretend to
know nothing of the phone call from Gaylene.

Dear Keri,

I'm very excited about the prospect of meeting you. Needless to say,
I'd very much like to have you participate in the documentary. Maybe
we could spend a little time together, talking about or doing whatever
compels you most, be it discussing environmental concerns or sneak-
ing off to go fishing. In terms of filming, I can assure you that we are
low-impact, high-respect, and of course would honor any concerns
you might have in terms of privacy and time. Thanks Keri.

Best, Holly

That night Hulme faxes back to the hotel.

Kia ora mi mi Holly,

Thanks for the faxes, your best chance is to catch me up on the week-
ends. Saturday afternoon or evening would be fine. I'm happy to talk—

I'm always happy to talk—but not willing to do anything else, camera-wise. Meantime, safe travel.

Na, Keri

Yeoww! I am personally thrilled, but am professionally dismayed *No cameras?* What the hell? Is this woman just indecisive, or does she have two sides?

We bolt out of Christchurch the next morning and head west over New Zealand's alps toward the west coast, which is flanked by the Tasman Sea. On the map, the tiny town of Okarito is a dot at the end of a squiggly coastal road that looks like it will take several hours to drive.

Old Sheila sputters to a stop in Okarito and we take in the town in a single glance. One church, one dock, one flock of white herons, and a smattering of small, private homes. Population: twenty-five; divas: one.

I prepare to make the half-mile walk to her house alone. Michael tucks a liter of Talisker whiskey under my arm. "Turn on the charm, or there's no show," he says, reverting to his natural pessimistic state, which I find oddly comforting.

I wonder if I'll get the same response Kerewin gave the little boy who appeared at her home in *The Bone People:* "Well in case no-one ever told you before, people's houses are private and sacrosanct. Even peculiar places like my tower. That means you don't come inside unless you get invited."

I march toward "the tower," determined to convince Hulme to go on camera.

I am sloppy with fear and excitement, and self-flagellation: I hate myself for getting us to a point in the production where the show hangs on one conversation. I stop dead at two signs that declare: UNLESS I KNOW YOU OR YOU HAVE CONTACTED ME FIRST, DO NOT COME IN, and UNKNOWN CATS AND DOGS WILL BE SHOT ON SIGHT.

Scared.

Ba-boom. Ba-boom. Ba-boom. My heart thumps as I walk up a heavily wooded path to her front door. I weave my way through thick Dr. Seuss–like vines, which take the edge off the bright day. I bang the metal knocker on the yellow door.

"Who is it?" bellows a decidedly grumpy voice from the other side.

"Hol-ly Morris," I squeak out.

The door swings open and there she is: Keri Hulme. All six foot one of her. "Heavy shouldered. Heavy hammed, heavy-haired," goes the description of Kerewin. She wears a loose, thick green work shirt and dark sunglasses that make you almost not even notice the curly crop of brown hair that lies on her head, like a helmet.

"Come in, *kia ora,*" Keri says coolly. I enter and walk into a modest living room, anchored with books—seven thousand of them, I've heard—from floor to ceiling. The room is peppered with statues of snails, humorous talismans of a book deadline missed by more than a decade (and counting). Hulme gestures for me to sit in a small wooden chair as she settles into a leather high-back throne behind what (I presume from the stacks of manuscript paper) is her writing desk. She rocks back, and a little forth, in the leather chair, eyeing me; puh-puh-puffing on a small wooden pipe.

"Help yourself to coffee," she says, gesturing subtly with the pipe. I stand and pour myself a cup.

"Would you like goat's milk in it?" she asks.

"No, thanks," I respond.

"Right answer," she says.

There is a bag of coffee hanging from the ceiling, "to keep it away from the rats," she says, "and I have a gun for them." So I wonder what the machete is for.

The next hour passes in bits, like a dreamy blur, spliced with possibility but gloppy with tension (mine). Hulme puffs, and turns the tables, and begins to interview me with a perma-sideways glance.

K: *What do you know of Waitangi?*

H: Morally complicated, renaissance, *rangatiratanga.*

K: *You work with family? Your mother?*

H: Wonderful and fraught, respect and boundaries.

Keri is fully exercising her look-me-in-the-eye clause, as Gaylene foretold. I volley with my hero, traversing a delicate line of wanting to be cautious and not take conversational risks (or mispronounce Maori words) but knowing that coming off like a sycophantic fan could be just as deadly. I'm certain Keri can smell a fake. "Play it straight." Kiwi soundwoman Jan's last words of advice echo in my head. "One note of insincerity and you'll be out on your can," she had warned, aware of her compatriot's infamous skittishness.

K: *Each backpack holds a book in progress; we have earthquakes here. Must be able to run.*
H: Mmmmm, practical.
K: *Whitebait?*
H: Translucent, magical, the high holiday of the avid angler.
K: *Te kaihau?*
H: Yes, I am a wanderer.

Knowing she is both media-shy and media-savvy, I explain that I have no agenda, am not after sound bites, and want a culturally aware, unplugged image of New Zealand to unfold in the show.

It is now or never.

I smile (though not too solicitously), squinch up my courage, and kick my foot in the door with a bit of invented courage: "It was unclear from your fax," I say with a boldness meant to eclipse my fear, "whether or not you're up for being interviewed."

One hundred years of pause ensue, followed by a millennial stare.

Keri squints, as if examining my *wairua,* soul.

I stare back, careful not to avert my eyes.

"Whitebait run in September you know," she says.

"Yes, I wish I could be here," I respond, honestly.

She breathes deeply, glances out toward the Tasman, then back at me.

"I'll do it," she says, finally. "But we must do it here. I won't go anywhere with you," she continues, dashing my hopes of our going fishing together. But she's agreed to go on camera and that is the most vital thing.

I excuse myself, too quickly, and sprint down the road to find the crew and get this in motion before she changes her mind. But it turns out once she makes up her mind it sticks, with grace. Playing it straight—no sycophantism, no begging, no false promises—had paid off.

"*Now, now, now,* you guys," I say, grinning and panting. "She's agreed, but we have to shoot inside."

After quick introductions, Liza and Jan scramble to set up their equipment. Worried that too many people might make Hulme spook, I've asked Simon and Michael to wait with Old Sheila. Liza is framing up, and I start the interview, trusting that she will roll as soon as she can. I ask Keri if there is an artistic vision or flavor unique to New Zealand. Keri keeps her black-rimmed dark glasses on and, I notice, has a habit of covering her teeth when she speaks.

"I think most emphatically and firmly there is. There is sort of a pessimistic streak. It's basically experience, I suspect. We know that bad things happen quite frequently in New Zealand. You get unexpected good; you look for the dark side of it," Keri explains, and I think of her four earthquake-ready books in progress.

"I think one of the contributing things to, as it were, a New Zealand art, whether it be theater or filmmaking or whatever, [is that] there's a dual cultural base, between two interacting cultures," she says. I wonder if the discordant intersection of cultures might be the source of what we outsiders consider offbeat, or quirky, brilliance.

"The other contributing factor is just the archipelago itself. We're a strange set of islands, and it doesn't take long for people to be molded into being New Zealanders."

Like Keri, New Zealand has a political and spiritual self-reliance that comes from being an island nation. It is a country where you do things your own way, rather than simply importing ideas from other places.

"One of the interesting things I find about New Zealand is that because we're a fairly secular society, we will explore things that possibly other peoples won't. We are still a young enough set of cultures to not be fixed in any way, young enough to feel that we can explore everything," she says.

This, too, could contribute to New Zealand's unconventional films; I ask her why she won't let *The Bone People* be adapted.

"I've consistently refused to sell the film rights for *The Bone People*. I don't mind it with short stories; several of my short stories have been written to films. It's slightly different when you're dealing with a novel. No, you can't transplant written word into visual and auditory form without generally suffering greatly. We have a novel that is layered, that is fairly tricky in various forms of metaphor and image. You can't easily transform that, and again you're getting into that process which I think is the reader's province. Some stories will reach much better inside a head than outside of it. I've obviated any opportunity of that happening in the next two novels because I've invented a set of people who are fairly impossible to film," she says, enticingly.

"Uh . . . how did you do that?"

"They're blue," she says with a touch of pride.

"They're blue. Care to expand on that?" I laugh.

"Well, don't you think the world needs some blue people?"

"So are you playing God?"

"Yes, of course," Keri says, running her nails across her lips and blowing. "My idea, though, is not just to rest for one day of the week but pretty well all of them.

"Everybody wants to play God and you do that by developing a set of humans of your own to play with. So I invented people who are roaming around the world and dripped them onto paper."

"And fishing?" I ask, knowing she has stated publicly that both fishing and family come before writing in her holy trinity. If she's God when she writes, what is she when she's at water's edge?

"Ah, fishing. It is, I suppose, my metaphor for life, death, and the universe. I have loved fishing ever since I was a very small child, and when I arrived over here on the west coast I discovered whitebaiting and I have become an *obsessive* galaxophile ever since. It's not so much a game of fish and fishing, it is life during the two and a half months of the whitebait season. I collect whitebait lore and whitebait stories and eat them a lot whenever I can catch them, which is why the novel that's coming out this year is called *Bait*." (Hulme has described *Bait* as "a funny novel about death.")

"Fishing is, it's an art form of a very special and nurturing kind. But it's a particularly civilized art form, too. You've got to be wholly aware of your surroundings and the fact that while you can cast quite deliberately to something, you never know what you will get, and the process of writing can be very big like that," she says.

Yes! I think. The marriage of fishing and literature is deeper than mere metaphor. The *act* of fishing is similar to the *act* of writing itself. The masochistic urge to wake up in the predawn hours and stumble with loaded thermos toward an icy-cold stream to catch something you ultimately let go . . .

"So . . . potential?" I say.

"Yes. Potential. The more you fish, the more directed you can become and the more open you can become for whatever is coming along . . . and that's how you can explore ideas that don't have the glamour or the sex appeal that as a young person you'd go for—there's other things you'd mine later on."

"Like what?" I ask.

"I think inevitably, the older you get as a writer, the more you start looking at the really big questions. You start looking at mortality in a lighter sense in that you start looking at the cycles of the world; the mortality of species; the vulnerability of environments, particularly when you live in a place like the west coast," she says.

"You've talked about being a nomad, but you aren't really, are you?"

"I'm not a nomad except in the head. I like comfort, and being a nomad can sometimes be exceedingly uncomfortable, in both the physical and the spiritual sense. . . . I don't think I've got the mental stamina for it, really," she says.

Personally I find the discomforts of the nomadic life bracing, and inspiring. But Keri must draw her creativity from somewhere else.

Then, for the first time, she takes off her glasses. She rubs her eyes. I notice that one of them wanders a bit.

"I think the riskiest thing that I do," Keri says, "it's not a physical thing at all, it's being open to and exploring mentally every field of knowledge whatsoever that entertains, interests me, or I come across. I'm willing to test against currently established truths of anything and everything," she says.

"You're an intellectual bungee jumper?" I tease, knowing Keri abhors the sport.

"*Boinng!* There goes the eyeballs. Yes, you're right. Put it this way: I am not devoted to comfort in the head, but I'll leap off cliffs and hope there's a sufficient updraft in the mental world. And so far there has been a sufficient updraft." Her smile breaks through and around the hand that tries to cover her imperfect teeth.

Hours have passed, and videtape packaging litters the floor. The sun bolts tangerine through the window behind Keri's desk and lights up the backpacks full of manuscripts. "Keri, can we go down to the beach and have a glass of wine?" I blurt out, a request devoid of fear or strategy.

"Why not," she says. I grab my still camera and we walk together to a deserted stretch of beach nearby. The day is unloading its final shots of glory; pomegranate red, Valiant orange, and indigo. Keri Hulme, two bottles of wine, my old Polaroid camera, and a roiling Tasman Sea all reaching a confluence at magic hour. This is what the late Spalding Gray referred to as "a perfect moment," LSD without the drugs—a blissful surge of contentment as all your stars align and the world seems to hum. Keri stands near the sea as I load my camera, but she doesn't touch the water.

I have traversed the dicey territory of meeting a person I have revered from afar, and survived to swoon about it. But Keri, of all people, would abhor the thought of me putting a diffusion filter on this moment. Let's just say Keri still represents all things diva to me.

I came to New Zealand looking for political estro-power and am left with an image of Keri standing next to the sea, firmly rooted to this quirky, independent set of islands. In the face of relative isolation, she, and her country, have developed the personal strength—mana, if you will—to go their own way.

We are eye to eye, swiping at sand flies.

"Red or white?" I say.

"Ah, white preferably for me," she says. I pour. Then I take a picture of Keri Hulme, and set it on the sand to develop.

"These little bastards here," Keri says, swatting, "they were supposedly put here so that humans don't get enamored with paradise—and you can sort of believe that."

6

CUD, SWEAT, AND FEARS

—

Aman iman. ("Water is life, and life is water.")

—TAMACHEK SAYING

Time has drained out of this reality, I think to myself as I shove a needle through yet another set of blisters on this, the third long day of walking through the sweltering central Sahara with Tuareg nomads on salt caravan. I never knew that nothingness could take up so much space. And, since I can speak exactly three words of the Tuareg's native language of Tamachek—*tanenmert* ("thank you"), *el ma tovlid?* ("how are you?"), and *iy uhen* ("hello")—I pass the hours ruminating on the concept of ethereal nothingness—which takes up a surprising amount of time. When my mind starts to bead up and roll off and disappear into this overwhelming landscape, like runaway mercury from a cracked thermometer, I latch onto some more tangible activities: counting the razor-sharp whiskers that pop out of my camel's muzzle, miming to my blue-swathed, all-male comrades, or tossing over in my brain how I could know so little about Niger, a West African country that is five times the size of Britain and sits just left of Chad.

The Scottish explorer Mungo Park traipsed through sub-Saharan Africa in search of the source of the Niger River in the early nineteenth century, although it was the French who eventually jimmied themselves into the position of colonialist power by playing tribal powers off one another. Since the country was not worth much—that is, there were only a few natural resources to exploit—the French bowed to political resistance in the mid-1900s, and Niger won its independence in 1960. France's colonial legacy, including language, remains among the educated.

And now, a Tuareg rebellion simmers. The Tuareg, a disenfranchised desert warrior tribe, have led a rebellion against the government for three decades, ever since the droughts of the 1970s when the corrupt government failed to pass along its international aid resources to the desert people. This violence between the government and the Tuareg (who some say are armed by Muammar Qaddafi of Libya), significant banditry, and a few coups d'état have made Niger destination non grata for travelers. A cease-fire between the government and rebels opened up a political window, occasioning our unlikely presence. A crew of three and I are here making a program for Pilot Productions. We have jumped through this current window of relative peace to walk through the Sahara with the "blue men of the desert," regal-looking men swathed in fabric pounded with indigo, who are concerned, mostly, with salt.

Political, geographic, and economic realities have conspired to maintain a way of life that has existed since Muhammad and have kept this spot largely unmarred by the tentacles of the transnationals. This is in contrast to Borneo, where the value of the rain forest has meant relatively quick liquidation, accompanied by swift change for the Penan. I am learning that this long, long walk that has happened for more than a thousand years does not pause for a political rebellion, and that if the camel lumbering beside you tries to take a chunk out of your arm, a twelve-year-old boy mysteriously appears and whacks it across the neck with a long wooden stick.

"We'll be there during the Salt Curée season," Vanessa, my cohort in Borneo, and now in Niger, had told me over the phone before our departure. "All kinds of festivals take place because it's right after rainy season. It's considered a time of plenty."

Plenty must be relative; seems to me it is simply the season least likely to kill you. The 115-degree heat is clean and dry and hard. To survive the desert you must regard it with proper respect. We breathe slowly, always through the nose, to avoid the blade in the throat that strikes when inhaling through the mouth. This section of the Sahara is called the Te Nere, which means "the void."

We are walking to the oasis town of Fachi to trade the dried tomatoes and onions that weigh down our camels for salt. The salt caravan leader, Oumarou, like his men, wears a blue robe, cinched with an ornate leather belt. He, and every other man, carries a sword, a legacy of the Tuareg warrior tradition. Oumarou leads us along an invisible path; his daytime compass is the angle of the shadows cast by his camel's ears, and how the winds sculpt the dunes. At night, he checks his naviation by the stars. Orion stays on the left cheek. We walk, leading our burdened camels, at a constant pace for ten, twelve hours a day. Our walk is filled with utter stillness and constant motion, and I sense that this is a place where even small mistakes have big consequences. This quiet caravan has little in common with our raucous orange-and-white Kiwi caravan. On this trek, there is no road, no gas; and there are no divas. The women stay in their home villages, in more fertile points of Niger, raising the children and growing the vegetables and spices that their mates haul, for months at a time, across the desert to trade for salt.

The Tuareg men's eyes are warm and eerie, with the slightly nondirected look of the blind; they beam out a sliver of light from behind black head coverings called *cheches.* Keri Hulme created a set of unfilmable blue men to protect her art from the compromises of the camera. These Blue Men are filmable, but it remains to be seen whether or not we are compromising them. My presence and that of the crew must be strange, but the men seem to take it in stride, literally. Our to-ing and fro-ing and as-yet-unsettled relationship with the camel persona seem to provide a bit of comic relief, given the laughs that slide out from under the *cheches. Taddezza tifellas. Iba nit akennas,* goes the Tamachek proverb. Laughter creates accord. Its absence creates dispute.

The *cheche,* or *taguelmoust,* is a scarf that covers the head and neck, leaving a slit for eyes and mouth. I dislike veils and at first firmly resist wearing one.

Stupid.

Like many Western women, I have negative associations with veiling—something I'm hoping to explore on the next *Divas* shoot, in Iran. But for now, we're here in Niger and anyone without sunstroke knows that the *cheche* is a savior from the punishing rays. It's wise not to let politics obscure pragmatism in the Sahara. I clue in late, but from then on Oumaruo patiently wraps and rewraps my mustard-colored *cheche* (using a technique proving too complicated for those of us raised with Velcro), salvaging some of my dignity and most of my bright pink skin.

"Tanenmert," I say to Oumarou, relieved.

"Niger's Islamic. Eighty-five percent of the people are Muslim. Men veil, and women don't, or at least aren't required to, which confuses the anthropologists," says Vanessa, who has taken to wearing a Yankees baseball hat and given up on the *cheche.* Men rarely remove the *cheche* in front of others, as it protects them not only from the sand and sun, but from the *jinn,* evil spirits that occupy the desert.

A friendly banter of Tamachek punctuates the early morning hours of walking, but by noon the heat rules, and the Blue Men fall silent. I am trying to stay true to the "amazing cultural experience" and not start a bitching loop in my brain about the increasing discomfort, but it is hard. My calves cramp. Sand whips into my eyes. The heat saps everything, even the energy needed to complain. Oumarou veers his steady gait my way and hands me a hollowed gourd filled with water. *"Aman iman,"* he says in Tamachek. *"Ishou."* ("Water is life, and life is water. Drink.")

I hand the gourd back, and when Oumarou turns away, my camel hocks a loogie on my arm. I am wiping the shockingly large glob on my pants when Chris, the quiet British soundman, walks up. Chris, a consummate pro, melts into the background during shooting. If he comes front and center you know something is wrong. "We are in the quietest place on earth," he says, adjusting the mic on my collar, "so quiet that you can't wear synthetics. I'm picking up tons of rustle. Only cotton from here on out, okay?"

The hours wear on. The crew drives, I walk. Only the pain from my blistered feet provides the edge that keeps me from succumbing to woozy, heat-induced delirium. Everything happens on the move. Water passes from goatskin sheath to gourd to man, and the walking never stops. A pungent mix of millet, goat cheese, and water is mashed together and run from man to man to me by a nimble little boy, the twelve-year-old son of Oumarou, who is constantly trailed by a little white goat, and the walking never stops. The flat, featureless sandscape pours out into infinity; the desert is elegant in its simplicity, and both liberating and dangerous in its reduction of life to a fundamental resin—simple lines, food, water, salt.

When the moon rises and the walking finally does stop, the camels are relieved of their three-hundred-pound loads and are fed. Despite their uncouth habits and famously pissy personalities, I'm coming to appreciate these efficiently built dromedaries that can survive seventeen days without water and regulate their own body temperature. Their sexy eyelashes, and a bit of a squint, allow them to plod forth in any manner of sandstorm.

We set up camp in silence smattered with camel groans of relief. The hay that has been on their backs is arranged in something like a Western "open-space cubicle layout." The Tuareg start fires with wood and dried camel dung. Small dancing flames bounce subtle hues of indigo around us. Meals of millet seem simple compared to the effort that goes into the tea. Tea preparation is a high art that includes a series of glasses of tea in varying strengths: "The first is drunk strong and bitter as life; the second one sweet as love; the third one mild like death," the Tuareg say.

We sit down one evening by his fire to do a "formal" conversation on camera with Oumarou. *Formal* here does not mean hair, makeup, and Barbara Walters. It simply means we are not walking while it is going on and we use some artificial lighting, that is, flashlights. Tim, the cameraman, has a respectful manner and warm rapport with those not used to being around cameras that is appreciated by all of us. He clips a mic on Oumarou, who is brewing up a batch of tea. Oumarou pours the thick liquid three feet from the kettle to a shot glass to another glass, back to the kettle, and back into a glass in a confusing caffeine jig that would rattle even a Seattle barista. The long-distance pouring creates a layer of foam and cools the tea quickly. I sip the second shot glass of thick, sweet tea that Oumarou hands me. I have convinced myself that Oumarou and I have bonded, though we have exchanged mostly gestures and smiles—not words—throughout the hours and days. Still, I have decided (unilaterally) that he is not simply putting up with us. But now, as the cameras roll and it comes time to actually talk, the difficulties of forced intimacy show themselves. The questions and answers go through three translations—English, to French, to Hausa, to Tamachek—then the answer comes, Tamachek, to Hausa, to French, to English. This also means an entire group of people participates in our "intimate" conversation.

"What do you think of the future of the caravans?" I ask.

"My youngest son has taken an interest in this life," he says, gesturing to his son, who is pounding millet. "And his son will do the same."

"Have you ever seen a camera before?" I ask after ours is clicked off.

"No, but ten years ago my eldest brother saw one," Oumarou tells me.

—

Cameras, and interference in delicate cultures in general, always brings up mixed feelings. A no-interference prime directive seems right and honorable, a lot of the time, but sometimes tradition or circumstance creates injustice, and interference seems justified. I think of how Ruchira Gupta's film gave visibility to the issue of sex trafficking, and how Pratibha Parmar's film *Warrior Marks* shed light on clitorectemies in Africa. I wonder if our shows—covering Borneo's threatened Penan, and now, the Tuareg—support the right cause by giving voice and exposure, or simply add to the white noise of cultural interference.

Irony may have scorched sincerity in my life, yet somehow the searing sun seems to be reversing the effect. It is rare that I feel honored or privileged in the moment—or, God forbid, actually utter such words, even if I feel them. But here and now I am keenly aware of this magical swatch of experience, and its precarious existence. Oumarou said that he expects his son and his son's son to live the circular life of the caravan. But that is unlikely. Ironically, it is the unrest and poverty of the region that have protected this way of life. If the country becomes more affluent, from foreign investment or other factors, there will likely be more trucks than camels carrying salt, and tourism may gain a bigger place in the economy. Out here, in the middle of the desert, to me, life feels gilded by being as it always has been. The oceans of sand and pure blue indigo make it easy to forget the punishing poverty of Niger that was so evident when we arrived in the capital city of Niamey.

Our arrival in Niger seems like months ago, although only a week has passed. We drove from Niamey to the holy city of Agadez. Agadez was founded roughly five hundred years ago and has long been regarded as the gateway to the desert. It is considered holy because of its many religious festivals and its great mosque, which was built in the sixteenth century and topped with one of the highest mud minarets in Africa. We hired a Tuareg guide named Aghali, whose *cheche* covered everything about his face except his aviator sunglasses and mustache. Aghali drove us through the naked Sahara in a beat-up old Land Rover piled high with firewood and camera equipment, and initiated us into this mostly flat, featureless scape where the winds' sculpting and unsculpting of the dunes was his only map. Reading the winds, divining by their direction, takes a special cartographer.

We bogged down in the sand frequently, despite having drained air from our tires for better traction. We dug and dug and Aghali told us the story of the Swiss couple who left their jeep to seek water, and died. It takes two days to die of thirst out here. "Never leave the jeep," Aghali says. Fulfilling the task we charged him with, Aghali eventually found the tracks of a caravan: hundreds of pancake-shaped indentations leading into the distance. Vanessa and I swapped excited smiles, and wondered at his navigation. We knew the caravans existed, but our production challenge was that we did not know where they were at any given time. These caravans only cross this ocean of sand twice a year, when the sands are firm enough to sustain them. Aghali carried on, following the tracks into a seemingly intangible expanse; our small expedition felt like a cohesive dream wandering into another dimension. We were fully vested in Aghali's skills. No caravan, no show.

The Tuareg have controlled sections of the Saharan routes since the seventh century and have often fought for that territorial right. Currently, there is intertribal rivalry among two primary tribes of the region, the Tuareg and the Fulani. But these desert tribes are also dependent on each other for commerce, so tensions stay at a low boil.

Two hours after initially spotting the tracks, a heat-jittery, amorphous black mass appeared in the distance.

Caravan.

We drove toward the mass and then Aghali and I jumped out of the jeep. We walked faster to catch up, then slower as we came apace with dozens of veiled, indigo-draped men leading hundreds of camels in a teardrop formation. The caravan did not stop. *"Efraiy a dassa a dai wadouwen?"* ("May we join you?") we asked the *madugu* ("leader").

The *madugu,* Oumarou, simply smiled, then swung his chin toward the distance. *"I walla."* ("Yes.")

—

In camp I watch as Oumarou walks among the dappling of fires, surveying the site, his broad chest thrust out and his sword still at his side. Silhouettes of folded beasts against the horizon provide the only definition between earth and sky, desert and camp. I crawl behind a bundle of hay into my sleeping bag under a rack of stars, the rest of the Milky Way a dusty night-light. Stars shoot to the rhythmic euphony of Oumarou's boy pounding millet, and to the gurgly, garage-band cacophony of camel digestion. A chunky sliver of the moon hangs, low and heavy, like the belly of a pregnant woman rocking on all fours. Despite the tea, sleep comes fast. Too fast. I do not want to miss any of this, but I am quickly swept away by the fabled sandman.

The next morning I am conscious of how pure and clear-headed I feel. Every day that I walk across this stretch of the Sahara, leading a camel with lovely eyelashes and an ornery persona, feels epic. The Tuareg nomads have no word in their native Tamachek for *tomorrow*. Today is today and tomorrow is . . . not today. Talk about living in the present. Because survival is so tenuous, the Tuareg culture moves straight to the point, in almost every respect. Appropriately, the Tamachek language is all consonants, no mealy-mouthed vowels. Like the cop Kiran Bedi in India, the Tuareg acknowledge and leverage life's transience. Walking this path of immediate existence is teaching me, too, about every moment.

Some nights I simply walk into the desert a half mile or so from camp and lie down to sleep. There is nothing to be afraid of, as here, in the middle of the desert where temperatures can reach 160 degrees, few creatures can survive. The desert's sterility is freeing. Day doesn't break in this desert. No birds or cicadas or garbage trucks to gong the collective morning bell. Instead, dawn creeps up. There is simply a silent lightening that mysteriously grows from imperceptible, to *there*.

Oumarou nods for me to help him one morning after I've walked in from the distance. He has me hold his camel's tether while he cauterizes its wounds (caused by the rub between hard, unforgiving saddles topped with heavy weight) with a sizzling piece of iron. This is a daily, predawn ritual. We load up the camels with hundreds of pounds of blankets, millet, hay, dried tomatoes, and onions, and set off to walk.

Because of the singular nature of our activities, the small crew, and our complete disconnection from the outside world—no e-mail, no satellite phone, and only two dodgy walkie-talkies—this shoot is calm, strangely free from Adventure Divas worries that usually permeate everything. Our financial debt has risen as fast as the economy has fallen. The energy of running a business on ideals and curiosity (rather than capital) has begun to sour. Jeannie is, understandably, tiring of being behind a desk and wants to divagate herself. The hotel in New Zealand is threatening to sue, and an avalanche of details is giving me the personality of . . . a camel. Maybe Adventure Divas wasn't meant to be; maybe we should cash it in. Out here, I see the beauty of simplicity.

Soft folds of taupe cover the distance in every direction; the huge blue sky clicks like a puzzle piece into the landscape's curved edges. My reaction to the emptiness is strangely devotional. I am falling in love with a place—which I have never done. The elements—the heat, the walking, the sand—are demanding, but they leave me raw and happy. I have a strange desire to submit to this desert. I have experienced many fine places in my travels, always wondering if I would ever be taken enough to stop, to shelve the nomada within.

Sometimes the relentless green growth of the Pacific Northwest feels demanding, as if it is taking up too much brain space. Psychologist Mihaly Csikszentmihaly says our consciousness has limits. That is, our central nervous system can only process so many bits of information—sounds, sights, emotions, thoughts—at once. "It is possible to process at most 126 bits of information per second, or 7,560 per minute, or almost half a million per hour. Over a lifetime of seventy years, and counting sixteen hours of waking time each day, this amounts to about 185 billion bits of information. It is out of this total that everything in our life must come—every thought, memory, feeling, or action. It seems like a huge amount, but in reality it does not go that far."

Here, in the belly of the Sahara, the stuff of consciousness is not cluttered, and the precious bits go a long way. An uncanny space-time relationship strips me of everything. Vanity. Ego. Time. Anxiety. Irreverence. Out of the corner of my mind's eye, I get a glimpse of what it must feel like to simply exist. And I guess this is what I mean by being in love. I have never been anywhere so desolate and I have never felt less alone.

It figures I would fall in love with a politically destabilized region, on a caravan that does not traditionally include women, in an environment that cannot sustain life.

But even love needs an oasis. When I finally see Fachi, it's like mainlining a fruit smoothie, and I realize how starved I have been for color. I am desperately happy to see this cliché come to life: palm trees in the desert sea, and its mirror-image mirage, tantalizingly close. I want to sprint toward it, but the Blue Men of the Desert keep us at their steady pace.

Fachi's buildings consist mainly of ancient mud-brick fortresslike towers with tiny rectangular windows. It is one of the oldest inhabited towns in the Sahara. There was once an enormous saltwater lake here, but it evaporated under the heat of the fierce Saharan sun, leaving behind an area rich with salt deposits. The Kanouri people, who control the salt deposits, are the descendants of slaves who have lived near and mined out the cliffs of Fachi since the eighth century.

Like thousands before us over hundreds of years, we are here to feed and water the camels, and to trade. Fachi has always been a lively intersection of cultures and peoples, and stopping here makes me feel part of the larger nomadic order. We walk a procession of six camels through Fachi's narrow streets, which are lined by low mud walls and surrounded by wind-sculpted trees. We are followed by a band of small children. *"Cadeau, cadeau"* ("Present, present"), they call to us, half-playing, half-begging, the legacy of a French school that once existed here but fell away after independence.

Our camels groan with relief as off come the tomatoes, onions, and millet that will be traded for salt. Landlocked Niger has no commercial salt mines or seawater for evaporation. Nor does Morton's have a holding here, and imported salt is too costly. Human beings need salt to live. Thus, in Niger, this oasis is vital.

Oumarou indicates I should go with a Kanouri couple whom he seems to know. Perhaps he trades with them. The couple takes me down to their plot of circular pans, disk-shaped formations in the ground, from two to five feet in diameter, which are filled with brown, briny water that evaporates in the sun, leaving the residual salt. The man and woman slowly wade into the water-filled pans and begin shaking the silty contents through a strainer. They are accustomed to working in 120 degrees. The woman hands me a strainer, and I step into one of the round bodies of water to help with the work.

"Ahhhhhhh!" I scream, as a dozen razor blades, or perhaps a school of piranha, lay waste to my feet. The intense saline content of the water sears my cuts and blisters. This is a pain I cannot take. The couple is amused, but sympathetic, and the woman nods toward some shade. I hobble away and duck behind the clay wall, and breathe through the pain. My livelihood may have its strains and psychic entropy. A life mining salt in the middle of nowhere is pure, and perhaps simple, but most certainly it is brutal. The couple works in the blazing sun until they have two calabashes full of rough animal-grade salt, and then we all walk up and out of the salt "mining" area to find the rest of our crew.

We get to Oumarou and the trading area just as the transactions are completed. Vanessa is calculating. "Thirty days of nonstop walking across the desert will earn each man approximately five hundred dollars," she says. "A hard way to make a living." The camels sigh with the practice of knowing martyrs, as the Blue Men lash heavy pillars of a dried salt-and-mud mix on either side of their humps and ready the camels for their return trip.

I dread saying good-bye to Oumarou. We won't be returning across the desert with them; we are on to our next story. Television shoots enable countless intense, brief relationships with extraordinary people. Mostly I am inured to this constant parting of ways with another human you know you will never see again in your life. Yet this time, reality hiccups. We do not know each other, really, and in my raw state I am probably heaping extra meaning where none is due. But his world has tweaked mine, unexpectedly.

"*In taoudet*" ("Safe travels"), I say from three feet.

"*Inshallah,*" Oumaru responds, with just a hint of a nod, and then turns east, Orion now on the other cheek, to lead his men on the walk back across the Sahara.

I climb back into the twenty-first century, Aghali shifts it into gear, and as we drive toward Timia, I feel time begin to fill the hourglass again.

The desert approaching Timia is different than the nothingness of the Te Nere. A hazy dense sky swirls pockets of dust, and volcanic craters pock the distance. Trees buck reality and insist on growing out of mountains of rubble, standing in defiance of an otherwise apocalyptic landscape.

Timia is home to the sedentary agriculturalists called the *kel oui* Tuaregs. We wend our way up a dry riverbed in the Land Rover, and when we arrive at Timia we are taken aback by its greenery, lushness, and fertility. We set up camp on the outskirts of the oasis and spend the evening discussing the plan for tomorrow's filming.

"How many cups of this do you think equals that first cup of Tuareg tea? Caffeine-wise," I ask Tim groggily the next morning, as we stir up our fourth cup of Nescafé.

"No idea, mate," he says, then adds, "Did you know Aghali killed a viper in camp last night?" He pushes his plastic cup, midair, toward a clump of scrubby bushes. This news sends a *craaaack* through my desert Eden. I have been free and safe at night because I believed I was. Tim shows me where the dead snake was tossed. It is black and limp, two millimeters from decapitated. "Snakes. It *had* to be snakes," I say. The Tuareg believe the desert is filled with evil spirits; I wonder if they assign anything to animal visitations.

The festival is in full swing by midmorning. Dozens of women swathed in indigo with bangles and black veils sit in tight circles rapping on the *tinde* drums and bellowing. All this a preamble to the day's main event: a series of camel races.

The contestants, who have walked days or weeks to get here, line up in ornate regalia, proud atop their camels. I am growing downright fond of the versatile camel. Not only can a camel carry half its own weight; its milk can feed forty human babies in inevitable times of drought. But today they are not wet nurses or pack animals; today each of these beasts is expected to behave like a thoroughbred. Today, they are honorable steeds whose good looks and speed may bestow status, and a bit of prize money, upon their riders. Frenetic drumming and ululating is the backdrop to an inaugural ceremony led by the village's blacksmiths. The blacksmiths seem to be the grand poo-bahs of most things ceremonial, probably because of their association with fire, the element of creation. In phase one of the competition they call out numbers one by one, and steed and rider, both layered in colorful blankets and fringe, sword swinging from the rider's hip, join a circle running around the blacksmiths. They are judged by their regalia and pedigree, white and leggy camels being considered the most beautiful. The drumming and ululating and throngs of onlookers keep the atmosphere at a heady pitch.

The blacksmiths bless the event, and one of them drops a sword that sets ninety camels and riders off in a hurricane of hollering and hooves for the first of three races. As they thunder past, I note a few significant differences between a horse race and a camel race. First of all, there is a hump to deal with; secondly, there are no stirrups; and third, well, despite the beating they're getting, the camels never actually break into a gallop. It's more of a fuel-injected hyper-trot. Ouch.

The racecourse wanders off into the distance, partly following what looks like a loopy riverbed. The race is twenty minutes long, give or take, and the riders quickly disappear into a cloud of dust and distance. After about ten minutes, news ripples through the crowd that a rider has fallen off and been trampled—which is somewhat serious as we are at least four days (by jeep, much more by camel) from even rudimentary medical-care facilities.

Because of the accident, half of the men drop out of the second race, preferring to save their necks for the last race, which has the biggest kitty. Attention turns to the injured rider, who has been brought back in from the course. He is quite dazed, but luckily he seems to have only broken an arm.

In a matter of hours all the Zen equity built up on the long desert walk drains from my soul. I, a competitive adult-child-of-a-professional-athlete-and-gambler, am planning to get myself into race three. From the moment I heard *race,* my serotonin flooded the zone and drowned out my culturally sensitive alter ego, who heckles: *Whitey! Woman! Culture skater! You just parachute into cultures—bopping around with as much imperialist swagger as the next guy.* My inner voice of condemnation now at bay, I begin to justify a potential cultural trespass. Adventure is a woman's right, I rationalize. And a willingness to take risk—well, that's very divalicious. As Keri Hulme exemplifies, we all must pursue our updraft—mental, physical, or otherwise. I humbly, and incorrectly, wrap a *cheche* around my head and walk up to the lead blacksmith.

"*Je voudrais monter sur le chameau,*" I say.

Blank stare . . . then slightly bewildered grin.

"Did I get that right?" I ask Vanessa, who is fluent in French.

"What?" Vanessa says. "You *can't*—You're joking, right?"

"You don't understand, Vanessa. Derby Day is a high holiday in my family. I was built for this."

"Derby Day?" she queries, Europeanly.

"As in *Ken-tuck-eee.*"

I repeat my request to the blacksmith, louder this time, fairly sure he understands French, and willing volume to lead to comprehension.

"Yes, uh, I think it's the concept that's the problem, not the language," says Vanessa.

A frenzied discussion among the blacksmiths ensues. My head swings back and forth, following the debate.

Clearly there is concern.

"Your insides," the blacksmith finally says to me in French, which I can mostly understand, "may damage the horns on the front of the saddle."

"My impaled liver is less important than the saddle?" I say to Vanessa.

"Trop chère. Trop chère," he says—of the saddle.

It's true; in this, one of the poorest nations in the world, a saddle is gold, and who am I to make value judgments?

"What are the chances of a liver transplant in Agadez?" I ask Vanessa, half-joking, and continue to lobby the blacksmiths.

"It *would* make great footage," muses Vanessa, tantalized. "But are you sure you want to do this?" she adds. Vanessa is both producer and director on this shoot. The producer in her realizes it is her job to keep me alive. The director in her feels that *this is the nutgrab.*

But I have gone inside my own head, regressed not to my secret happy place, but to that focused, pulsing headspace I used to go to at track meets before the gun went off, in basketball games before the whistle blew, in touch football as the Hail Mary was lobbed.

I barely hear Vanessa saying, "You don't have to race . . . but . . . but . . . if you're gonna do it . . . do try to face camera around the last bend."

The crowd parts and I see before me a ten-foot-tall, fifteen-hundred-pound white camel swathed in multicolored blankets and layers of leather fringe. The camel wears an intricate saddle of silver, leather, and carved wood, which is topped with a lethal trifecta of horns.

"Lots of luck," Vanessa says, nudging me toward my steed.

I am handed the reins to the beast. "Shhhhh, shhhh, shhh," I say to him, imitating my fellow jockeys, and he kneels with a cranky, homicidal shriek. I climb aboard my massive camel and line up with ninety or so other contestants, all aggressively jostling for an inside position, yelling at one another and their camels, regalia clanking, crops gripped as tight as the tension in the air.

And this is when it hits me like a tsunami that, this time, I have gone *too far*. I should *not* rip through the Sahara desert on a giant camel competing against veiled men with sharp swords who have done this drill since the time of Muhammad.

Oh, why can't I be content with life's calmer glories? It's not just that I need a new notch in ye olde adventure belt. It is a deep-seated, almost irrational fear that I will miss out on an experience within my grasp that I have passed up because of fear. But here, in the middle of the Sahara, as the sword is about to drop, the *truly* sick thing is: I WANT TO WIN.

Aaaaaand theyyyyyyre offff . . .

The next fifteen minutes are a blur of survival tactics, rapid-fire cussing . . . and wholesale regret. My rusty horseback-riding skills do not translate, and my dream of winning (or at least placing!) is trampled within moments.

I just want to live.

My camel runs fast, a tenth-gear trot, and I am, shamefully, gripping the horns in order not to be flung over the top of the seven-foot-long curvy neck, or skewered like a holiday pig, or both, in rapid succession. I *do* want to live, but my father's DNA sears through my blood and *mostly* I don't want to come in last, so I try to do like the jockey just ahead of me who has one leg contortedly wrapped around the camel's neck to stabilize himself, the other foot quivering the camel's nape—a sort of Saharan accelerator. I wrap my leg and thump my camel haphazardly with my filthy, blistered bare foot, and he responds like Secretariat at the Belmont, determined to wear the Triple Crown. He lurches us ahead several lengths and passes two contenders. I'm dying to turn my head and look and gauge our lead, but I know that when Lot's wife fled Sodom and Gomorrah she looked behind her and—*poof*—was turned into a pillar of salt. In Niger this strikes me as a real possibility. I don't look back.

I'm in the final stretch, eating dust along with two riders behind—one of whom is gaining fast on me—when suddenly the rhythms click and I'm

Lawrence of Arabia, no hands, yelling to my camel, the power of a crumbling empire behind me. My bum and the camel's hump are in perfect sync and we are charging toward the finish, neck and (very long) neck with a taupe-colored camel whose rider is a peripheral blur of indigo. With a final gasp, we place second (to last) by a nose and throttle past the finish line, where we are rushed by a dozen ululating women who surround the camel and smudge indigo on his face.

The women seem particularly thrilled at our performance, which is a bit of a mystery to me since we finished nearly dead last.

"You are the first woman ever to enter a camel race in its history. They can't believe you actually finished," the lead blacksmith walks up and says, revealing the significance of my trespass into a five-thousand-year-old tradition. "This girl over here says she wants to race next year," he adds, pointing to a young woman of about fourteen smiling our way.

"Really?" I smile back, sharing an odd moment of global sisterhood, but also worrying for her. It's one thing for a privileged traveler to buck mores, and entirely another for a local girl to do so.

Who's to say: Arrogant traveler inappropriately messes with status quo? Or, a lesson in having to cross the starting line, in order to move it. I jump off the camel, and twist my bad ankle when I hit the ground. I stand, all my weight on one leg, and begin to unsaddle my steed. Villagers are beginning to peel off and return to their homes across the oasis. The girl just watches me.

7

BEHIND CLOSED CHA-DORS

—

Dear Inga la Gringa,

I'm going to a Muslim land. Do I really have to wear a veil?

—Perpexed About Persia

Dearest Perplexed,

Your closing, "Perplexed About Persia," leads me to deduce that the "Muslim land" to which you refer is Iran. This is pretty important, because the religion observed in Iran is not the same as that of Turkey, which in turn is vastly different from Islam as practiced in Afghanistan, or Oman.

So . . . Iran.

You need to wear a veil in Iran.

Iran is a theocracy, that means a religious government. Rule of law in Iran is that it is illegal for women to be in public without a head covering. Veil yer ass up.

With love, Inga la Gringa

Veil politics may have been only in my head in Niger, but *veil,* a four-letter word in the lexicon of some people's feminism, was sure to be a flashpoint in our next location.

I was sprinting toward this final shoot of our premier season with the scattered, determined energy of a greyhound on its last day of racing: tired but enthusiastic, skeptical yet still loyal, slightly lame, and wondering if retirement meant Sundays in the park or a shot of sodium pentobarbital. (And frankly, not sure which I would prefer.)

Jeannie was in Iran scouting, and I was to go there along with a crew, a few weeks after her return. But after several bureaucratic delays and extra fees, I was getting nowhere with our Iranian journalist credentials. One day our contact who was trying to shepherd the visa process along from Tehran called. The real problem had reared its head. "Today the official intimated that you have too many single women on the crew. American single women are considered a special liability. That's why the visas are not being granted."

"Thanks. Uh, right. Okay, let me think. I will call you tomorrow," I said, and hung up the phone.

"It's not looking possible to get the whole crew in," I droned to Jill, sodium pentobarbitally. Jill was our website's managing editor, and her years as a salty beat reporter always made her my preferred commiserator.

Jill clicked her mouse, pushed our new home page live, then checked the e-mail. "You'd better figure out how to get there, if only to go retrieve your mother. Check it out."

TO: IRAN CREW
FROM: JEANNIE
SUBJECT: RE: FASHION QUESTIONS

If you're asking about clothes, the visa problem must be solved—excellent! I think it's wise to take one all-black cover-up, that is, scarf and manteau (manteau is a French word for coat—sort of like a loose overcoat) for meetings with officials as a sign of respect. Otherwise, conservative colors (though not nec. black) are OK. Despite having to cover up, am having a GREAT time—Iranians are so hospitable!—Jeannie

Jeannie's optimism jibed with our public reality. To outsiders, it appeared we had it made; we'd imagined and achieved an ambitious goal. Episodes of the series had started broadcasting on PBS, and our tiny empire thrived online, with chat rooms, advice, streaming video, and behind-the-scenes info on the series. "Confident, quirky and beautifully filmed," said the *Chicago Sun-Times*. Hundreds of e-mails were pouring in:

> I stumbled on your show and love it! Women have been waiting for it for years! So many shows are male-oriented and we never find out about the people behind the cultures. I've struggled with moving away from Chicago for my whole life. After watching the show I've decided it's time to move *onward*! Thank you, thank you, thank you!
>
> Leah

> Absolutely the finest armchair tour I've ever had the pleasure to see! You deserve enormous credit for dealing with a political minefield without preaching or prevaricating. The women you featured are inspirational!
>
> Greg

But, since we spent our time making TV rather than raising the additional underwriting we desperately needed, the truth was we had a lot less money than anybody knew (a dirty little secret Jeannie and I held close); we were receiving fat, litigious, fire-related envelopes from New Zealand; and now we were having trouble getting visas to our last location.

Too many single women, *pffft*.

This was no time to retreat, I thought, pacing the office. I read that in Iran, the political lines are always moving and the rules of the game are constantly shifting, which creates an atmosphere in which social improvisation and sociopolitical agility are survival sports. Time to think Iranian. I returned to my desk, grabbed the phone, and started swapping out the crew, women for men, Americans for Brits—thus, integrity for pragmatism. Seven days later, only twelve hours before our flight departed, a FedEx package arrived containing our visas. *Khoda ra Shokr.* (Thank god.)

—

The politically charged air neutralizes Tehran's infamous pollution, and it feels as if I am sucking pure, sharp oxygen on this, our first day in Iran. The thrill of being here makes the brown baggy smocklike wrap that shrouds the contours of my body and the itchy moss-green synthetic scarf that covers my hair almost bearable. The black Georgia work boots don't do the look any favors. The crew and I hop into a van to begin our tour of Tehran.

We wanted to come to Iran because it felt critical that our first season cover the Middle East; that we explore divadom in a region where religious, often regressive traditionalism and meddling imperialism from countries like the United States both exist and sometimes collide.

Furthermore, we felt that the Western media was leaving out much of Iran's complexity. One of the stories not being told in the West, we had heard, was that beneath their veils and behind closed doors, Iranian women were anything but shrinking violets. And that, in fact, women in Iran experience freedoms that are unique in the Middle East.

We're all crammed in the van, and Vresh, our Armenian-Iranian driver, is expertly navigating Tehran's main drag. Julie Costanzo is producing; a mild-mannered Brit named Orlando Stuart is the cameraman; Persheng Vaziri and Maryam Kia are Tehran-based producer-translator-fixers; and Parviz Abnar, who handles sound, rounds out our crew. We are on our way to meet Shahla Sherkat, founder and publisher of a magazine called *Zanan,* which means "woman" in Farsi. But first there is a particular building I want to see.

"Here's the American embassy—well, here *was* the American embassy," says Persheng, who left Iran for New York as a teenager but now spends half her time in Tehran. "We're *not* supposed to film here," she adds, nodding toward a few soldiers wielding Kalashnikovs.

This building marks my first memory of Iran. It was on November 4, 1979, when images of blindfolded hostages started pouring from the Middle East following the return of Ayatollah Ruhollah Khomeini, who would go on to lead the country's conservative, Islamic government. Islamic militants (i.e., politicized students) had seized the American embassy in Tehran and held fifty-two American hostages.

I remember watching those images and thinking how scary it must be to be blindfolded and surrounded by deafening chants. I also remember how careful the Iranian students were in helping the hostages down the front stairs of the embassy so they wouldn't trip.

We drive slowly by the embassy, later referred to as a "U.S. den of espionage." The compound is currently a training center for Islamic guards and spreads over an entire city block; a six-foot-tall brick wall forms its perimeter. The wall is freshly painted with sloganry: WE WILL MAKE AMERICA FACE A SEVERE DEFEAT! There is an image of the Statue of Liberty with a skull face; there is a handgun painted in the red, white, and blue of an American flag. DOWN WITH AMERICA. I find these anti-U.S. images more intimidating than those in Cuba. Perhaps this is because Cuba's propaganda is from a political era that seems benign, almost kitschy to me, whereas in Iran the symbols, on some level, feel loaded with contemporary meaning.

"Roll film," I say to Orlando, our cameraman. "Well, uh, on second thought let's use the small video camera," I add, grabbing it from the backseat.

"This is the place where the four hundred-forty-four-day seige happened in 1979—" I say to camera with a bit too much emotion for a real journalist, "and we're not supposed to be filming, so we're doing so very quickly. We should go faster. Can we speed up?"

The hostage crisis was more than twenty years ago and those images on the embassy steps have *been* Iran to most of us in the West. Like Cuba, little of the reality of Iranian life had been reported in the media since. Even when Iran was bestowed the dubious honor of membership in the tripartite "axis of evil," the media image still did not widen measurably.

I had heard Iranian friends call Los Angeles "Tehrangeles," partly because more than a half million Iranian expats live there; but as we continue driving I begin to understand other similarities between L.A. and Tehran. First: traffic. Tehran's four-lane traffic is crammed with drivers who seem to consider transportation a competitive sport and dents badges of honor. Second: The rich live in the foothills and the less wealthy people fan out across the plain. Third: smog. "The Alborz Mountains are right there, but you can rarely see them," says Maryam, pointing into a haze. Except for the bundles of fresh, bright flowers for sale that dot most street corners, it's an aesthetically unpleasant city that seems to be the victim of some poor architectural decisions.

We pass the fifth giant sign that displays the same two faces: Ayatollah

Ayatollah Khomeini   *Ayatollah Khamenei*

Khomeini, the now-dead founder of the Islamic revolution, and the current "supreme leader," Ayatollah Khamenei. Unlike Cuba, there is commercial advertising in Iran (we just sped by the familiar, colorful Microsoft flag), but mostly the prevailing images are guys; big guys, fierce guys, bearded guys, and most of all *dead* guys—martyrs. The two supreme leaders dominate, but their images vie for space with these lesser-known martyrs, hundreds of thousands of young men who died in the war with Iraq that began in 1980 and ended in a virtual stalemate in 1988.

Glorification of martyrs has become a political tool to assuage and convince a population that losing their sons was worthwhile. Even now, parents of each of these men receive a stipend from the government, which is extremely significant in a country with a 20 percent unemployment rate. This payout buys support for the "mullahs," which is how most people refer to the minority conservatives who rule. Even more colloquially, the mullahs are referred to as "they" or "them." (As the shoot would progress I would come to understand the fear inspired by, and omniscient qualities attributed to, these ubiquitous pronouns.)

"The mullahs can run a religious revolution but not an economy," sighs Maryam good-heartedly between translating signs for us: THE BEGINNING, THE

END, THE APPEARANCE, THE DEPTH OF EXISTENCE IS GOD—THE QUR'AN; IT IS OUR
DUTY TO THANK THE MARTYRS—SUPREME LEADER; and, AMERICA CANNOT DO A
DAMN THING. I notice that Maryam must have brown shoulder-length hair, as a
bit has fallen from beneath her royal-blue cotton scarf. We haven't spent time
together outside of work, and so have not yet seen each other unveiled.
Maryam, an Iranian who spent much of her youth in London, quickly tires of
translating and rolls her eyes at me, as if to say, *We look right through this propaganda, why can't you?*

Persheng, tall, thin, and dressed in something that looks like an oversized
raincoat, is also worried that we're a little too focused on the Islamic signage.
She pulls me aside when we stop to get a close-up of a sign with a silhouette of
a fully covered woman. The sign encourages good *hejab* (the Islamic dress
code). In Iran, women are required to wear a head covering—a veil—starting at
age nine, but not the full chador (a head-to-toe, tentlike garment; *chador* actually translates to "tent" in Farsi).

"You're not going to use this footage just to play into people's fears and
stereotypes, are you?" says Persheng, having noted our "scary" collection of
b-roll. I think she's worked with Western crews in the past who wanted a fla-
vorful, but not necessarily real, story. She wants me to know that Iran is not all
terrorists and veils.

"No, no," I say. "I understand that it's just government manipulation.
Don't worry. But the show has to acknowledge those fears and misperceptions
in order to move beyond them, right?" I explain.

Despite the glowering religious icons looming above, the country does not
feel scary, and we've yet to experience any anti-American sentiment from a
three-dimensional human. On the contrary, we've been greeted with warmth
everywhere we've gone. Earlier we were chasing down a rumor of a wall said to
be covered with anti-U.S. slogans. We arrived at the location and asked the old
security guard about it. "Oh, I painted over that years ago," he said with a dis-
missive laugh and a sweep of his hand. "Please, please sit and have some tea
with me, and perhaps a pipe?" he said, nodding toward a hookah.

The story of Iran's Islamicist revolution, and especially its impact on
women, is not simple. In the 1970s, before the revolution, Iran was run by
Mohammad Reza Pahlavi, who succeeded his father as shah in 1941, and
Tehran was experiencing rock music, reefer, and miniskirts along with much of

the world. Wearing *hejab* was actively discouraged by the government. But while a wealthy minority lived the high life, the masses lived in poor conditions with high illiteracy and little health care. Like Batista in Cuba, the shah was an autocrat installed and propped up by the United States (read: CIA), and he stirred up a great deal of popular resentment. Workers and middle-class students protested against widespread offical corruption and the lack of jobs. Religious conservatives railed against "Westoxification" of their country. Some women, both religious and secular, who wanted the regime *out*, took to wearing veils as an act of political defiance.

Many political factions participated in the resistance to the shah—not only Islamists, but leftists, communists, and feminists as well. But as the anti-shah forces gained strength, it was the more conservative elements of the opposition that came to the fore.

In January 1979, the shah was forced out of the country as the result of a massive popular uprising. Two weeks later, Ayatollah Khomeini returned from exile in France and joined with secularist anti-shah forces in the formation of a new government. Over the next few years, faced with a hostile United States and a bloody war with neighboring Iraq, Khomeini and the theocrats consolidated their power. As Maryam is fond of saying, "The deal was done." A band of conservative religious clerics slipped into the void of what was essentially and originally a *political*—not religious—revolution.

For Iranian women, the revolution has been a mixed bag. A "jihad against illiteracy" and greater access to education have created opportunities that were previously unavailable to most Iranian women. Sixty percent of Iran's university students are women now, compared with 25 percent before the revolution. But Khomeini also put in place a system of draconian family laws and strict dress codes for women. Veiling was no longer optional but mandatory.

In the twenty-five years since conservative theocrats took power, there has been a slow, staccato walk toward political reform. Women have successfully protested for more freedoms and for the relaxing of some veiling requirements. On May 23, 1997, the reformist religious cleric Mohammad Khatami was democratically voted into office as president. But, since the religious supreme leader trumps the elected president in the Islamic Republic, Khatami was less able to bring reform than a now frustrated populace had hoped. Some blame Khatami for the slow change; others think his hands were tied by the reigning theocratic powers. He was reelected in 2001, but faith in Khatami continued to plunge. (And in July 2005 ultraconservative Mahmoud Ahmadinejad was elected president.)

Nonetheless, Khatami's election in 1997 ushered in an era of relative freedom for the Iranian press. At any given time, there are about fifty nongovernmental publications on the street in Tehran. But publishing remains risky business. Recently there has been another of several waves of crackdowns by the conservatives; scores of publications have been shuttered, and many of their publishers are under indictment.

While my first-amendment instincts cry out at this censorship, I know that my own culture also has forces that get in the way of a free and robust press. Here in Iran it is the government that impedes; in the United States, it's profit-driven media conglomerates. In the United States, news judgments are frequently not based on what people need to know, but what they are perceived (through polls or ratings) to enjoy consuming. Thus, a market fundamentalism—a tyranny of profit—determines what is news. As Neil Postman says in his now twenty-year-old (yet still prescient) critique of television, *Amusing Ourselves to Death,* "Censorship, after all, is the tribute tyrants pay to the assumption that a public knows the difference between serious discourse and entertainment—and cares."

The role of the press in Iran's reform movement is critical to understand, so I want to meet Shahla Sherkat, one of Iran's best-known publishers. Last year she was sentenced to four months in prison and a three-thousand-dollar fine—a significant amount of money in Iran, undoubtedly more than a year's salary for her—for attending a conference of international journalists and arguing in a public setting that *hejab* should be a matter of *choice,* rather than law. Sherkat remains hard at work while her case is on appeal.

Sherkat's magazine *Zanan* has a circulation of more than 100,000 and rides a dangerous wave of feminism and politics. For more than a century, through shahs and clerics alike, Iranian women have struggled for more liberty. *Zanan* marks a contemporary chapter in that struggle and the magazine is credited with turning out the critical women's vote for President Khatami, the only candidate who called for greater freedom for women and for the government to move to a less strict interpretation of sharia, or Islamic law.

We walk up to the second floor of an unremarkable gray cement building in midtown Tehran and into the *Zanan* offices, which are filled with a dozen young women in conservative black and gray *hejab*. Early-nineties PCs hum with activity and stacks of magazines accent the waiting area. I am struck by the spendy graphic sophistication of the covers, and by how politically frank they are. One of them has been enlarged and hung behind Sherkat's desk: a red and black image of a woman pulling the veil back to reveal her lipsticked mouth. Sherkat greets us with a reserved smile and a Western handshake. Forty-something Sherkat, who has dark, intense eyes, is dressed conservatively in a tan gown with a full black head scarf. We set up to interview her at her desk, behind which are shelves bulging with feminist books from publishers around the world.

Once a revolutionary student who hit the streets to bring down the shah, Sherkat now regards herself as a reformist journalist. By way of introduction to the magazine, she takes me through past issues.

"This issue features an interview with Mrs. Khatami. It was published especially for the elections," she says, holding up a cover with a smiling first lady. While Sherkat and her magazine have supported Mrs. Khatami's husband, they turned critical of him when, after elected, he appointed only one woman to his cabinet.

"This one," Sherkat continues, holding up another issue, "is about runaway girls in Tehran and how homelessness is becoming a problem; this one is about AIDS." Other issues the magazine covers include domestic violence, rhinoplasty, patriarchy, feminist films, and temporary marriage. The latter, a loophole in Islamic law, allows a couple to marry for as little as a few hours. Some condemn it as legalized prostitution; others defend it as a way for unmarried women to have sex in a country that prohibits it.

Her magazine, now in its twelfth year, is still being published, despite a prison sentence over her head for speaking out against the legal enforcement of *hejab*.

"What do you think Western feminists misunderstand about Iranian feminism?" I ask.

"And also, what do they understand?" she responds warmly, a small, sly smile bringing her face to life.

"Yes, well . . ." I stumble, reminding myself not to lead with my Western guilt.

"Does This Woman Wear a Chador?"

"Sir, Have You Ever Hit Your Wife?"

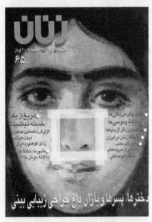

"Girls, Boys, and the Popularity of Nose Jobs"

"Where Are These Girls Running To?"

"The Political Rights of Women in Iran"

"Women, Why Do You Buy Gold?"

"Basically I think the Western feminists don't know that an Iranian feminist movement exists. Some people think that women in Iran still remain at home hiding behind the veil. But, as you may have noticed, women are present and active in many layers of social and political life in this country," Sherkat tells me. "This is not something granted to them by the government, but rather the will of women themselves, which has forced the government to accept their participation in various aspects of life in the society. I am a Muslim, I have Islamic faith, and at the same time I am doing the work that I do."

Sherkat sees no conflict between her religious faith and her feminist faith. She explains that women in other Islamic countries, however, such as Saudi Arabia, are often denied more rights, such as driving and voting, than are Iranian women. *Zanan,* she says, tackles issues relevant to Iranian women's lives. Many of those issues are previously unexposed in journalism and certainly are not discussed in public.

But I want to know more about the overall tension between reformist journalists and the government. As of April 2004, there were eleven journalists behind bars, several of whom have never been charged or tried. Several major daily newspapers have been shut down and websites are heavily censored.

"So how do you survive in this atmosphere? I mean, it's hard enough to publish a magazine anywhere," I say, knowing from my own experience that feminist publishing is a difficult racket.

"Journalism in developing countries is like walking on a tightrope, it requires a tremendous balancing act—never mind publishing a magazine that is exclusively targeted toward women. Sometimes you encounter an extremely valuable article with a potentially strong impact on the readers, one that can all by itself result in greatly positive influence on the society as a whole. I may decide to publish such an article," she says, "even if it results in the closure of the magazine," she says matter-of-factly.

She continues: "There are also times when the costs of publishing a piece outweigh its benefits, and can cause problems for a magazine that has been around for ten years and may even survive for another ten. In this case we decide not to publish such an article."

Near the end of our talk we discuss the coming elections, and Sherkat turns the tables. She's been pretty sober up to this point, but she gets a playful crinkle around her eyes and asks me, "Which of our two countries do you think will have the first woman president?"

I know she's challenging the presumption that the United States is more liberal on women's issues. And it's true that although Shirley Chisholm and Geraldine Ferraro and Hillary Clinton come to mind, it does feel implausible that the United States will have a woman president anytime soon.

"Forty-six women are candidates for this term of the presidency. We have an article about it," she says, handing me an issue still hot from the presses.

Who knows. Maybe Iran, like Pakistan (Benazir Bhutto) and India (Indira Gandhi) and New Zealand (Helen Clark), will be led by a woman before the United States is.

On the way out, walking past the young women who work for Sherkat, I don't focus on their gray and black chadors as I did when I came in; instead I notice the subtle sheen of pink on the lips of the graphic designer, and the researcher's lavender toenails.

It would be six months after we left Iran before Sherkat's appeal was settled and her prison sentence for publicly challenging *hejab* was commuted. The fine still stood. The mullahs got the money. *Zanan* is still publishing.

The next day Maryam continues our education in the boundaries of *hejab* by taking us to a "happening" coffee shop in northern Tehran. We linger around a cascade of outdoor decks vibrant with young women and men sipping café glacé and making eyes at one another, just like in any mall-of-youth in the world. Sixty-five percent of Iran's population is under twenty-five—which means an entire generation has come of age since the revolution. Like twenty-somethings the world over, members of that generation are interested in defining their own lives morally and politically. The decks are surrounded by trendy stores featuring high-ticket Western items and designer knockoffs. This is tony Tehran and we are among the Westernized elite, who find the clerics' dress code oppressive and push its boundaries. Only one woman here seems to be honoring the most modest interpretation of *hejab*. She is a lone woman, with a baby, and is wearing a black chador. She stands out as not fitting in.

"Capri pants visible at two o'clock," I stage-whisper to Orlando, our cameraman, so he can film a daring, tall brunette with glistening peach lipstick, toeless sandals, and painted toenails. "And check out that ingenue." I nod toward a twenty-year-old with a fiery red veil perched five inches back on her head. "How does she manage that?"

"Bobby pins," says Julie.

Personal acts of defiance, such as wearing makeup, revealing an ankle, letting bangs tousle out from underneath a carefully positioned scarf-cum-veil, give a pretty clear indication what these woman think of living under sharia as interpreted by *them*—the mullahs. Despite it being against the law, Iranian women wear a lot of makeup, much more than American women do. I love this beauty revolution. "How do they get away with this?" I ask Persheng.

"They don't, always," she responds. "I have a friend who went too far when she was camping up in the Alborz. She was caught with her veil off and sentenced to flogging. Seventy lashes. Luckily, she was able to buy them off and get a more lenient flogger who wouldn't hit so hard."

Legislating women's powerlessness (via, in part, a dress code that makes them invisible) seems to be the centerpiece of the theocratic leaders' struggle to maintain their own power. From Saudi Arabia to Afghanistan to Turkey, the degree of political freedom a population experiences in general is directly expressed in the degree of control over women. But this is certainly not a tactic limited to Islamic societies. Tightening the reins on women and overall political freedom happens whenever fundamentalism lurks. Case in point: the Bush administration's agenda to limit civil liberties (the Patriot Act) and revoke a woman's right to choose.

"You guys are obsessed with the veil," Maryam sighs. She shakes her head and finishes her *qahvé Turk* as we shoot through a second tape at the coffee shop.

"You're obsessed too much with it," she says, waving her hand. "It's finished. The deal is *finished*. I mean, it's more than twenty years now."

"Would you wear the veil if you didn't have to?" I ask.

"Of course not," she says, looking at me as if I am a confused simpleton. "Would I wear it? What a thing to ask."

While Maryam would not choose to veil, many Iranian women would for a variety of reasons: to honor the Qur'an's code of modesty, to avoid harassment from men and keep from being overly sexualized, to keep the sun off.

Maryam is right that the veil is just a scarf, a piece of clothing worn throughout the Muslim world and beyond. Obsessing about it instead of, say, the repressive marriage and family laws of Iran, may seem misguided. But in making the veil mandatory, as Iran's theocracy has done, the veil becomes a powerful and institutionalized symbol of oppression. And for better or worse, TV is a visual medium, and the veil is a powerful image. So I toss Orlando a third tape.

Resistance to the mullahs' monoculture is not limited to the big cities or urban sophisticates. Jeannie came back from the scout trip with a story of a folk painter and rice farmer named Mokarrameh Ghanbari. Ghanbari, she told us, was challenging Islamic art taboos in a way that had made her a sensation in the tiny village of Darikandeh, on the Caspian plains. We leave behind the haze and head for the hills to meet her.

We drive through the Alborz Mountains, passing the highest peak in Iran, the 18,300-foot volcanic Mount Demavand, which has been muse to hundreds of Persian poets. The Caspian plains are the heartland of Iranian agriculture and run the length of the country's northern border, stretching between the Alborz and the Caspian Sea.

Julie and I are used to being in production overdrive and assumed we'd make it to the Caspian in five hours. (That is, unless our tires melt in the outrageous heat.) But every hour or so our Iranian team pulled home-field rank and stopped for tea and pistachio breaks at one or another of the open-air roadside eateries with thatched roofs. When it comes to road trips, the Persians' three-thousand-year-old culture becomes apparent. Very civilized. We Westerners had to curb our eat-and-run ways. And we Westerners were outnumbered four to three.

The road through the Alborz, like most that breach mountain ranges, follows one stream up to the divide and another back down to the plain. Along the way we pass a huge dam. "My father oversaw the electrical production of that dam," says Persheng. Persheng's parents now live in Manhattan. The Iranian diaspora, like the Cuban, is largely made up of the country's well-off and educated who chose to (and were able to) leave.

The descent out of the Alborz is much steeper and curved, and the trucks, fueled with cheap gas and testosterone, play chicken on the two-lane highway. I secretly thank Allah for the alcohol ban. Because the Caspian fog creeps up these canyons, they are more lush than those of the ascent, and the steep downgrade makes the views more spectacular. Despite the occasional spike of adrenaline through my body, I begin to relax. "A fast-moving car is the only place where you're legally allowed to not deal with your problems," says Douglas Coupland, extolling the virtues of road trips. And, I'd add, in Iran, a fast-moving car in the mountains, away from the watchful eyes of the morals police, is one of the few places you can let your scarf slide back enough to allow a bit of fresh wind to cool the scalp.

Julie and I slouch in the backseat of our van, doing just that, trying not to let our Iranian crew see us. I notice some pink silky fabric hanging out from under Julie's dark gray manteau. "Are you wearing your pajamas?"

"Yeah. It was the coolest thing I had. It's like having to wear a coat and hat in Manhattan in August. Hotter than hell here," she replies, flashing me her pajama hemline. We giggle like girls who've just talked their way out of gym class.

The Caspian plain is created by countless streams that run from the mountains to the sea, in many parts creating the perfect conditions for growing rice. "The best rice in the world is grown here," says Persheng. "When Iranians want cheap rice they buy the stuff imported from California."

During the Clinton administration, Secretary of State Madeleine Albright lifted the trade embargo with Iran for limited items: rugs, pistachios, and caviar. Ahh, the power of luxury goods. The way that American companies get around the embargo, and sell rice to Iran, for example, is that the U.S. parent companies do not directly participate in the trade; foreign subsidiaries take all responsibility and U.S. companies simply take a piece of the profit. Coke, Jergens, Halliburton all do this.

We reach Nowshahr, a scenic town on the shores of the Caspian in the same province as Mokarrameh's village.

"You can feel the sea before you see it," Jeannie had told me of the Caspian during the passing of the baton back in Seattle. "It's humid, not like the desert air of Tehran. And the orange blossoms," she swooned, "reminded me of California when I was a kid."

When we pulled up along the sparkling, blue-gray Caspian, I see chunky, brightly colored wooden fishing boats playfully galloping out to meet the sturgeon. The rocky shore is lined with many men, but I zero in on the handful of women pumping their shoulders underneath floral patterned chadors, casting out lines from thick twelve-foot rods. I suck in what feels to be the greater freedom offered by the Caspian region, though I know that this freedom is partly illusory. While we had slipped away from the watchful eye of the largely Tehran-based theocracy, Iranian rural areas can be hotbeds of conservatism and religious fundamentalism.

When we find Darikandeh, it isn't hard to pick out Mokarrameh Ghanbari's home once we get within eyeshot. Her tall metal front gate is painted with friendly, blue and white toy soldiers wielding big guns.

She is dressed in a white veil and a black sweater that hangs over a patterned red skirt and she greets me at the front door with a lip rub on each cheek. She's five feet tall, seventy-six years old; small and roundish in that layered, peasant way.

"Salam, khosh aamadid." Mokarrameh greets me, grasping both my hands in hers. *"Madaret kojast?"* ("Is your mother with you?") she asks, remembering Jeannie's earlier visit.

We step into Mokarrameh's house, and in one glance I take in more color and joy than I've seen in an entire week. Bright blood-red and jet-black Persian rugs cover the entire floor of her living space and the walls are covered, floor to ceiling, with paintings, many of women swathed in cheerful fuchsia and greens and yellows. A grown-up playhouse. This exuberance and personal flair is a strikingly different Iran from that found in the public hotels, offices, and street corners we've experienced so far.

Mokarrameh shuttles around her living room, leading us from one painting to the next with a bounce. She touches her gray bun of hair, covered by the white veil, with girlish nervousness and frequency.

Mokarrameh's painting was born out of a bout with depression. A friend gave her paper and colored pencils to express herself and once she started, she couldn't stop. Later, her son gave her paints, and today he is still her supplier. Initially the walls of her home were her canvas, and as her depression lifted, she moved onto the doors and windows. Many of her paintings are on the back of discarded wallpaper.

Strict Islam forbids the use of the human figure in religious images (only Allah creates) and discourages figurative sculpting or painting. Mokarrameh has had visits from the Komiteh Emdad (revolutionary guards) because of her work, which includes shapely ladies with skin showing. I am especially drawn to a vibrant painting of a slightly busty mermaidlike figure in a gold, sparkly gown, but even it is benign by American standards. One wonders if the rumor of an old village woman painting—a class- and gender-defying act—brought the authorities to see her as much as the "heretic" nature of her work did.

As we speak it becomes clear that nothing was going to keep Mokarrameh from doing her art: neither her lack of formal education, nor the revolutionary guards.

"I didn't go to school and I am not literate," Mokarrameh tells me, "so I do not know enough, and I only look at a few pages of Qur'an as an inspiration, but I cannot really read Qur'an. I don't lie. I don't think Islam says that drawing shouldn't be done. I don't think there is anything wrong with it," she says in respectful defense of her passion.

"I started painting at sixty-four. For four years I would only paint at night. If I had an unexpected visitor, I would hide everything very quickly. If they saw the paint on my hands, I would try to pretend that it was nothing and hide my hands and change the subject!" she says with a giggle, hiding her small, thick hands under her thighs.

Every painting has a backstory and she is eager to tell them all. Mokarrameh shows us a leggy woman in a bejeweled dress beside a handsome dark-skinned man. "The man and woman are lovers and now they are going to marry, even though the bride's father disapproves," she narrates.

"But now he gave in," she says of the father, with a note of triumph, as if she both created and changed a bit of history through her painting.

When Mokarrameh began painting, just about everyone in the village was against it, as much out of fear of the unknown as out of religious conviction.

"Now it is different. For the past two or three years, I have been painting freely. I can leave the doors open and paint in freedom and nobody considers it strange anymore," she says earnestly, her arms and chin swinging up and to the right in a gesture of victory.

"I have had some people and guests coming from other cities and they ask me, 'Don't you get scared at night with all of these strange paintings around you?' and I say, 'No,' and they say, 'You're lying,' and I say, 'No, I swear. God created humans, is he scared of his people? And I have created these paintings and I am not afraid of them.' " Mokarrameh's paintings aren't strange or scary, so my only guess is that the "fear" question comes from others' perceptions of how odd and forbidden it must be to be surrounded by human images of one's own making. Like Keri Hulme and her blue people, Mokarrameh (though I suspect she'd hardly look at it this way) is also "playing God" by creating her own universe and peopling it.

While we are talking, a neighbor stops by, clutching a chicken by its feet. Its red head dangles, and its unhappy clucks are muffled by the thick cloth of the woman's black chador. Mokarrameh takes the chicken and hands the neighbor a painting. These days most of Mokarrameh's neighbors have her paintings, as gifts or currency. Seems the local community has acclimated to the painter next door.

"Painting isn't all I've done," Mokarrameh tells me. "I was a seamstress for ten years, and I started when I was fourteen. I did the makeup for the local brides for fifteen years. I have delivered many children—at least twenty-five of them. I was a chiropractor and fixed a lot of bones and limbs."

I look toward Persheng in hopes of getting her to explain Mokarrameh's chiropractic skills. Turns out she practiced the "old way" of setting broken bones and fixing sprains, learned only by experience, rather than med school, and from information passed from one healer to the next. There are always people in villages who are believed to have a unique "touch," or healing power in their hands. Apparently, Mokarrameh is one of them.

Mokarrameh's son has joined us for the day, in part to help translate. He translates from Mazandarani, which is a local dialect spoken in the northern parts of Iran, into Farsi for Persheng, who then translates into English for us. This son is one of nine children, and because he is single, he is the most involved with Mokarrameh's day-to-day life. He supports her artistic endeavors, but not without some occasional reservations.

"One night," Mokarrameh tells me, "he walked in as I was painting and asked me, 'Mother, what are you painting?' I said that it was Adam and Eve." She walks me over to a three-by-eight-foot painting of the famous couple.

Only tiny leaves delicately cover their genitalia.

"He said, 'Why would you paint a member of the human family naked?' "

"I told him when God created us we were all naked!—and then my son didn't talk to me for ten days. The revolutionary guards also questioned me about the painting. I was so angry with my son," she says with a mischievous little smile, "that I painted two more naked Adam and Eves! . . . But he's okay with it now," she concludes, nodding toward her son, who smiles a bit sheepishly and shrugs. I wonder if he ever regrets giving her those paints.

Mokarrameh takes my hand and walks me over to a huge painting that dominates one of her walls, which she describes as a family portrait. It depicts a large round wooden table, around which are seated a dozen of her family and friends, there to celebrate a wedding. She starts to explain who is depicted.

"This is Manoochehr, Mr. Jon, Mr. Haj, Monir, Mahastee, she is my *havoo*."

"Your what?" I ask.

"My *havoo* is the one sitting on the bottom."

A *havoo* is a woman's husband's other wife, Persheng explains. In Islam polygamy is still legal on the condition that the man treat all of his wives equally and be able to support them. Mokarrameh's husband had three wives and apparently treated them all equally badly.

"I had two *havoos* but I really liked my older *havoo*. The middle one has died."

"I can't tell you everything now because you're filming," she whispers conspiratorially. "But in the old days—it wasn't like today, people having boyfriends and girlfriends. They used to marry you and take you off by force. My husband was a *kadkhoda* [a very powerful leader of a land or village]. He liked me very much but I didn't want to marry, and after one whole year they married me by force," she says matter-of-factly.

"Is your husband in the painting?" I ask, wondering what a *kadkhoda* looks like.

"I didn't want him to be in there. That is where he was," Mokarrameh says with a small smile, pointing to an empty gray smudged spot between images of two of her sons, "but I whited him out."*

All the way back to Tehran, Julie is curled up, battling one of the migraines she endures every few years. The loose cloth layers of her charcoal-colored manteau are squinched around her body. She looks like a sad, gray ball. Tiny groans occasionally breach the folds.

---

* Mokarrameh Ghanbari passed away in October 2005.

"The Caspian is famous for bringing on migraines," says Maryam sympathetically. "It's the light. And the barometric pressure created when the moist ocean air hits the mountain air."

The only stops we make are for Julie. Along the roadside, I hold back her veil, and a few layers of material, so she can barf unobstructed. Truckers toot their horns. We make it back in a record five hours. At the hotel, Julie pulls the red velour curtains, collapses into bed, and holes up in her dark room for twenty-four hours. "I am so sorry, Holly," she says through her pain, which is made worse by feeling that she is not doing her job.

"Julie, don't be ridiculous. I spent two days unconscious in India, remember? It happens. We all go down now and then."

"Did you see . . . see that woman. In the Caspian. Black chador, with the baby. She was at the coffeehouse too," Julie says, quietly and gravelly from under the covers.

"What?" I say, wondering if she's a bit delirious with pain.

But she's fallen asleep, having succumbed to the migraine pills.

I leave three bottles of water at her bedside, and ask the man at the front desk to check in on her every few hours. His eyebrows rise with concern.

"She'll cover up before you go in. Don't worry," I say.

Orlando, Persheng, Maryam, and I drive across Tehran to Al-Zahra University, a women's college, to talk to the chancellor, Dr. Zahra Rahnavard. I wanted to meet an insider who could explain how theocracy could coexist with the kind of self-expression I'd seen in women like Shahla Sherkat and Mokarrameh Ghanbari.

Dr. Rahnavard is an academic and a sculptor, and was one of President Khatami's trusted advisers. "This interview is a big deal," says Persheng. "She's close to Khatami, but she's also one of the most respected intellectuals in government right now. And she must have written a dozen books. She's very establishment and religious, but she agitates for reform in her own way, I guess."

Dr. Rahnavard's office is large and filled with windows and chadored assistants scuttling about. Her small sculptures pepper the room and I notice that none of them is a human figure. She stands behind an intimidating large wooden desk, the top covered with glass (all fitting for her academic and intellectual stripes), and greets us. "Welcome, it is a pleasure to meet you," she says in English, although she will choose to do the interview in Farsi so she will be more fully able to express herself. I wonder, though, if, like Castro, she declines to speak English as a matter of principle. Shan't speak the language of Mr. Imperialist is Castro's position.

It is hard to imagine that this formal woman dressed in a conservative black chador was a political rabble-rouser said to have worn miniskirts before the revolution. (Then again, I once wore a cheerleading outfit; we all change.) There was some initial disagreement within our (secular) crew about whether or not we should interview Dr. Rahnavard. While faith seems to be a part of the fabric of many, if not most, people's lives here in Iran, being religious and actively intertwining religion with politics is an ideological stand that is discomforting to some. (Of course this intertwining happens in places like the United States—come on, John Ashcroft!—and Ireland too, although in those countries it is more informal and less institutionalized.) Like Shahla Sherkat, Dr. Rahnavard participated in overthrowing the shah's regime, but unlike Sherkat, Rahnavard is now working within the theocratic government, albeit as a reformer. Despite the debate among the crew, in the end it seemed important to hear from an establishment diva—a self-described devout Muslim and feminist who might offer us a greater understanding of Iran's intersection of religion, government, and, in Rahnavard's case, art.

"How do you negotiate being an artist and a politician at the same time?" I ask Dr. Rahnavard.

"In the name of God, the compassionate, the merciful," she starts, a preamble that alarms me, but that is not uncommon in Iran.

"If you are asking, 'How can a president's political adviser be an artist?' This in itself reveals that, in reality, the reformist politics are based on cultural and artistic aspects. And the wave of reform that has begun sweeping over our country in answer to our people's needs for more liberty and democracy—of course within the boundaries of religious teachings—these reforms have a cultural aspect to them, and because of my artistic character, I can approach politics in a more poetic and free way."

So, Dr. Rahnavard believes art, democracy, and Islam can thrive in peaceful coexistence, and as an artist herself, she feels she can bring them together.

Dr. Rahnavard has worked to reform the system from within, in several different ways. Her best-known reformist stance is her belief that women should be able to wear bright-colored *hejab*. Sanctioning bright colors in Iran is the equivalent of issuing a nose-ring mandate at home. I ask her if she thinks we in the West misinterpret *hejab*.

"I think that the West's understanding of *hejab* has not been correct. *Hejab* is an Islamic requirement and not something that the Iranian government has introduced. It is written in the Qur'an and observed in the whole world of Islam. I believe that the interpretation of religion and Islam that exists in Iran is one of the most interesting and intellectual interpretations in the world of Islam regarding women and religion."

Well. There is debate about *hejab* being an Islamic requirement. Apparently there are only two places in the Qur'an that suggest such modesty, both oblique and open to interpretation. And Dr. Rahnavard 's argument seems to sidestep the fact that while veiling may be a historical tenet of Islam, the government's enforcement of it by law (that if broken lands you in jail and gets you flogged) makes it political.

But Dr. Rahnavard is an expert, a consummate politician, and the author of several books on the subject of *hejab*. I feel a bit of a political dilettante in the face of a powerhouse, so, after briefly considering challenging her assertions, I prudently decide this is a time for active listening. One thing is for sure, the story of women and Islam in Iran is endlessly fascinating and clearly evolving. And players such as Dr. Rahnavard—people who bridge the clerical and secular worlds—might just be at the crest of the next wave of change.

"What is the biggest risk you have taken?"

"One of the biggest risks I have taken has been entering the world of religion because I chose it myself and it was not practiced in my family. When I entered this world, I felt that I had entered a beautiful and superior world. I was criticized a lot by my family and friends but I insisted on following the beautiful Islamic beliefs that I had gotten to know."

I don't get even a hint of that creepy cult vibe I often get when people are extolling their religious devotion.

"But I must say when we talk about religious beliefs in our country, there are at least two different kinds of beliefs: One is of the extremely backward conservative traditionalists and the other, of innovators that have an intellectual understanding of religion. My religious beliefs are of an intellectual nature because I have observed freedom, beauty, and art in religion. I believe that an ideal democracy can exist in religion if we approach it correctly," she says with calm confidence.

"What do you mean?" I ask.

"Religion can only be in harmony with democracy when we accept that it rises from the heart of the people. When it rises from the heart and holds love in it, everything will naturally start and end with the people. The important thing is that governments leave people free in choosing religions of their own will. If it is forced, then they will not succeed."

Love? Freedom of religious choice? Democracy? This is a kind of Islamic thinking we don't hear enough about in the popular press. But what Dr. Rahnavard describes is hard to understand for a West that sees Islam only in monolithic religious terms, rather than as integral to the traditions, culture, and everyday life of much of the world.

That Dr. Rahnavard changed from secular to religious after the revolution, and took this stand against her family's wishes, is fascinating. Maybe she was influenced, like many of her generation, by the writings of philosopher Ali Shariah, who proposed Islamic behavior as an antidote to mindless Western copycatting. In any case, something happened to her spiritually between the miniskirt and the chador. Perhaps she decided that in order to make change, she needed to do it from within the establishment. Perhaps her religious conversion made her able and willing to operate within the theocracy. One thing is clear: Despite her conservative *hejab* and formal manner, Dr. Rahnavard's position on the relaxing of *hejab* is radical, given her establishment status. I wish we could have had dinner at her home, or gone to her personal art studio, rather than talk with her in this office. Public guardedness and political savvy are necessarily a way of life here. Getting behind closed doors helps tell a fuller story, but that's pretty difficult, with a camera, in Iran.

Or in D.C. for that matter.

Dr. Rahnavard leaves for her next appointment, and we stay a few minutes longer so Orlando can shoot b-roll of some of her small sculptures in her office. I notice a lone business card under the plate of glass that covers Dr. Rahnavard's wooden desktop. I walk over to see who gets this coveted position, then nudge Orlando to zoom in: It is the business card of the *New York Times* bureau chief in Iran. I show it to Persheng. "Politicians are politicians," she says, "and for some here, chadors are power suits."

The next day we pile into our white van, which Vresh has waiting for us outside our hotel. Armed with a pound of pistachios and nine lukewarm orange sodas, we are happy to leave the congestion of the city behind and be road-tripping to the city of Shiraz to meet some entrepreneurial lady cabdrivers. On our way we stop at the tomb of his holiness, the mausoleum of Ayatollah Khomeini, which is forty-five minutes outside of Tehran.

The mausoleum suddenly rises like a mirage out of the flat, arid landscape, as if insisting that it *must exist.* I will be here, dammit, the structure seems to say.

The mausoleum has been a work in progress for ten years and although still unfinished, it already looks past its prime. Many consider it an eyesore and not in the tradition of the beautifully crafted mosques of Iran. We pull into a parking lot and the whole scene reminds me of a Six Flags amusement park—a giant complex grossly bowing under the weight of its own ideology. But, unlike Six Flags, here there are no trolleys to take us to the front gate, so we have to lug our equipment a quarter mile.

Maryam and Persheng have the honor of doing battle with officials who do not want us to film inside. The rest of us pass through metal detectors and are quickly pulled aside by a posse of black-chadored women who hustle us behind private curtains for a very thorough once-over. Having been in production for months on end, always battling exhaustion, having given up a personal life, this frisk by dexterous women in black—up, down, around, exploring folds and nooks and crannies—is by far my most intimate moment in many, many months. They don't coddle you with "I'm going to touch your calf now, okay?" rhetoric, like American airport security. These very serious women pat and search with gusto, and with the erotic bar as low as it is, I relax and quite enjoy the moment.

"Where's Holly?" I hear Orlando ask Julie on the other side of the curtain.

"I don't know, she went behind the curtain about five minutes ago. Maybe they're working over her gear."

The atmosphere inside Khomeini's mausoleum is part mosque, part picnic, part memorial. Women tend children and pray on the left side of the large room; men are aligned on the right, facing Mecca and prostrating themselves. In the back and on the edges children play, women chat, and men gossip. A lone old man sings a loud, elegiac tune to nobody in particular. A few men sleep in the far back. Scores of people cluster at a room-size glass cage at the fore of the vast interior of the building, which holds the tomb of Khomeini. The glass chamber, surrounded by a fence, emits an eerie green glow and mourners in black look at his closed sarcophagus, praying and wailing and clinging to the fence. Offerings of Iranian bills are pressed with a prayer through the links in the fence.

There were ten million people at Khomeini's funeral in 1989. I remember television images of the crushing crowds that stopped the progress of the hearse. I also remember how creepy it was when people ripped off pieces of the shroud, hoping for a holy relic.

The mausoleum is a place of pilgrimage and deep feelings, especially, it seems, to the formerly disenfranchised who gained access to power for the first time after the revolution. (A similar power shift happened in Cuba after its revolution.) But for the most part, it seems the Khomeini cult is a fading minority. An old woman comes up to us and sings the praises of Khomeini, but after the initial pitch, she realizes we are not a government television crew and starts to complain about her dire conditions and difficulty making ends meet. Persheng gives her a thousand tomans and she goes away. I can't help thinking that the millions of dollars being pumped into this shrine might be better spent in this country where half the population lives in poverty.

I walk outside to meet the rest of the crew. The Middle Eastern sun beats down on Sky Dancer, who is perched on the hood of a car. Julie is using the Flexfill (a silver disk used to reflect light on interviewees) to bounce a glow onto her pink cheeks, and Orlando is taking still pictures.

"That's it, Sky darling, show us some sass," he says in pitch-perfect British lech.

It is a slightly perverse scene to be taking place here. We are honoring a leggy, buxom, six-inch American doll with big, unveiled, blue hair. In Texas, "the bigger the hair the closer to God" might hold true, but not in the Islamic Republic of Iran. "You know, the shah's granddaughter was a Dallas Cowboy cheerleader," I say to Julie as she repositions the Flexfill.

"Nooo!" she responds.

"Yeah, swear," I say. "She could get three months in jail for that cheerleading outfit here."

I glance two auto rows over and see the woman with the baby from the coffeehouse in Tehran, sitting in a car. A surge of adrenaline zips up my spine. "Julie," I say, nodding toward the car. Julie's eyes widen. "I *knew* we were being followed," she whispers. Persheng scans the parking lot suspiciously and her eyes stop on the woman. "Yeah, I saw her when we were leaving Dr. Rahnavard. We've got a minder. Let's get out of here. Now."

We cover up Sky Dancer and continue south to Shiraz, a city once famous for its wine, which is now only drunk behind closed doors. Thankfully, somebody transplanted the Shiraz grape to Australia, where it flourishes.

We are not going to Shiraz to taste wine, but to visit the Ladies of Paradise cab company, run by demi-diva Zahra Moussavi, an entrepreneurial taxi magnate. The Ladies of Paradise cab company grew out of a transportation need for women and female students who were not allowed to ride alone with male drivers or were not comfortable doing so. We pull up outside the Ladies of Paradise office in Shiraz and see two covered heads bent under the hoods of cabs, cranking on things with white-gloved hands that stand in contrast to their black chadors. One of the people with her head under a hood is Zahra Moussavi.

"I started with five drivers two years ago, now I have thirty," says Zahra, a lively woman with a quick smile, dressed in a conservative chador. She walks us to meet her staff at HQ. In a small room we find seven high-spirited ladies, all dressed in black except for the white gloves, sitting around the dispatcher's radio and talking to one another.

"What's your favorite part of this job?" I ask the group with the help of Maryam's translation.

"That we can drive fast and take the ladies where they want to go!" says one woman, smiling. All heads nod in agreement.

"In America there are a lot of bad jokes about women drivers. Is that the case here?" I ask.

The women don't get my gist, so Zahra explains to them. "You know, like when they say, 'Don't forget the brake is in the middle . . . and the gas is in the kitchen!' " All the women laugh, and a few white gloves slap black-clad thighs.

Zahra offers to drive us an hour out to the twenty-five-hundred-year-old ruins of Persepolis, which is one of the seven modern wonders of the world and offers a symbolic representation of Iran's regal past. Orlando, Maryam, and I gladly accept and hop into her Peykan. Along the way Zahra explains that while she is the boss and founded the company, she still had to get her husband's written consent before she could start the business. While it is common for women to drive in Iran (unlike in Saudi Arabia, for example where it is illegal), it *is* highly unusual for a woman to own a cab company. Then again, it's unusual for a woman to run a cab company anywhere in the world.

I admire her entrepreneurial spirit, which is not unlike that of Islam's top prophet, Muhammad, who was a merchant. Zahra is in good company, sharing both capitalist and spiritual savvy with Muhammad, who scholars say was sympathetic toward women and forwarded ideas like banning female infanticide and granting inheritance rights to women. Indeed, before he was a full-time prophet, Muhammad worked for his wife Khadijah, who was fifteen years his senior, and he is said to have adored her. (He never took a second wife until after Khadijah's death, at which point he took several.) Over time, scholars say, Muhammad's concepts have been perverted by law and government. Makes sense. Certainly Khadijah didn't have to get her husband's permission to start *her* business.

"This is the entrance for this palace that was built for the first time by Darius the First," Zahra tells me. "We bring many passengers here," she says as we pull up to Persepolis and park in an empty gravel lot. "The palace was built from stone by hand and it took them many years using hammers and chisels."

Persepolis was once a magnificent complex of palaces that was the summer capital first for Darius, and subsequently for a number of other kings. Even though a fraction of the original city remains, these ruins are much more impressive than any others I've seen. "Puts the Acropolis to shame," says Orlando, as he pans across a bas-relief of a lion devouring a bull. Giant pillars lunge toward the sky and are capped, seventy-five feet up, with intricate sculptures. Slabs of the rocky mountainside are cut away for huge terraces. An ornate staircase once led to the royal apartments, which had two official entrances and one secret doorway that opened into the harem. Only thirteen of the original seventy-two pillars still exist, but Persepolis is still awesome.

I realize how much I have been fixating on the "cold, impenetrable" images of the Islamic Republic back in modern Tehran and everywhere in the media: the looming clerics looking down from billboards, the silhouetted signs commanding the exercise of "good *hejab*." But here, in Persepolis, I see Iran as

Persia—a rich, pastiched culture originally made up of tribes of people from northwest Asia who settled here three thousand years ago. Together these tribes started what became the Persian Empire.

Persepolis was largely destroyed around 330 B.C.E., when Alexander the Great first pillaged and then burned it down over the course of eight years. In recent decades these ancient ruins have created a quandary for ruling clerics because they represent a pre-Islamic imperial past that the theocracy has not been keen to embrace. Nonetheless, with a small but budding Iranian tourism industry, Persepolis has become a source of much-needed income.

Persepolis is in austere silhouette by the time we leave and drive back to Shiraz. Zahra tells us she ends most of her days at the mosque. "You can join me, but," she says, not unkindly, her eyes cast down toward our feet, "we must stop somewhere first." She stops the Peykan at a store and runs in. Two minutes later she returns and hands me a pair of socks. While we (as Westerners) can get away with bare feet in sandals (though it is technically illegal) in Iran, bare feet are neither acceptable nor respectful in a mosque. Before we enter the mosque Zahra cinches up my scarf, extra tight, and pulls it down my forehead, making absolutely sure not a single strand of hair is showing.

I follow Zahra into the mosque's walled, stone-floored courtyard, which is brightly lit on this dark, moonless night. Women on the left, men on the right, separated by a curtain, which ever so slightly flutters in the evening breeze, allowing worshippers, should they so choose, to take tiny glimpses into each other's domain. I follow Zahra into the left side, the women's side, with the camera and fall back as I've always done when it is time for communion in church.

A constant, incantatory prayer accompanies the scene: *Allaho akbar.* (God is great.) And then in lower tones: *Besmellah rahmane. Alhamdollallah rab'el alamin.* (In the name of the compassionate God, the God of all worlds.)

Halfway through the prayers I notice Zahra stand and begin to make her way through the lines of women who are tapping the crowns of their covered heads, not in unison, but with a common spiritual undulation, toward Mecca. As the line of heads rises, Zahra scuttles down the aisle sliding business cards onto the ground in front of them. And as the heads bow, they do so right onto THE LADIES OF PARADISE. Target marketing, Muslim style.

"Are you networking at mosque?" I whisper to Zahra, slightly incredulous.

"Yes," she smiles, and tilts her head with a laugh.

Allaho akbar. Besmellah rahmane. Alhamdollallah rab'el alamin.

The Persian sun beats through the white eyelet curtains that cover the windows of the hotel restaurant back in Tehran two days later. It is a May afternoon, ninety-eight degrees, and we are having lunch: chicken kabobs and orange sodas all around. "Chestnuts Roasting on an Open Fire" croons over the hotel sound system.

"Any luck with Operation Beauty?" I ask Persheng, who has been trying all week to get us permission to film in a beauty parlor.

"It's very difficult," Persheng explains to me, "no headscarfs means no cameras." Beauty parlors are one of the few public spaces where women can be unveiled.

"I called the parlor that I've been going to since I was a teenager. She's supposed to call me back tonight. We'll see," adds Maryam.

Wherever I travel I try to spend a bit of time at the beauty parlor as I find that it is a hotbed of frank information and, here in Iran, it would seem, ground zero for the beauty rebellion. Furthermore, it's a chance to make an entry in my catalog of masochistic beauty regimens the world over. In my youthful, unshaven, Birkenstocked days of yore, I condemned beauty parlors with a Khomeini-like fervor. "Dens of corruption," I might have called them, as the ayatollah called any place espousing Western values. At best, I thought beauty parlors were the realm of The Vain and The Bored. I attributed their nefariousness to the beauty standards pressed on American females (fashion magazines being the worst offenders) that keep them barfing up dinner and hating their bodies.

But times change, and now any sort of orthodoxy tires me out. Now I consider beauty parlors the estrogen-charged answer to the Elks Club.

That night we get the green light from Maryam's beauty parlor connection, but it's going to have to be a top-secret operation.

"She says we can come in the morning, though we have to be discreet," she tells me over the phone. I call Orlando's room. "You've got the morning off. No men allowed in beauty parlors. I'll be right over to get the camera," I say and hang up.

The next day we are staked out around the corner from the beauty parlor in our nondescript white van.

"Cotton," I say to Julie, mopping up the sweat that trickles out from under my polyester veil. "Why didn't Jeannie tell us to bring cotton?"

Our cell phone rings and it is Maryam, who has gone ahead of us into the plain brick building with drawn curtains. On her cue, Julie and I scurry across the street with our equipment hidden under our layers.

We are buzzed through the first giant white metal door and into a bleak off-white foyer reminiscent of 1950s institutional architecture. The first door clanks behind us and locks with a not-very-customer-friendly *thud*.

"So 'Women of Cell Block H,' " I whisper to Julie.

"I know. In the name of God, who knew beauty was criminal?"

Another startling buzz; the sound of a cascade of locks; a second door opens slightly and a set of eyes peers out at us.

We're in.

The shop owner wears a blue smock and pauses from the hot iron to hand us glasses of tea and a plate of cookies. Someone flips on the sound system, and upbeat Persian music fills the parlor. The room is filled with smiles and chatting and not a trace of reserve. As we have discovered repeatedly in Iran, once behind closed doors the famous Iranian hospitality and warmth come forth. The coverings and scarves that draw the line between public and private hang on a row of pegs on the wall.

I start shooting.

"You can only film from the neck down," reminds Maryam, which strikes me as somehow ironic. Customers are poised under stunning 1950s pink egg-shaped hair dryers, finger- and toenails becoming fuchsia and cherry red and purple. Hair is being worked over with a vengeance I haven't seen since the mid-eighties, and even then usually reserved for local TV anchors. A bin of pastel-colored hot rollers flanks every beauty station.

"Why go to all this trouble if you just have to cover up?" I ask Persheng.

"But our faces are not covered, and that explains all the makeup—often heavy makeup—not to mention the nose job craze. And the scarves get pushed back enough to show off the highlights on the hair," Persheng says. The bits that do show become ever more important. And of course, women are often unveiled in private homes.

Manicures, pedicures, and a deep commitment to hair removal animate the parlor's landscape. I walk around shooting b-roll of body creams, hair products, and an impressive range of "muscle massagers," which look suspiciously like mid-century vibrators. Julie is getting the fuzz on her upper lip removed using a Middle Eastern method called threading. A long white cotton string resembling dental floss hangs around the beautician's neck, and the strands cross in front of her chest. The beautician finesses this intersection of the threads, twisting them together at a rapid-fire pace, creating a friction against the face that pulls out the hair.

"Islam," she says with a nod toward her handiwork, meaning "this is how we do it here."

"Look Iranian," I say to Julie as I zoom in on her full-blooded Italian upper lip, which is magically going bald.

"Does it hurt?" I ask, wincing for her.

"Uh-huh," she responds in a slightly higher than usual pitch. "It's like a row of fire ants is mowing its way across my lip."

We go down a metal spiral staircase into a basement full of a dozen gurneys, the ladies on them in varying degrees of repose. The two chatty beauticians in the room go from woman to woman, carrying out procedures with the speed and levity of Trapper and Hawkeye in the M*A*S*H operating room.

"Your turn," Julie says, grabbing the camera. I drop my drawers and climb up. A five-foot-three-inch, kindly, unveiled Iranian woman hugging a small bucket of what looks like gurgling crude oil comes my way. I prepare to be waxed, Persian style. The woman cuts five-by-seven-inch swatches of translucent cellophane-like material, which will affix to the wax. I sense a silent flinch from across the room, and prepare myself as she ladels gobs of hot copper-colored wax onto my legs.

"If you ask a woman in her twenties," Julie says, "what one thing she would want to have if she were stranded on a desert island, the answer is—"

"Yooowww," I screech as my gentle waxer rips out all the hair on my right

inner thigh. I am part Greek; we give the Middle Eastern women a run for their money when it comes to fur.

"Lipstick," says Julie, "and if you ask a woman in her thirties . . ." Julie continues.

"What? What?" I say, clenching for the next sear of pain.

"Tweezers."

Understandably, none of the Iranian women would agree to be filmed getting waxed. Julie and I climb back up the spiral staircase, dazed and hairless, debating the ethics of passing off an American thigh for a Persian thigh in the show. When we emerge from downstairs Persheng tells me that when we send a tape of this show back for the Iranian divas to see, it can't include the waxing sequence. Otherwise it will never get through the censors.

"Oh," Persheng says, tapping her watch, "we've got to get going to meet Pooran," reminding us of our meeting with an Iranian poet and scholar. With that, we throw on our manteaux, cloaking a half-day's worth of hard-earned beauty, and trade beauty politics for poetry.

"Poetry for Iranians is religion, a religion as powerful as Islam," writes Elaine Sciolino in her book *Persian Mirrors.* Even the pious in Islam may have a volume of poetry on their coffee table next to the Qur'an. In Iran, poetry is revered, and poets (especially talented, dead ones) are rock stars. People flock to the graves of poets in Iran the way Americans go to Graceland. We first learned of this phenomenon in Shiraz, when we visited the tomb of the fourteenth-century lyric poet Hafez. Here in Tehran, we'd heard people, especially women, go to the grave of Forough Farrokhzad.

Forough has come to represent the creative, rebellious, self-determined life and is an icon for many Iranian women. Imagine a cross between James Dean, Sylvia Plath, and Eve Ensler. Her legendary status grew when in 1967 she was killed in a car crash at age thirty-two. We will visit Forough's grave, but first we will go see her sister Pooran, who's less well known than Forough (except among intellectuals), but is reportedly just as independent-minded.

We arrive at Pooran's house in central Tehran, carry our equipment through a fenced-in garden, and buzz the door. Pooran is portly, with abundant brown hair pulled back into a bun, and she wears a long dark gown. Her face has loads of sparkle and a paradoxical heaviness. In addition to being a writer and editor, Pooran is the keeper of her sister's flame. Pooran immediately warms to us. ("I like Americans," she would tell me later, "they are simple.")

She leads us to a comfortable couch and we drink coffee and chat as Orlando sets up the camera. Pooran's house is Westernized, like many in Tehran, in a style circa 1952.

The inscription at the front of Hafez's tomb in Shiraz said that "the grave of a poet is a place where you can smell love." So I dive right into the love thing. "As a scholar, and the sister of a beloved poet known for her sensual writing, you must have some insight about the Iranian approach to love." Pooran responds without hesitation (and Persheng translates).

"In general all Iranians are in love, in other words, *hot-blooded*. The reason is the sun that shines directly over Iran. And when the sun shines so strongly the cells move more rapidly. And when they move more rapidly, love is more passionate," Pooran explains emphatically, with her soul, as much as her voice and hands. And here I've been complaining about the heat. "And when love is more passionate, it gives rise to poetry."

"In reality most Iranians are poets," Pooran continues. "Even those street peddlers who during my childhood sold beets and ice cream, their chants were rhythmic and they spoke with poetry. If you pay attention you can see that Iranians can come up with poems instantly and the reason for it is love that is inside them."

"Your last book is about poetry, isn't it?" I ask.

"Yes, it is about the path of poetry by women from the fourth century [the tenth century A.D.*] until my sister Forough. I have studied how women poets lived, because the male-dominated society did not allow women to speak at all so the women were forced to live behind closed doors and would compose poetry. The fact is, we only had around four hundred women from the fourth century until Forough who were able to write poetry but, because women had no identity, most of them wrote the poetry from the words and perspective of a man. Women had not yet gained their historical identity so they did not have the audacity and bravery to write poetry in their own words," she explains.

"And where does your sister fit within the canon?" I ask.

* Iran follows the Islamic calendar, which starts with the birth of Muhammad in 570 on the Christian calendar.

"My sister Forough in reality started a new school of thought, meaning that for the first time in Iran she wrote from a woman's perspective. Forough speaks plainly and simply and is frank and sincere. She is brave and candid."

Forough is widely regarded as a charismatic genius, an artist answerable to her own ethic. She urged her sisters to rise up and "uproot the roots of oppression," and she made some unconventional personal choices, including divorcing her husband and giving their son to his father so that she could pursue her poetry. She shed light on the oppressions endured by Iranian women, and urged them to take action to change their situation. Forough's poetry was banned for years for its sensuality. Case in point, an excerpt from her poem "Another Birth":

> *Life is perhaps lighting up a cigarette*
> *in the narcotic repose between two love-makings*
> *or the absent gaze of a passerby*
> *with a meaningless smile and a good morning.*

Pooran smooths the lap of her black gown and goes on to explain the culture in which her sister created. "Eastern people—not just Iranians, but Easterners in general—always live under a kind of mask. They never show their true selves, but rather, like an onion with many layers," she says, miming the act of peeling, "you have to keep peeling away layer after layer to uncover the real person. Forough was just herself; there are no skins."

All that Pooran is saying jibes with the experience we have had here. The onion explains a lot, actually. For example, Americans hear that Middle Easterners "lie," but it's more like they tell you what they think you want to hear. It almost falls into the category of a courtesy. But this is a communication dance that plain-spoken Puritan-bred Americans have a hard time following. The reason Pooran likes "simple" Americans is that no onion peeling is necessary.

"What do you think are some of the myths about the East that the West has?" I ask, noting that Pooran, like her sister, communicates with unusual directness for an Iranian.

"When people from the West come to interview me I've realized that they look at us from a different perspective, as if they have come to visit a woman from a thousand years ago. This is not the case at all. We have certain rules here, and naturally owing to our upbringing we have learned to accept those rules, but the truth is something else."

I wonder how many layers Pooran will pull back.

"The intellectual aspect has always been more important to me. It is always during the hard times, under pressure, that growth takes place. The women in Iran have gone through an amazing period during this past twenty-five or so years. They have taken an intellectual journey. In spite of the destiny that may have been decided for them, they went in the opposite direction and have achieved tremendous growth."

Pooran shows me around her house. The walls are covered with framed photos of her late sister and of their brother Fereydoun, also dead. Fereydoun was killed a few years ago, allegedly by fundamentalist Islamicists in Germany for being bisexual and outspoken against the Islamic Republic.

"My brother was the love of my life and his sorrow is always with me; it's always alive with me."

The untimely loss of two of Pooran's siblings has not made her cower but, rather, has made her pursue all that is poetic in life.

"I am not afraid of anything. I am traveling a path," she says, arcing her hands into the air in unison, as if daring fate to double down.

"We create fear, it doesn't exist, it comes from our own weakness. I'm not weak, not at all," Pooran says, her chin slightly lowered, slowly moving side to side, creating emphasis. "Not even my brother's death scared me. I grieved, but I wasn't frightened. I *never* fear."

Cameras and veils fall by the wayside, and Pooran serves us a meal of *shormeh sabzi,* a delectable feast of lamb, herbs, and lemon. I watch her pretty young brunette assistant flirt with Orlando; Julie and Pooran dance a bit to Kurdish folk music, then meander through Pooran's vast library of books. As we leave, Pooran gives me a pair of bear hugs. Before the first she looks me in the eyes and wishes me well with my work; before the second she says warmly, "Yes, I like Americans." And then she writes down directions to her sister's grave for us.

Unlike the tomb of Hafez, visiting Forough's tomb is discouraged by *them.* Every day people sneak into the cemetery where Forough is buried and light candles and recite her poetry over her grave. The wrought-iron front gate of the cemetery is locked with a thick, rusty chain. A small, stooped old woman comes to the gate and denies us entrance.

"*Emrooz ta'tile,*" she says, crankily. Go away. Closed.

I pull out ten dollars. I've never greased palms to get into a cemetery before, but the woman snatches it with a speed that indicates she is clearly well versed in this quid pro quo.

"*Doorbin nemish,*" she says. But no cameras. We return the DigiBeta camera to the van and tuck the PD 150 under Persheng's manteau.

We walk through an old, wooded cemetery and weave between flat tombstones in various degrees of disrepair. We amble through windy, overgrown paths until we spot a small cluster of people gathered deep in the cemetery. "Must be Forough," I say to Persheng, who slides the camera out from under her wrap. We approach the women and a man who are gathered around Forough's grave, which is marked by a large white marble slab lying flat on the ground, covered with beautiful Farsi engravings. The women ladle water from a bucket and wash the tombstone with their hands. One of them lays six red roses on the fresh, clean surface.

A woman with dark hair, wearing a mint trench coat, white headscarf, and fresh lipstick, begins to read from one of Forough's volumes.

> *I shall wear*
> *a pair of twin cherries as earrings*
> *and I shall put dahlia petals on my fingernails*
> *there is an alley*
> *where the boys who were in love with me*
> *still loiter with the same unkempt hair*
> *thin necks and bony legs*
> *and think of the innocent smiles of a little girl*
> *who was blown away by the wind one night.*

The next morning, back in our hotel's restaurant the instrumental theme to *Titanic* bleats on for the seventh time in the last two hours.

"If I had to work here and listen to this incessant tune I'd go nuts," I say to Julie, scratching my temple with a pinky under my gray scarf.

While in Tehran we've stayed at this hotel and, naturally, we've bonded with the proprietors. Tired of the *Titanic,* I ask if we can put a few of our CDs on the hotel sound system. The men agree and point us toward the stereo cabinet. Julie slides in a CD and presses play: when Suzanne Vega comes on—maelstrom.

"Nemishe! Ejazenadareem!" ("Oh my, not allowed! It is illegal!") the men yell as they run for the sound system. Waiters come dashing from the restaurant; cleaning ladies freeze wide-eyed. We have been actively looking for a woman who will sing on camera, and know full well that women's voices are not to be heard publicly in Iran, yet we still inadvertently transgressed. Honest to God, it was an accident. We hadn't even connected *that* rule with *our* Suzanne Vega.

"The police may come. Bad. Very bad," says the manager, yanking the CD out of the player, his discomfort eclipsing his kindness for the first time. He has met so many of our requests—Internet access, bottles of water, black coffee—and here we have put him in jeopardy. We apologize over and over again.

The Suzanne Vega incident illustrates that it's not just hair but a woman's voice that can be dangerously tempting. Julie and I want to find someone who can explain the laws about women singing, and maybe even sing on camera.

We have two days of shooting left and, realistically, only one chance at landing such a singer. Pari Zanganeh. Zanganeh is an icon in Iran. Her performing career thrived in the seventies but then was practically stopped dead by the revolution. Yet her popularity as a folksinger remains strong. Zanganeh maintains a sort of phantom career; her fans play her old records behind closed doors, and she is recognized as if she has a televised concert every Saturday night.

I was initially reluctant to put her in the show because she is famous, wealthy, Shah-associated, and, according to Jeannie, who met her on the scout trip, she has a tiny white fluffy dog with a jeweled collar. But aristocracy would do in a pinch. She's agreed to meet us for an hour.

The whole truth is that Pari could have easily left Iran with the revolution and continued her skyrocketing career in the United States, what with its large expat community. (In fact, Pari does frequently tour the United States and sings to huge crowds.) But Pari chose to stay in her native Iran because she loves her country, and she loved her mother, and her mother wouldn't leave.

Julie, Orlando, Persheng, and I walk through a tall metal gate, step onto the manicured grounds of the Zanganeh estate, and marvel at the white-columned mansion in the foothills of the Alborz. The small white fluffy dog comes tearing toward us, yapping. We walk up the stone path, past a pool, and under a white latticed arch and knock on the front door. The door swings open and Pari stands there, looking very sophisticated in dark glasses. Pari was in a car accident in her twenties that left her blind. In addition to her singing career, Pari has raised loads of money for blind children, and she writes kids' books that are published in Braille. She is wearing a black-rimmed hat atop coifed sandy-brown hair, a white linen blazer, black skirt, and pearl earrings, and her lips are topped off with a cinnamon shade. The big, black, square sunglasses give her a slight Jackie O look.

Pari greets us with a smile and gracefully ushers us into an elegant living room with parquet floors, white furniture, and a piano against one wall. Framed photos of herself and other unveiled women adorn the house. We have been in Iran long enough to feel how risqué this is. As we set up the cameras it occurs to me that Pari is the first person to be interviewed without a head scarf; she just wears the hat. I wonder if this will get her in trouble with *them,* and what kind of power protects her when she bends the rules.

Over tea and sweets Pari begins by telling me, in English, about a series of small concerts she has recently been allowed to perform.

"So you're saying you can perform as long as it's only for women and it's in a private space?" I say.

"Yes, since four years ago we have been allowed to sing for ladies, which is a great occasion for me. We go step by step in Iran."

I've got an understanding of how stifling the rules can be for women here, but I want Pari's take. She lives in such a different world than, say, Mokarrameh Ghanbari or Zahra Rahnavard. I want to know how the public quelling of women affects the heart and soul of a performing artist.

"Well, it has been like this since the changing of regime in Iran. The women are a little bit . . . how can I say . . . the activities of the ladies are restricted a little bit."

A bit? A lot is more like it. Clearly, even Pari must be judicious when choosing her words.

I tell Pari about our hotel lobby incident. "Can you explain the thinking— the philosophical defense—behind women not being allowed to sing?"

"It is hearing the voice of women singing solo that is forbidden. One thing is, I think the government—even if they themselves have discovered that it doesn't harm the human behavior—they are somehow trapped with this idea that the voice of women is tempting. Tempting towards the sexy feelings of men. By seeing my hair or hearing your voice they just go crazy, huh?" Pari laughs at the absurdity of this.

Fear of voice seems to stem from the same place as uncovered hair. Iran's president in the nineties, Ali Akbar Hashemi Rafsanjani, was considered a moderate but that did not stop him from saying, "It is the obligation of the female to cover her head because women's hair exudes vibrations that arouse, mislead, and corrupt men."

"They do everything they can to protect themselves against sex and women," Pari adds with a good-natured snort.

Whether she is performing abroad or at home, Pari tells me, she prefers modest dress. The Islamic restrictions may go too far, but the other extreme—sex-obsessed—can be just as oppressive.

"In the United States, my God, they advertise for cheese, even for cheese, chairs, tables, I mean handkerchief, dress. If they want to make it appealing: 'sexy cheese,' 'sexy dress,' 'sexy chair.' Everything is with the word *sexy*. How to sit sexy, how to talk sexy, how to wear sexy," she says with an exasperated laugh, crossing her sexy stockinged legs.

"You've got our number," I concede lightheartedly.

As a parting gift, Pari goes to the grand piano and belts out a rousing operatic number, tempting the world with the full-throated voice of a diva.

During our time in Iran I asked one of the women we interviewed (I won't name her here as her comment was dangerously frank) if she would be willing to go without head-covering while we filmed. I knew the answer would be no, but I was curious what her response would be. Perhaps it was unfair of me to ask.

"*They* will kill us," she had responded with a look of terror. And like every diva, with the exception of Pari (who wore a hat), as the cameras went on, she donned the veil. Fresh flowers and hospitality, humor and intellect dominated our private interactions in Iran, but that spirit was often obscured by veils and cameras and fear.

As a "simple" American who best understands the syntax of straight talk and the premium of individuality, I was confused by Iran (oh, that onion), humbled, but, most of all, struck by the many women who are indeed anything but shrinking violets.

Whatever its reforms, the theocratic regime creates a fear-based atmosphere, in the face of which publishing articles about patriarchy, appearing on camera in a hat instead of a veil, or expressing the artistic vision within you represent exponential acts of courage.

On our last day in Iran, Vresh drives us forty minutes outside of Tehran so we can capture an image that three weeks ago would have struck me as incongruous, but now seems plausible: women hang gliding. A half dozen gliders are congregated on the top of a plateau, choosing their own covering; tossing aside old-fashioned shoes for heavy black boots, strapping on thick helmets. The yellow sails lie on the ground behind them, separating us, occasionally whipping up in the wind and obscuring our view of one another.

I've tried to see through the veils, peel back the layers of good manners that hide more complex sentiment, lift the scrim of public discretion that implies complacency. Beyond the docile, shrouded image of Iranian women, there is passion: women who live by poetry and sing behind closed doors, and whose risk-taking bears great consequence.

One by one the hang gliders sprint toward the cliff, thick-heeled boots still peddling in those first moments of takeoff. I watch them sail off the cliff, like so many Sky Dancers blazing through the air, exhilarated, the ironies fluttering in the wind like the chadors, revealing blue jeans underneath.

"*Veil* may be a four-letter word," I say to Julie, "but so is *diva.*"

We shoot film until we have nothing left and Tehran begins to light the sky in the distance; then we call it a day.

EPILOGUE

—

Hatching vain empires. . . .

. . . Who shall tempt, with wand'ring feet

The Dark unbottom'd infinite abyss

And through the palpable obscure find out

His uncouth way . . .

—JOHN MILTON,
PARADISE LOST, BOOK II

TO: JEANNIE
FROM: HOLLY
SUBJECT: BOA CONSTRICTOR

hey Mom,
I've decided Adventure Divas reminds me of the first page of *The Little Prince*—remember?—the simple drawing of the "cowboy hat" turns out to be a boa constrictor that swallowed an elephant. Don't know what our next step should be, business-wise. Let's just tread water for the moment. It's nice to be at a booty-appreciating latitude, the caipirinhas are perfectly bittersweet, and at some point in each day the surf is always up. More soon. love, Hol

We returned from Iran knowing that our footage held great importance. The culture of fear and reactionary politics that took over the U.S. post-9/11 was formidable; our footage held the opportunity to put a human face on a region increasingly characterized as "terrorist," and we jumped on it.

The planes hitting the towers of the World Trade Center was a dramatic, deadly meeting of the fundamentalist and imperialist camps—camps our pilgrimage had set out to ignore in search of an alternative (if sometimes subliminal) empire, divadom. But ash from that cloud of fear eventually settled on us, too.

The adventure travel industry, where much of our original money came from, had dried up. Our little Adventure Divas empire, built on halter tops and hope, foundered along with the rest of America. We had been standing in still water for months when I fled to Brazil.

Right now I am writing these words in a blue spiral notebook, sitting cross-legged on a boulder just north of a sleepy fishing village in the Brazilian state of Bahia. After years of crossing the globe in overdrive, I'm holed up—free from obligations, deadlines, or film crews—trying to finish this book, learn to surf, and decide if our enterprise can continue.

"Surfing is work, so we don't surf on Sunday," said instructor Benjamin yesterday. Bahia's tropical-paradise setting has been a salve, but the magical image of surfing that first caught my attention was manifesting as rote work: sore shoulders, an infected toe, a bruised hip and ego. So far the week had been one of hard knocks, each tough lesson built on the previous day's wipeouts.

Last week, in preparation for surf camp (and for sitting on this boulder in one of Brazil's physics-defying bikinis), I, driven by my *when in Rome* zeal and somewhat forgetful of the agonies of Iranian wax, found myself spread-eagled in a beauty parlor. A squat, white-smocked woman named Gabriella plopped down a small metal bucket. Towels protected her hands from the heat.

"*Relaxa. Respire,*" she said, and ladled on thick wax, then began to search out and uproot virgin hair from places that theretofore had received little depilatory consideration, most notably . . . My Package.

riiiiip

sssseaaar . . . ahhhh!

peeeelll tugggg

"*Terminado,*" she declared after an hour. "*Americanas. Demoram muito. Sao muito peludas,*" she said, and shook her head. Americans. Take long. Lots of hair.

I looked south: *Bald, bald, bald—bald as a Ping-Pong ball.* Except, that is, for one exquisitely carved, perfect strip of glimmering copper hair, perched atop my mons, proud, like a tiara.

A friend had written down a question for me in Portuguese; I leaned over and handed it to Gabriella.

QUAL EH A COISA MAIS IMPORTANTE EM DEPILACAO? (What is the most important thing to know about waxing?)

Gabriella stopped and considered the question for a moment. Then she said, *"Saber o que quer tirar antes de colocar a cera."* Know where you're going before you put the wax down.

I've been thinking a lot about this advice, as I try to make sense of the last few years. Did I know where this was going before I put the wax down with Adventure Divas? Not really. We jumped in and began to root out, and uproot, with no assurance of a final result and little idea how daunting, and exhilarating, our task would be.

Sometimes in life a confidence, or runaway idealism, or just-the-right-time-of-month hubris presents itself and leads to pure action; that was the genesis of Adventure Divas. We were laser-focused on our goals. Before we snuck into Cuba, I put it in a speech: "We're sort of in that no-man's-land of developmental wisdom—too young for hindsight and too busy for foresight—but we have been around enough to trust our instincts."

With divas in our sights, we did succeed in exploring cultures through the eyes of people whose independence, talent, and vision are transforming lives, communities, and political landscapes in their respective countries. We were inspired by a new brand of role model: the self-determined woman who grapples with fear, lives passionately, and, in doing so, improves the world around her. We tried to put a face on the accepted (but yet-to-be-fully-acted-on) socioeconomic fact that the progress of nations depends upon the empowerment of women.

But did we measure and map global feminism? Our data would probably not satisfy the Academy. Gathering empirical evidence to prove something as elusive as a tidal change on the horizon is tough, and not something Adventure Divas was built for. But divadom—that global realm of potential inhabited by so many of the women we met—does exist. It speaks many different languages and doesn't (thank goodness) gather in a circle to sing 'Kumbaya.'"

And by broadcasting divadom's stories, I hope, in a small way, we helped light that rocky path between imperial grasping and fundamentalist entrenchment—illuminating the way not with a hundred-watt flood lamp but with the flashlights and votive candles of individuals who work to slay ignorance and fear, and chase—as Keri Hulme put it—life's updraft.

"Um, dois, tres, quatro, five, six, seven." Jumping jacks on the soft white sand have been surf camp's morning ritual, and the exercise inserts a much-needed dose of visceral to the stasis of writing.

"Center yourself, paddle, paddle—now—turtle dive!" instructor Adriano has encouraged as I've practiced balancing on the longboard. I wish like hell I'd not skipped so many yoga classes, which I'd been taking, whenever possible, since the India shoot.

Day after day *"Abaixa mais"* (stay low) wafted across the din of surf (usually right before I tumble off my board) as I tried to learn surfing's fundamentals "on the inside"—that is, on the already broken whitewater waves near shore. But even on the inside, I've been struggling.

"You need to pay attention," Adriano imparted kindly as he bandaged a cut on my foot.

Today, on this welcome day of rest, I sit cross-legged and scribbling. The buxom, green South Atlantic, like a crisp mountain range at dawn or the infinite Sahara, is a siren that commands my attention, and I hope it will deliver some 20/20 vision with which to make decisions about the future.

What of this television business? Nefarious opiate of the imperialist transnationals or underutilized power tool to be co-opted? "The Master's tools will never bring down the Master's house," said the poet Audre Lorde. Perhaps. The jury is still out.

And what of me? Desk jockey turned nomad. A transitional nester like our cousins the orangutans. In the end, all journalism is subjective and all pilgrimages are personal. I set off to make documentaries and spread divavision, but what I took away was a deeper understanding of individual agency around fear, templates for happiness in service, tutorials on courage in the face of oppression. More often than not, it was the wanderings off the path—into a staring contest with Bornean snake, or into a contest of wills with a glistening twelve-pound Cuban bass or an alpine abyss—that locked in these lessons from the divas.

I also found out that road life is not simply a means to an end; it's who I am. Most countries have their nomadic people and maybe I'm among them. Every night spent shivering under a scratchy wool blanket, every rat I ate in the name of cultural sensitivity and "that TV moment," every bittersweet parting of ways confirmed my suspicion that I am one of those visceral learners (who sucks at bubble tests). I have to lay my hands all over something to understand it; burn myself to know it's hot. I need to feel the fear of a gut-wrenching drop to see the summit clearly. Being in motion, not knowing what's going to happen next, not only suits me, but has become an unlikely vehicle for faith. "Salvation is being on the right road," said Martin Luther King, Jr., "not having reached a destination."

And so it goes. If there's one thing the divas have shown it is that to indulge your passions fully is to know yourself completely. Only then can you treat the rest of the world—its people, its ecosystems, its politics—with proactive wit and compassion.

That, you might say, is the nutgrab.

Ah, the nutgrab. When I got back from Iran I explained to Jeannie that although the shoot had been a logistical challenge—what with the Big Brother government and itchy fabrics that got in the way—we had successfully found the nutgrab.

"The what?" she said with a laugh.

"You taught me the term—y'know, the TV thing. The most important ideas crammed into one concise notion."

"You must mean *nutgraph*—the journalism term. I like that though—*nutgrab*—gets 'em by the balls, you know."

What? *Nutgrab is nutgraph?*

Oh my. I'd trotted around the world feigning credibility, all the while bandying about a locker-room perversion of journalistic jargon. One could draw a profound Buddhist *What-you-think-is,-isn't* lesson from this. Or perhaps one should simply know where she's going before she puts the wax down. In any case, the nutgrab snafu seemed an apt example of the working relationship my mother and I had developed over the past few years—an odd, loving, highly functional miscommunication.

"*Did you hear the big news?*" Adriano asks as I meet up with my surfing comrades on my last day of camp. "The fishermen caught three massive tiger sharks last night," he says, enthusiastic (and tells me I can get some for dinner at the fish stall down by the water).

"Yeah?" I say, only mildly concerned as there are never shark attacks in these waters. (And one doesn't have to be a child of karma to know a surfer should not eat shark. I decline.)

We tie down our boards on top and pile into a van to drive to a beach called Engenhoca, which means "genius machine."

"It's called that because the waves are always working," says Benjamin, moving the long VW gearshift into third. This is a graduation day of sorts for me. Today I get to go "to the outside"—that mysterious area beyond the break that elicits hushed murmurs of "tubes," "curls," "positive adrenaline," and "serious drops." Surfboards tucked under our arms, we walk half a mile down a winding dirt path through playful, swaying clusters of palm trees. We strap on our leashes, which will anchor us to the surface should we get thrashed about, and make our way out beyond the break.

Benjamin quizzes us on wave-break direction, and for a while we half-heartedly paddle toward unpromising swells. The waves *are* working today, but quietly. Nearly an hour passes; I am happy to bob and watch the waves roll into the divinity-kissed beaches.

Benjamin yells something I can't hear over the lively ocean.

I turn my cheek and rest it on the wet board, and look over the expanse of water. Usually I'd be scanning for fish, wanting a glimpse of a sleek fin darting about, but, funnily enough, right now it seems to be enough just to believe they're there.

Benjamin hollers again, louder and excited this time, from under his floppy khaki hat. "Ready to catch some green?" This time I hear him. He nods toward a fast-gaining set for which I am perfectly positioned. A wash of fear surges through my shoulder blades into my gut.

But then, my heart springs into gear.

I turn the board, wave now at my back, and paddle fast and hard. Faster and harder and stronger than I ever have. For two strokes strange, hulking synchronicity overtakes me.

Upward dog, then, measured and quicklike, I fling my feet perfectly into position. I am up! *One. Two.* Awkward and thrilled to be riding the power of the wave. *Three. Four.* Magic seconds.

I sssssurf.

—Just as fast, the moment is gone. I hurl off the board into the sea and am churned around for what feels like minutes, but is not. My right hip scrapes along the rough bottom; it hurts, but I know it will only bruise—not bleed and bring the sharks. All goes oddly quiet and calm; then I am pushed up, up, up, with the happy inevitability of a cork easing from a wine bottle. When I breach the surface my eyes sting at the salt and fresh light. I fumble for the board, grab the rails, haul myself, ungainly and panting, onto the fiberglass, and paddle out to practice some more.

ACKNOWLEDGMENTS

—

The Adventure Divas enterprise—the TV series, the website, and this book—has been an exercise in gratitude, hard work, and camaraderie from the start, and individuals all over the globe helped make it possible. The size of my appreciation is reflected in the epic length of these acknowledgments.

The divas who appear in this book, and the many others who appear in the television documentaries but could not be included in these pages, continue to be a driving inspiration: Iramis, Dori, and Janet of Instinto, Gloria Rolando, Lizette Vila, Carilda Oliver Labra, Assata Shakur, Emilia Machado, Kiran Bedi, Alice Garg, Anuradha Pal, Bachendri Pal, Ruchira Gupta, Ela Bhatt, Shubha Mudgal, Marilyn Waring, Rt. Honorable Helen Clark, Sima Urale, Hinewehi Mohi, the Land Girls, Tania Stanley, Gaylene Preston, Keri Hulme, Tahmineh Milani, Mokarrameh Ghanbari, Shahla Sherkat, Azita Hajiyan, Pari Zanganeh, Pooran Farrokhzad, Zahra Rahnavard, and Zahra Moussavi.

Huge thanks go out to the early believers who got us off the ground: Andy Meyer, Jack Slevin, Ken and Cindy McBride, Johnny Morris, Bill Wheeler, Tina Arapolu, Carolyn Broquet, Steve Marts, Warren Franklin, Matt Bien and Paul Goldberg of Pure Audio, Michael Gross, Kate Thompson, and my long-time dear friend Laura Slevin.

To those who stoked the furnace at Divas HQ, much credit is due: Stacy Lewis and Jen Senkler were integral at launch time; a heartfelt spin of Sky Dancer to Rena Bussinger, Heather Reilly, and Susannah Fotopulos for their smarts and commitment; Jill Hodges made our web presence read, rumble, and dance; and, as mentioned above, essential creatives Michael Gross and Kate Thompson came early and stayed late.

The road and post folks offered up much appreciated humor (and some-times Cipro and coffee), along with their considerable talent: Thanks to Simon and Val Griffith, Jan McKinley, Susan Thomas, Steve Cammarano, Cathia Geller, Jim Wilson, Sophia Zubiria, Jen Brown, Lois Shelton, Paul Mailman, Pamela Yates, Maryam Kia, John Chater, Parviz Abnar, Doug Dunderdale, Liza Bambenek, Dan Davis, Orlando Stuart, Felicity Oram, Ellen Forney, Michael Cozzi, and Carrie Akre. Flying Spot postproduction and DataWeb also de-serve thanks.

Special thanks to Julie Costanzo, Persheng Vaziri, Catherine Murphy, Cheryl Dunn, Nassim Assefi, Pramila Jayapal, and Vanessa Boeye, who not only made it happen on the road, but also helped me recount it on the page.

Countless others contributed, among them Lara Kidoguchi, Katie Dreke, Nick Boorman, Denise Olivier, Neide Cooley, Kathleen Gasperini, Karen Wetherall Davis, David Geller of Whatcounts, Knoll Lowney, Claire Garoutte, Hal Jones, Laura Puckett, Joe Bolden, Mark Van S., Firouzeh Nourzad, Sholeh Seydali, Babak Khiavchi, Yasmine Rafii, Parisa Sadeghi, Puja Vohra, Teri Hein, Mike Frankfurter, Jim Dow, and Paige Meili. Also, hats off to the many interns, and to the contributers to www.adventuredivas.com.

PBS provided invaluable exposure and creative freedom. Enough cannot be said for Mary Jane McKinven, the brilliant, committed executive without whom *Adventure Divas* might never have hit the airwaves. Big thanks are also due to PBS's John Wilson and Sandy Heberer for their ongoing support.

REI and its CEO, Sally Jewell, provided essential underwriting; and thanks go out to the executives at National Geographic with whom we worked while on the road, especially Jacques Grenier and Mark Nelson. That loveable Australian, Ian Cross of Pilot Productions, brings the world into our homes every day, and I feel lucky to be a part of his operation.

Hang-ten to the one and only David Fox: who wouldn't be grateful to have a smart and loyal barrister who always has my back *and* lets me in on the best surf breaks? Thanks, too, to my agent Alan Berger of CAA, for his integrity and support through the thicket of the television industry.

This book began after the cameras clicked off, and it, too, has been informed by many people.

Respect and gratitude to my literary agent, Leigh Feldman of Darhansoff, Verrill, Feldman: the word *diva* could have been invented for this excellent advocate, who knows exactly when to soothe and advise—and when to deliver a full-court press—all with absolute charm and intelligence.

At Random House/Villard Books, Bruce Tracy and Katie Zug kicked off this venture and my fabulous editor Stephanie Higgs deserves a magnum of Mumm for her tenacious work in the face of ever pushed deadlines, for hammering away at my mixed metaphors, and for valiantly shepherding this book through the publishing process. Thanks, too, to publicist Jen Huwer, Beth Pearson, and all the talented production staff at Random House, as well as Robin Desser of Knopf for her early encouragement.

Editorial wisdom came from far and wide: Andrea Chapin, Blase Reardon, Michele Mortimer, and Howard Chaffey gave valuable input; and very special thanks to Jennie Goode and Lindsay Knisely, kindred grrrl spirits who, time and again, kept me on point.

To those who fed and walked me at all the right times throughout the writing process: Sunny Speidel, Betsy Whitaker, Inga Muscio, Johanna Striar, Evelyn C. White, Ewen Thomson, Jenny Leah, Sarah Stimson, Scott Friskics, my ever-supportive siblings—and the late, great Boo Radley, who left so many gifts.

TV relishes image and chaos, but writing requires quiet and space. In Brazil, a big *obrigada* to Monica and Rich Drennan, for use of their tropical getaway, and to expat John McGlocklin, for his advice and companionship in South America and beyond.

The Cottages at Hedgebrook writer's residency in Washington State provides incredible space and facilitates creativity. Co-founders Sheryl Feldman and Nancy Skinner Nordhoff deserve huge credit for their visionary action that now makes it possible for so many other women to realize their own creative and political visions.

I am indebted to valued friends and former colleagues from Seal Press, Faith Conlon and Ingrid Emerick, who gave the Niger prose its first airing, and to editors Susan Fox Rogers and Maria Finn Dominguez, each of whom published early material from the Cuba chapter.

Giant appreciation to my dad, Johnny Morris, whose support and go-for-the-gold approach informs many endeavors in this book and my life.

A sloppy French kiss to Michael Kovnat, whose brainy curiosity, patience, and zealous fact-checking brought home the final chapters in this book, and with whom I look forward to sharing all of the chapters and adventures to come.

And last, a galaxy of gratitude and love to Jeannie Morris, my mom. She has been a partner, co-conspirator, and invaluable positive spirit, in all things Adventure Divas, from day one. And she hardly ever told me to comb my hair. Yo Jeannie, we did it.

RESOURCES

—

Visit www.adventuredivas.com for more about the women featured in this book, to purchase videos or DVDs of the documentary series, for travel resources, and for information on DivaTours.

Below is a listing of the books, films, and other media created by the profiled divas. When available, a specific distributor, retailer, or website is listed. Some general sources for rare, out-of-print, and foreign language materials include: Alibris (www.alibris.com), BookFinder (www.bookfinder.com), Powell's Books (www.powells.com), Biblio (www.biblio.com), Amazon (www.amazon.com), Bibliofind (www.bibliofind.com), and eBay (www.ebay.com).

CUBA

CARILDA OLIVER LABRA

SELECTED BOOKS OF POETRY

Se Me ha Perdido un Hombre (*I Have Lost a Man*), 1993

Dust Disappears (selected poems translated into English), 1991

Memoria de la Fiebre (*Feverish Memory*), 1958

Canto a Matanzas (*Song to Matanzas*), 1956

Canto a Marti (*Song to Marti*), 1953

Canto a la Bandera (*Song to the Flag*), 1950

Al Sur De Mi Garganta (*At the South of My Throat*), 1949

Preludio Lirico (*Lyric Prelude*), 1943

WEB

Selected poems published online (in Spanish) at www.palabravirtual.com

INSTINTO

ALBUM

Cuban Hip Hop All-Stars, Vol. 1, 2001

FILM

Cuban Hip Hop All-Stars, 2004

WEB

www.papayarecords.com

GLORIA ROLANDO

FILMS

Los Marqueses de Atarés, 2001

Raices de Mi Córazon (Roots of My Heart), 2000

El Alacrán, 1999

Eyes of the Rainbow, 1998

My Footsteps in Baragua, 1996

Oggún: The Eternal Present, 1992

WEB

www.afrocubaweb.com/gloriarolando.htm

ASSATA SHAKUR

BOOK

Assata: An Autobiography, 1987

WEB

www.assatashakur.org

LIZETTE VILA

SELECTED FILMS

Otra Mujer sin Rostro (Another Woman Without Face), 2004

Voces . . . Sueños, Amor, y Paz (Voices . . . Dreams, Love and Peace), 2003

Romanza de un Ulma (Romance of a Soul), 2003

Contra el Silencio: Una Mujer (Against Silence: A Woman), 2002

Mujer Alma de Maravillas (Woman, Soul of Wonders), 2002

Una Mujer sin Rostro (Woman Without Face), 2001

Yo No Soy un Santo (*I Am Not a Saint*), 1999
Gracias a la Vida (*Thanks for the Life*), 1998
Cambiando Vidas (*Changing Lives*), 1993

INDIA

KIRAN BEDI
BOOKS BY
As I See It . . . , 2003
What Went Wrong?, 2001
Government.net, 2001
It's Always Possible, 1999
BOOKS ABOUT
Kiran Bedi: The Kindly Baton by Dr. Meenakshi Saksena, 2000
"I Dare!" Kiran Bedi: A Biography by Parmesh Dangwal, 1995
WEB
www.kiranbedi.com

PHOOLAN DEVI AKA "THE BANDIT QUEEN"
BOOKS
India's Bandit Queen: The True Story of Phoolan Devi by Mala Sen, 1991
FILM
Bandit Queen (directed by Shekhar Kapur), 1995

RUCHIRA GUPTA
DOCUMENTARY
The Selling of Innocents, 1997
Available for noncommercial use from:

> Ruchira Gupta, Executive Director
> Apne Aap Women Worldwide
> 22 Ballgunge Park Road
> Kolkata-17, India
> E-mail: ruchiragupta@hotmail.com

For broadcast use contact:

> Associated Producers
> 110 Spadina Avenue, Suite 1001
> Toronto, Ontario, Canada
> Phone: 1416-4800453

ORGANIZATION

Apne Aap (Women Worldwide), an initiative to end sex trafficking, founded by Ruchira Gupta.

WEB

www.apneaap.org

ALICE GARG

ORGANIZATION

> Bal Rashmi Society
> A 48 Shanti Path
> Tilak Nagar, Jaipur, 302 004
> Rajasthan, India
> E-mail: rashmi72@sancharnet.in
> Phone: 0141-2620861
>   0141-2651523

ANURADHA PAL

ALBUMS

Shanti (*Spiritual Essence of India*)

Stree Shakti (all-female percussion ensemble, led by Anuradha Pal, that performs traditional and innovative music)

Anu: A Tabla Solo

WEB

www.anuradhapal.com

IRAN

FOROUGH FARROKHZAD

SELECTED POEMS

Tavallodi Digar (*Another Birth*), 1964

Esian (*Rebellion*), 1958

Divar (The Wall), 1956

Asir (The Captive), 1955

FILM

The House Is Black, 1962 (available from www.iranianmovies.com)

WEB

www.forughfarrokhzad.org

POORAN FARROKHZAD

SELECTED WORKS

Encyclopedia of Women Culture Makers in Iran and in the World

The Eternal Women

Zane Shabane Mo Ood

Atash O Bad

Dar Entehaye Atashe Ayeene

WEB

www.ketab.com

MOKARRAMEH GHANBARI

DOCUMENTARY

Mokarrameh, Memories and Dreams, directed by Ebrahim Mokhtari.

Available from:

        First Run Icarus Films

        32 Court St., 21st Fl.

        Brooklyn, NY 11201

        Phone: 718 488-8900

        E-mail: mailroom@frifi.com

WEB

www.mokarrameh.com

ZAHRA RAHNAVARD

SELECTED WORKS

The Beauty of Concealment and the Concealment of Beauty (Translated text
    online at www.al-islam.org)

Imperialist Roots of the Abolition of Hejab

The Revolt of Moses

The Hijrah [Emigration] of Joseph
Tempests and the Tulips of Shahrivar
The Stories of Ali and Mash Medina
Philosophy of Islamic Art
Strongholds Behind the Front Line
Mourning at Hira
The Social Strata from Qur'anic Point of View
The Rise of Moslem Women
A Hero from the Qur'anic Viewpoint
Insight into the Qur'anic Verses
Islamic Government

SHAHLA SHERKAT

MAGAZINE

Zanan (Women), Shahla Sherkat, Editor
E-mail: info@zanan.co.ir

WEB

www.zanan.co.ir

PARI ZANGANEH

ALBUMS

Shah Pari
Goleh Ghessehaa
Gozashtehaayeh Noh (Reviving the Past)

NEW ZEALAND

KERI HULME

SELECTED BOOKS

Strands (poems), 1992
Te Kihau (The Windeater), 1986
The Bone People, 1985

HINEWEHI MOHI

ALBUMS

Oceania II, 2002

Oceania, 2000

WEB

www.maorimusic.com

GAYLENE PRESTON

FILMS

Perfect Strangers, 2003

Titless Wonders, 2001 (available from www.gpprods.com)

Punitive Damage, 1999

War Stories Our Mothers Never Told Us, 1995

Bread and Roses, 1993

Ruby and Rata, 1990

Kai Purakau (documentary about Keri Hulme), 1987

Mr. Wrong (aka *Dark of Night* in U.S.), 1985

WEB

www.filmarchive.org.nz

www.gaylenepreston.co.nz

MARILYN WARING

BOOKS

Three Masquerades, 1996

If Women Counted: A New Feminist Economics
     (original title: *Counting for Nothing*), 1988

DOCUMENTARY

Who's Counting? (produced by the National Film Board of Canada), 1995

WEB

www.bullfrogfilms.com/catalog/who.html

ADVENTURE DIVAS

SEARCHING THE GLOBE FOR WOMEN
WHO ARE CHANGING THE WORLD

Holly Morris

. . .

A READER'S GUIDE

QUESTIONS FOR DISCUSSION

1. The Adventure Divas team set out to take divavision to television, "to storm the bully pulpit and launch a cross-media empire." (xv) Was this fool-hardy or inspired? Is Audre Lorde right when she says, "The Master's tools will never bring down the Master's house" (268)? How much of the media you consume is generated by corporate-owned multinationals, and how much is independent? Explore how that affects what information you are getting.

2. Mother-daughter issues crop up throughout the book. Could you, or *would* you, work with your mother or daughter? Why do you think it is that when daughters hear that Morris and her mother work together they say, "Oh my god, I could *never* do that," and when mothers hear of it they say, "How wonderful! I'd love to do that"?

3. Adventure Divas media tries to "put a face on the accepted (but yet-to-be-fully-acted-on) socioeconomic fact that the progress of nations depends upon the empowerment of women." (267) Can you think of examples or counterexamples? Do you think there will be a geopolitical "tipping point" that will usher in wide-scale change in terms of women's status?

4. Readers either love or hate menstrual humor. Which camp are you in? Why does the subject provoke such strong feelings?

5. *Divadom* is a term used for the network of women the Adventure Divas enterprise pursues and the global realm of potential they and their work represent. How is imagining an alternative paradigm—one that is perhaps taking form on the horizon—useful, or is it? How can imagination stoke political and personal change?

6. Are you happy? Ever thought about ditching your day job or revolutionizing your life in some way to chase a long-standing dream? What would it look like? What would happen if you tried and succeeded? How about if you tried and failed?

7. Morris writes, "Adventure is about hurling yourself at the unexpected; it's how you walk to the corner store, *and* how you walk the Australian Outback." (xiv) Is there value in making every day an adventure? Is leaving "an underrated form of liberation" (55)? And why *did* Thelma and Louise die?

8. In Cuba, Morris suggests that "booty consciousness" may be an "alternate seat of power." (16) Do feelings about one's butt correlate to larger notions of power?

9. Do you think it's appropriate for film crews or journalists to visit "fragile" cultures such as the rain-forest-dwelling Penan in Borneo (75) or the Tuareg, desert nomads in Niger (205)? Does reporting on the status of these cultures help or hurt their causes? Does it do more good or more harm? Is there a way to do it responsibly?

10. Lizette Vila raised the notion of "machismo Leninismo" in Cuba. What do you think she meant? How does machismo play out differently in different cultures?

11. Morris explores different kinds of fear in the book—fear of political persecution, of losing loved ones, of failure (or success), of snakes. How do the divas tackle, transcend, use, or repurpose fear in their lives?

12. When asked about a strong ethic of "giving back" and grassroots activism in India, journalist turned activist Ruchira Gupta says that in part it comes from the Freedom Struggle, India's fight for independence. "Life is not just about living for yourself; we have to contribute something back to society. It's almost as if the thread of the freedom struggle is going through us." (125) What could we identify as the dominant ethics of the United States? What historical events or aspects of our national character shape how we treat one another and how we act in the global community?

13. Black Panther in exile Assata Shakur says, "We do not have the right, in the name of social justice, to bore people to death." How can fun be infused into causes of social justice and political action? Is that a worthy goal? Why or why not?

14. The book explores feminist realities in Iran as well as Westerners' discomfort with veiling. Is there necessarily a conflict between Western notions of freedom and Islamic concepts of modest dress, or *hejab*? If so, can they be reconciled?

15. Morris refers to a particular quandary in the "life after God" generation (meaning an American generation with many people not engaged in any formal religion or faith). They have a "need for ritual, the want of existential explanations, the affirmation of common truths" (101), but they feel duped if they buy into the available options. Can one craft a spirituality based on individual values and personal ethics? (In other words, how do you achieve one of life's nutgrabs without feeling like you're drinking the blue Kool-Aid?)

HOLLY MORRIS is the founder of Adventure Divas, Inc., a multimedia production company, and is executive producer and writer/director of the award-winning primetime PBS documentary series *Adventure Divas*. She is the former editorial director of Seal Press and the editor of two fishing anthologies, *A Different Angle* and *Uncommon Waters*. Her writing appears in *The New York Times, Ms., Outside,* and numerous anthologies. When she's not writing, or producing television documentaries, Morris is a correspondent for television series such as *Lonely Planet Treks in America, Treks in a Wild World, Globe Trekker,* and *Outdoor Investigations*. She can be reached at www.adventuredivas.com.